INFLATION

INFLATION

A Guide for
Users and Losers

MARK BLYTH and
NICOLÒ FRACCAROLI

W. W. NORTON & COMPANY
Independent Publishers Since 1923

For information about permission to reproduce selections from this book, write to
Permissions, W. W. Norton & Company, Inc., 500 Fifth Avenue, New York, NY 10110

For information about special discounts for bulk purchases, please contact
W. W. Norton Special Sales at specialsales@wwnorton.com or 800-233-4830

Manufacturing by Lakeside Book Company
Book design by Daniel Lagin
Production manager: Julia Druskin

ISBN 978-1-324-10614-2

W. W. Norton & Company, Inc., 500 Fifth Avenue, New York, NY 10110
www.wwnorton.com

W. W. Norton & Company Ltd., 15 Carlisle Street, London W1D 3BS

10 9 8 7 6 5 4 3 2 1

Mark dedicates this book to his wife, Jules,
who actually read this one as we were churning it out,
and to his daughter, Vivien, who might read it one day.

Nicolò dedicates this book to his parents, Alba and Franco,
and his siblings, Cecilia and Pietro, for their continuous
support and for being the best family one could wish for.

Contents

≍

INFLATION

Introduction

≡

WHY WE NEED TO RETHINK WHAT WE THINK ABOUT INFLATION

We listen to opinions that make us feel good, instead of ideas that make us think hard.

—Adam Grant

In the summer of 2021, Nicolò Fraccaroli approached Mark Blyth suggesting that they write a book on inflation together. Mark asked him what such a book would do. They could write such a book, but why bother? What was there to explain that we don't know already?

Back in the 2010s, Nic and Mark both wrote books on austerity, the policy of cutting government spending, often in a recession, to make the recession go away. After bailing out the global financial system in 2008, politicians and pundits soon began to fret about the inevitable inflationary effects of all that "spending," and by 2010 they successfully argued for a general policy of budget cuts to head it off. Both books basically said, "This is not going to work out as they think, and it may well be a disaster." A decade later, after much resistance, this became the consensus among economists.

Before inflation appeared in 2021, governments seemed to have learned the lessons of the financial crisis and the austerity years of 2010 to 2016 and had fought COVID-19 with an impressive bout of public spending. Then, when inflation—which we define in this book as "the increase in the prices of goods and services over time"—showed up in COVID-19's aftermath, the claim that inflation must result from all this "excessive spending" instantly gained traction. Economist Larry Summers claimed in a speech at the London School of Economics that due to excessive pandemic spending "we need five years of unemployment above 5 percent to contain inflation—in other words, we need two years of 7.5 percent unemployment or five years of 6 percent unemployment or one year of 10 percent unemployment," to bring down inflation. Such arguments reminded us of policymakers' arguments in favor of austerity in 2010. While the COVID response initially looked exactly like the opposite of austerity, we began to feel that history was repeating itself. In 2008 to 2009, spending to fight the crisis was the name of the game. By 2010, austerity was the only game in town. We began to wonder if the fight against inflation was really just "austerity by other means" a decade later.

Our suspicions grew as the debate over inflation's causes and consequences got more heated throughout 2021. Prominent economists disagreed vehemently on the causes of inflation. This was no technical discussion for ivory-towered academics. It mattered because identifying the causes of inflation was key to deciding on the next step: how to *fight* inflation. By early 2022, one inflation-fighting strategy in particular began to garner a lot of attention: that, as the Larry Summers quote above exemplifies, the only way to stop prices from spiraling out of control was to generate a large economic recession.

The thinking went that central banks must raise interest rates, thereby increasing the cost of investment and debt servicing. This would have the effect of destroying people's jobs as the economy slowed down, which would get rid of inflation. Otherwise, people will begin to expect prices to keep rising, and that very expectation would make inflation rise further as wages and prices chase each other up in a "spiral." Unemployment is bad, but it is the only thing that will stop the development of this "wage-price spiral" of inflation, which is worse.

Just as the austerity spending cuts were portrayed as the hangover after the spending party that we all had to endure, now "everyone" would have to suffer this recession as the inevitable cost of excessive COVID-19 spending. This was, we were also told, the only solution. If we failed to grit our teeth and suffer that recession now, we were probably on our way to a hyperinflationary nightmare such as the ones we find in places like Argentina, Venezuela, Zimbabwe, or even the German Weimar Republic, which supposedly paved the way to Hitler's electoral success.

To us this drumbeat sounded an awful lot like the "therapeutic austerity" claims of the 2010s that asked everyone to suffer for the greater good, but from which no good came. This argument for raising interest rates to attack inflation ignored the fact that, just like austerity, belt tightening in the form of rising rates really only hurts those whose pants are tight to begin with. That is, we don't all suffer recession and unemployment equally. So, was fighting inflation really just "austerity 2.0"—a form of "monetary austerity"? Was hyperinflation really a risk that our governments were running? And was it true that "there is no alternative" but to intentionally generate a recession and unemployment to escape the inflation trap? It turned out that we had quite a lot more to say than we had initially thought. "The further we looked into it," as David Byrne from the Talking Heads once put it, "the further things stick out."

Specifically, we are all taught that too much money causes inflation. But it turns out that the old dictum by Milton Friedman that "inflation is always and everywhere a monetary phenomenon" is true only in the way that "shootings are always and everywhere a ballistic phenomenon." Clearly you can't have a shooting without bullets, but that doesn't tell you why it happened or who was likely to get shot.

Furthermore, the whole notion that you need a big recession to cure inflation has not just been disproven by current events—inflation fell while employment and growth increased in many countries, especially the United States. But we also found in our research that this piece of conventional wisdom has surprisingly weak theoretical and empirical support. As we will show, there is no direct relationship between inflation and unemployment, whereby central banks can trade off one "bad" against the other. We also found that the notion that people have a particular type of "expectation" of future prices that central banks can use to steer the economy is really dubious too. Finally, if you estimate the harm done by inflation to peoples' life chances and the harm done by unemployment, the unemployment harm outweighs the inflation harm by six to one. Are we then harming ourselves through a self-enforced recession to achieve a far lesser good?

Delving further into these issues, we kept coming back to the 1970s, the last time that the rich countries of the world had a big inflation. The then head of the US Federal Reserve, Paul Volcker, pushed interest rates up in order to cause a massive recession and kept them up until inflation subsided. But what if the real lessons of the 1970s lay elsewhere? What if Volcker's hike was actually too much and too late? What if inflation was falling anyway and for totally different reasons? If so, was our policy today similarly flawed, but (so far) we got lucky?

Given that Nic and Mark both had prior experience in debunking the case for therapeutic recessions during the austerity period of 2010 to 2016, it made them think that they might after all, have something new and worthwhile to say on this topic. There was another common element in the inflation and austerity debates. In both cases policymakers used off-the-shelf "economic playbooks" in their response to both crises, which can be a dangerous thing to do.

If you watch American football, you will know that standard "plays" from the playbook are very useful if one wants to act quickly in a familiar situation. But relying on such standard plays also prevents us from seeing solutions "off the playbook" that better fit unfamiliar territory. With austerity, the economic playbook came, in the main, from the 1920s, and the play was "cutting public spending to deliver economic growth." It didn't work for the simple reason that if we all (the state, firms, and consumers) cut spending at the same time there will be no income generated from which to save, and from that no savings to invest. Without investment you can't have growth, which was what austerity was paradoxically trying to achieve.

In 2021, policymakers dealt with inflation by returning to a playbook written out of the experience of the 1970s. But quite why the obvious policy solution to a massive increase in natural gas prices and a shift in demand from, say, restaurants to "if I'm going to be stuck in here on Zoom for the foreseeable future, I need a new couch right now" (what we actually faced in 2021) was to make the cost of borrowing money more expensive—especially for those who were already the most credit constrained—is far from clear. This, in turn, got us thinking about whether the 1970s inflation playbook is accurate. And if it is not, how did we get stuck with it? Are rising interest rates really the best way to deal with rising prices? Are there viable alternatives? Was this the only play in the playbook? Were we risking a recession—in the midst of rising populism and political polarization—for no good reason?

In the coming chapters, you'll find the answers to these questions and more, based on the existing evidence that we have, both from past experiences with inflation and from the latest research. We'll show, for instance, that hyperinflations are really the exception, not the rule, and that so-called excessive public spending can, at best, explain only a small part of the inflation story. We'll see that there are some alternatives to rate hikes out there, but to see them you have to want to look out past the light of the proverbial drunk's lamppost.

THE ELEPHANT GAME: INFLATION STORIES AND SHIFTING THE BLAME

The truth is that there are always alternatives to rate hikes, otherwise we wouldn't be debating the causes of inflation. By late 2021, we began to realize that those debating the causes of inflation were, unconsciously or consciously, playing a version of the famous "Elephant Game." The Elephant Game is a mental party trick in which you imagine a group of blindfolded individuals locked in a room with a strangely passive elephant. They each approach the elephant from different angles, trying to figure out from touch alone what they face. The one grabbing the trunk thinks it's a large snake. The one rubbing the leg thinks it's a tree. Only when they are freed from the darkness do they see the elephant for what it is.

We became interested in why some people are so sure that they have a snake, and others that they have a tree. That is, we are interested in the different inflation stories that emerge, not only to explain the phenomenon of inflation, but also as political weapons in the battle to shift the costs of inflation onto someone else. Why is this important? Inflation creates winners (yes, there are some) and losers, as well as abusers. As a consequence, different inflation stories portray different heroes, victims, and villains, telling us who caused the problem, who will be hurt by it, and crucially, who has to pay for it.

We will show you that there are four main stories, or genres, that dominated the debate. Each of them identifies a different villain that caused prices to go up: the government, the workers, the disruptions from the Ukraine war and COVID-19, and greedy corporations. Identifying a villain is not just a matter of blaming and shaming. It tells you what to do to combat inflation. For example, if the villain is the government, you just have to slash its spending. If the villain is global supply chains getting gnarled up, it's not clear that cutting spending or raising rates will do anything about those problems. But doing so may well compensate certain groups whose assets are impaired by such shocks.

Each of these stories has a different set of policies attached to them to bring prices back to normal. Some of them agree with the 1970s playbook and advocate for creating a recession. Others propose alternative solutions, such as price controls, that were perceived as hopelessly heterodox when the inflation debate began, but were actually implemented by not-so-heterodox governments later on without much fuss and with mixed results. Similarly, this time around, when central banks raised rates, they actually failed to cause a recession, and in many countries employment went up, not down. Central banks celebrated that they had caused an "immaculate deflation" (or a 'soft landing,' as they prefer to call it) without causing a recession. But that was not the play in the playbook. So did they cause the outcome or just take credit for the result? We have some answers to that too.

We will try to convince you that there really is no single timeless and true story about inflation. Rather, we want to show you that some explanations are better than others, in particular cases and in particular periods. You could argue that prices went up because of government spending or corporate profits, but that might be only the tail, or the leg, of the inflation elephant. Each of these inflation stories are partial stories. One could argue that they are partial simply because the protagonists of particular stories were a bit hasty in rushing to conclusions rather than waiting for more solid evidence to pop up, which might be true in some cases. After all, we need some certainties, and cementing the dominant interpretation of "what's going on" and "who is to blame" is a large part of creating that certainty. But as political economists we also know that interests can play an important role in shaping any economic narrative. This is no conspiracy theory. No one intentionally engineered a global inflation. But once that inflation arose, some didn't see just a problem. They also saw an opportunity.

If you're a politician from the opposition party, it is convenient to blame inflation on the reckless spending of the incumbent government. If you're a big supermarket chain, it is convenient to blame the higher prices you're charging to your customers on higher electricity and transportation costs. And it is telling that central banks argue for the need to control wages (which is the government's task) by invoking the specter of an out-of-control wage-price spiral barreling toward hyperinflation, rather than controlling prices (which is the central bank's task). This is not simply opportunism and greed. It's simply part of the inflation game, a game whose rules are hidden to the many for the advantage of the few. One of these rules is that while inflation is harmful, it also presents opportunities for some. Those opportunities exist because of one specific characteristic of inflation: it creates winners, losers, users, and in some cases, abusers.

INFLATION'S WINNERS, LOSERS, USERS AND ABUSERS

In this book we want to show you that inflation is not what most policy-makers, or most people, think it is. Rather, inflation has multiple causes and just as many manifestations. It also has deep distributional implications. Basically, the question that we should be asking is, Who wins and who loses from inflation? It's odd to think of there being "winners" or "users" of inflation, since we are repeatedly told by the press, by politicians, and by central bankers that no one benefits from inflation. That, however, is far from true. As we shall see, some people, some corporations, and even some countries, most certainly gain from it.

Think of Saudi Arabia buying the world's most expensive soccer players to start a professional league with the superprofits that it gained in 2021–23 from the rise in oil prices. It exemplifies inflation's winners, who found themselves better off from higher prices on the assets they own and make money from. But there are also inflation's users. Those are the pundits and politicians who use inflation, or more specifically, particular stories about inflation, as political weapons. They use such stories to convince us that what is causing inflation is factor X rather than Y, and because of that, the solution must be policy A rather than B. In other words, inflation has real costs, and the storytellers don't want their constituency to pay those costs. So they tell you a story that's going to allow them to shift those costs onto someone else.

Once you start to think of inflation as a problem of distribution—who gets what, when, where, and why—we can see why the claim that no one benefits from inflation is deeply wrong. Surely there are inflation's losers, and inflation bears real costs for them. In a world of deep inequalities in income, wealth, and life chances, where, for instance in the United States, "roughly 40 percent of Americans have trouble paying for food, medical care, housing, and other utilities," millions of people were already struggling before inflation devalued their incomes even further. For many people, two years of 10 percent inflation could push them into homelessness. For such groups there are clear reasons why stopping inflation is a priority. But stop for a moment and consider the following. A large component of the income squeeze that we saw over the past few years was comprised of increases in the cost of fossil fuels. Thinking about fossil fuel–driven inflation shows us how the losers get played by the winners and the users.

As noted above with the example of the Saudi soccer league, the rise in inflation has been a godsend to fossil fuel companies and carbon-heavy economies, who prior to 2022 were facing increasing pressures from governments, activists, investors, and consumers to wind down their carbon-based operations. Since February 2022, with the world carbon short due to Russia's de facto gas embargo in Europe; Saudi Arabia's reluctance to pump more oil in order to keep prices up; and US shale producers' worries about generating another "boom-bust" cycle, prices and profits were booming, especially in the 2021–23 period. And with that boom, these countries and companies, and the politicians they fund, began to openly push back against the green transition that the whole world needs. They, as inflation's winners and abusers, were able to weaponize the pain caused by inflation to challenge the future costs of decarbonization in the name of inflation and protecting the losers, thereby saving their assets at the expense of everyone else. In short, inflation is a game of moving costs around. In this book we show you how that game is played.

We will show you who won and who lost from inflation, and who took advantage of it. We'll also show why it is often difficult to tell who the real winners are, while the losers remain quite clear. But in this grim landscape there is some hope. We'll see that different countries experienced quite different inflations, and that in some countries policymakers did make a difference. Governments, or the state more broadly, can transfer resources from winners and users to losers. They can and did (sometimes) redistribute the gains from inflation by the former to alleviate the burden on the latter. They can stymie the actions of inflation's abusers. We shall argue that inflation wars are indeed class wars of a certain type, but the hopeful news is that this is mainly by default rather than by design, and that we can do better if we understand inflation better, which is the point of this book.

BUT ISN'T INFLATION GOING AWAY? THE "LONDON BUS" PROBLEM

Actually, we don't think it is going away. To jump ahead a little, we argue that most of the time inflations are caused by supply shocks. Oil prices jump, wheat prices rise, supply chains collapse. That sort of thing. Yet, as we will discuss in detail later, most of our conventional ideas about inflation focus on imbalances in the labor market or in the growth of the money supply. That creates a problem, because if you are on the lookout for accelerating wages and loose monetary policies, you will discount the effects of supply shocks and firms keen to protect (and extend where possible) their profits. That will be a problem if we can reasonably expect more of these types of supply shocks in the future, which we think we can.

We come to this conclusion by developing a different understanding of the 1970s, the period that informs most of our thinking on inflation. Our version stresses supply shocks rather than monetary factors, and from that we draw a sobering lesson. Yes, this particular bout of inflation may be dissipating, but it will not be the last. In a tightly coupled global economy where the effects of, for example, climate change on food webs

and agricultural supply chains are just beginning to be felt, we can probably expect more such shocks in the future.

As we discuss more fully in the conclusion, add climate change's
effects on insurance costs; increasing geopolitical tensions that result in
tariffs and sanctions; and increasing nationalism leading to greater pro-
tectionism, and we may be moving into a world characterized by the
"London Bus" model of inflation. That is, there aren't any for ages, and
then they all come along at once, backing into one another and making
things cumulatively worse. This is why you should read this book about
inflation now. What we have seen from 2021–25 is a foretaste of the new
normal. We are going back to a more inflationary world, but not for the
reasons you usually hear in the papers and from pundits. To survive that
future, we need to think differently about it.

THE REST OF THIS BOOK

In the first chapter we tell you the five things they don't tell you about
inflation. We start by detailing different types of inflation—the good,
the bad, and the ugly—and then show you how inflation measures are
constructed and why the old adage of "sausages in, sausages out" really
applies here. We discuss what an inflation index is; how it's put together;
the surprising things it does and does not measure, like housing; and
why this arcane statistical stuff is really important. In short, what counts
is what is counted; there is no "true" measure of inflation out there, and
politics plays a big role in deciding what is and is not inflation.

The second chapter asks why we always turn to interest rates as the
way to tackle inflation. We review what raising interest rates did, and crucially did not do, in the past, and examine alternative policies to interest
rate rises. We discuss why, among these alternatives, the price control
policies applied to tame inflation in the 1970s are seen as a failure, and
how such price controls fared this time around in economies as diverse
as Spain, Hungary, Germany, and Scotland.

The third chapter details the various inflation stories that attempt to explain what causes inflation, who is to blame, and who needs to pay for it. We argue that there are four main genres that see the culprit of inflation in the government's fiscal stimulus, workers' claims for higher wages, supply shocks, or greedy corporations boosting their profits. Each points the finger of blame in a different direction, with accordingly different solutions and implications.

The fourth chapter discusses how likely it is for inflations like ours to spiral into an actual societal breakdown in the form of hyperinflation. We discuss what hyperinflation is and isn't, looking in detail at the cases of Venezuela, Zimbabwe, Argentina, and interwar Germany. We come to the reassuring conclusion that hyperinflation is very rare, despite how often it's used to score rhetorical or political points.

The fifth chapter asks: Why didn't we see this inflation coming? This chapter starts by setting up what we call the "settled history" of the 1970s in economics that forms the basis of our current anti-inflation playbook. We use two lenses to analyze this history: the supposed "fall" of Professor Phillips's famous "curve," a popular framework to interpret changes in inflation, at the hands of mainstream economists in the 1970s and '80s—despite the fact that we still use it today as the framework to understand inflation; and the rise of independent central banks as part of the new regime of price stability that was built in reaction to 1970s inflation. We then discuss the core ideas of the new regime of price stability that was constructed in the 1980s and '90s. This chapter highlights how that settled history has profoundly shaped our ideas about what inflation is, how to deal with it, and why we didn't see it coming.

The sixth chapter asks, Are inflation wars class wars? Having detailed what it is, where it came from, how we think about it, and crucially, *why* we think that way, we now dive into the core distributional issues at stake. Here we strip out the essentials of rival inflation narratives to detail who wins, who loses, who uses inflation to protect their profits, and who uses inflation to abuse others in the form of predatory rent seeking.

By looking more critically at inflation we answered many of the questions with which we began. But doing so also prompted new questions that are worth considering, and we do so in our conclusion. Is our future going to be more inflationary? Or is this inflation just a one-off event, and are we instead about to return to a low-inflation world? We lay out two possible futures—one of a return to low inflation due to deflationary forces in the global economy, and one of structurally higher inflation going forward. While we see the current moment as mainly a supply-side shock that will dissipate, we argue that inflation will not go back to the extremely low levels we have enjoyed for much of the past thirty years. Rather, we suggest why a structurally higher level of inflation may be in store for us in the future, and if it is, what we should do to prepare for that world. But to get started, let's dive into what inflation is and how we know we are in one.

1

≷

FIVE THINGS THEY DON'T TELL YOU ABOUT INFLATION

The only man I know who behaves sensibly is my tailor; he took my measure anew every time he saw me whilst all the rest went on with their old measurements and expected them to fit me.
—George Bernard Shaw, *Man and Superman*

NUMBER 1: THERE ARE DIFFERENT TYPES OF INFLATION: THE GOOD, THE BAD AND THE UGLY

So let's get started on our journey to understand what inflation is, why it's (often) not what it seems to be, and why our explanations of inflation are limited at best. Let's start with how we would know that we are in the midst of an inflation as opposed to a situation where some particularly noticeable prices (rents, fuel, houses) are going up without affecting everything else. To understand that we first need to define what inflation is.

Inflation is a general and sustained rise in the level of prices on average. But let's dig into what that actually means. You might think that we have inflation when prices are too high. But that begs the question, High in relation to what? Prices are very high in Switzerland, for example, which is a country with very low inflation (1.4 percent in June 2024). To use a common example, in Switzerland a Big Mac costs around $6.00. In Turkey, where inflation hit over 75 percent in May 2024, Big Macs are still much cheaper and cost around $2.60. So which one is expensive?

The key thing to understand here is that inflation is not really about how relatively costly things are, but about how their prices are changing. We talk about *inflation* whenever prices are going up and about *deflation* when prices are going down. If yearly inflation is 10 percent, that means if you paid $1.00 for a coffee last year, this year you'll likely pay $1.10. By focusing on changes, inflation gives us a picture of our purchasing power, which in the case of this cup of coffee, just fell by 10 percent. Similarly, you probably guessed that Big Macs in Switzerland cost more because people get paid higher wages there than in Turkey. But if we suppose that wages remain constant and both countries experience, say, 100 percent inflation, then Swiss and Turkish consumers will face a similar increase in the price of their McDonalds, even if it costs $12.00 for the Swiss and $5.20 for the Turks. Which one hurts more is quite a different question.

In short, what really matters when we talk about inflation is *how much*, *how quickly*, and *how broadly* prices are changing. *How much* focuses upon the magnitude of the change. We may not even notice if prices increase by 1–2 percent from one year to the other, but we'll definitely worry if prices double in a year. We care about *how quickly* inflation increases relative to our wages. In theory at least, if the price of fuel doubles but our wages also double, we would not be quite as alarmed, as this would be, as economists put it, a "nominal" rather than a "real" change. The numbers moved, but the relationship between wages and prices did not. Yet, as we shall discuss shortly, people often confuse nominal and real changes, which makes inflation's real effects different from our subjective perception of them.

However, if speed of change doesn't get you, then the *coverage* might. Inflation is only an inflation, and is only really a problem, when it affects many items that we consume at the same time. Remember, inflation is a rise in the general level of prices on average. The word "average" is important here. For example, if the beef for the burger in Turkey becomes too pricy, consumers can always switch to chicken or lamb. The problem arises when inflation affects all items and you can't substitute out. This is why we care about *how broad* inflation is and why it is best defined as a general upward movement in the level of average prices. Building on this insight, and possibly inspired by Sergio Leone's spaghetti Western movies, the governor of the Bank of Italy (then member of the board of the European Central Bank), Fabio Panetta, has usefully defined three types of inflation: the good, the bad, and the ugly.

Inflation can actually be *good* if it's moderate. Moderately higher prices are generally a sign of a growing economy where wages, in theory at least, rise in line with workers' productivity. In such a world, even if prices increase, wages are catching up, and people can afford the same amount of goods, if not more. For this reason, the goal of most central banks, including the US Federal Reserve and the European Central Bank, is not to lower inflation at all costs, but rather to maintain a stable and positive inflation rate, usually around 2 percent.

Bad inflation stems from negative supply shocks that push prices up and depress the economy. This is what we have faced recently when, for example, COVID-19 shutdowns and the war between Russia and Ukraine sharply reduced the availability of goods and the supply of oil, which spiked both consumer and energy prices. This type of inflation is considered bad because it impacts not just the good itself, oil or gas, but it also bleeds into the prices of other related items, squeezing incomes further. However, inflation is not yet *ugly* as long as prices fall back to normal levels once the shock dissipates, in this case when substitute sources of energy are found or supply chains are diverted.

In theory at least, inflation gets *ugly* when, to use the language of economics, inflation "expectations" get "de-anchored." We will talk about this much more later on, but it basically describes a situation where people keep expecting prices to go up because they have already gone up, and given this expectation, businesses raise their prices in an anticipatory manner, generating inflation in the process. Prices have, as economists say, "lost their anchor." If this happens, economic theory predicts that people will buy items now rather than tomorrow, because they expect prices for such items to cost more tomorrow. They'll also ask for higher wages to cope with these higher expected future prices. In doing so, however, both demand and wages rise, pushing firms to charge higher prices for their limited supply of goods, which is also more costly to them because they have to pay higher wages. And so prices and wages push each other upward in a cycle.

This situation is very difficult to escape. But as we shall see in chapter 4, it is also a very rare event. The inflation experienced in the US and the EU from 2021 to 2024 was not driven by such a "wage-price spiral." Moreover, it seems that especially in the United States, the economy and employment have both grown while interest rates were increased, and yet expectations remained steady. This, as we shall see later on, does not accord with the theory that inflation is caused by the de-anchoring of people's expectations of future price movements. But it does suggest that it is important to know which type of inflation we are facing, since each type suggests very different policy responses. So, how would we know which type we are facing? To understand that we need to see how inflation is measured.

NUMBER 2: HOW INFLATION IS MEASURED

The US Federal Reserve defines inflation as "the increase in the prices of goods and services over time." It reminds us that inflation "cannot be measured by an increase in the cost of one product or service, or even several products or services. Rather inflation is a general increase in the overall price level of the goods and services in the economy." The Fed actually monitors inflation by looking at different "price indexes." Price indexes are statistical constructs that add differently priced items, weight them in relative importance, and benchmark them to some time or price point. The Fed can then "track the index" value over time to give us an overall picture of how that general level of prices is moving. While there are many possible price indexes that the Fed can use, the Federal Open Market Committee (FOMC), the central bank's main governing body, focuses mainly on one of these indexes, the price index for Personal Consumption Expenditures (PCE). The PCE is a measure of the prices of goods and services purchased by consumers in the United States, and it is prepared by the Bureau of Economic Analysis. This is preferred over other indexes because it covers a wide range of spending categories, it is updated more frequently, and according to the Fed, better fits with the central bank's dual mandate to achieve price stability and full employment. Nevertheless, the Fed also monitors the Consumer Price Index (CPI), which is broadly similar to the PCE, but generally records higher inflation rates than the PCE due to the different ways (different formulas, weights, and scope, among other things) in which they are measured.

The data used to construct the CPI index in the United States is collected by the Bureau of Labor Statistics through a monthly survey that measures the prices of a basket of eighty thousand goods and services that represent what Americans buy on a daily basis. This basket includes, among other things, the cost of an apple, the price of gasoline, the fee for cable TV (even if no one has cable anymore), as well as the cost of a doctor's visit. The sample is selected to represent the consumption of urban Americans, which is 93 percent of the US population. Information on prices is collected through online web scraping, surveys, as well as information gathered from retailers via their supermarket scanners.

The Bank of England computes inflation based on the price of a basket of things that people frequently buy, which is regularly updated by the British Office for National Statistics. The basket contains over seven hundred goods, ranging from a loaf of bread, a bus ticket, a new or used car, and a foreign vacation. Inflation is the change in the price of the overall basket, which is called the Consumer Prices Index (CPI). The rate of inflation is based on the comparison between "the cost of the basket—the level of CPI—with what it was a year ago. The change in the price level over the year is the rate of inflation."

The European Central Bank says that inflation "occurs when there is a broad increase in the prices of goods and services, not just of individual items; it means, you can buy less for 1 euro today than you could yesterday." The index used by the European Central Bank is also based on a basket, like the CPI, but it is called the Harmonized Index of Consumer Prices (HICP) because all countries use the same harmonized methodology to make price changes comparable across Germany, France, Italy, and all the other countries that are part of the European monetary union.

And Why Is It Measured Like That?

Now, given all that, you might have seen in the news in 2022 or 2023 that in many countries inflation was "x" percent higher than the previous year. But given all these different ways of calculating inflation, can we be sure that we are really measuring the same things? Indeed, despite such reports, do *all* prices really seem higher to you? You might get a quite different impression chatting to your friends as opposed to reading the website of your national statistical agency regarding how inflation actually affects your life.

You may, for example, use a car very often, while your friend bikes to work, so inflation will look higher to you as gas prices have gone up a lot in the past year. But then you'll recall that your friend is upset that her rent has almost doubled and now she'll need to use what's left of her savings to pay her rent. You, in contrast, own your house with a fixed-rate mortgage. You are an inflation winner because inflation reduces the real value of your debts. If inflation is 10 percent and your mortgage is 5 percent, then the real interest rate you are paying is negative 5 percent. You are in effect paying your loan back in "devalued" dollars or euros, while your renting friend is being squeezed for more money. Inflation experiences therefore differ widely. How then can we build a common measure of inflation given all these differences?

Countries try to capture these different contexts and summarize them into a single index. Such an index should give us a picture that is broad enough to describe the trend of prices in an economy and how they're affecting the consumption of its citizens. To capture this, statisticians and economists think of inflation in terms of "consumption baskets." You put together a basket of goods and services that is representative of the general purchases of the population, rather than any specific individual, and identify their prices. These prices are then collected into a single indicator, the CPI that we mentioned above. This indicator gives us a number for each year, month, or even day. That number represents where prices stand in a country, where the price change of an item—the bit we are interested in measuring—is the ratio of its price at the current time period to its price in a previous time period (multiplied by 100). Inflation is therefore, as we noted already, simply the rate of change in this index.

Also, as we touched on above, when you are measuring and summing the changes of eighty thousand items, not every item in the basket should have the same importance, or "weight," since some items have a bigger impact than others on the overall price level. Let's say that we have the cost of both a hamburger and a package of pasta in the same basket. In the United States, changes in the price of hamburgers will have a higher impact on the CPI than changes in the price of pasta since Americans tend to spend more on hamburgers than pasta. The opposite would likely hold if we were to measure the CPI for Italy. Indexes are therefore never static. As consumption changes, so do the items in the basket. And as our economies change and we consume more services and fewer material goods, for example, so must we pay more attention to services inflation.

Indexes also allow us to break out different discrete measures. The main distinction you may hear made in this regard is between *headline* and *core* inflation. The indexes we have described so far measure headline inflation. However, analysts and central banks often prefer to look at the trend of so-called core inflation, which is headline inflation minus the prices of food and energy. The reason for doing so is that food and energy prices change a lot—in economic jargon, they are highly volatile, as they can change sharply from month to month or year to year, making it harder to discern the underlying inflation trend.

Headline and Core: The "Experience" Problem with Averages and Indexes

This distinction rings hollow for those most affected by inflation. You can average things, but no one lives on an average. If the current inflation is mainly driven by food and fuel costs, excluding them from the index seems a lot like cooking the books to find a lower number, even if doing so makes statistical sense. Ostensibly, headline CPI is used to compare price changes over years, whereas core CPI allows statisticians to better study monthly inflation. But core and headline clearly report different inflation rates (generally due to swings in oil prices), so the incentive to refer to one measure over another is not just due to the desire for better reliability or comparison. Economics is about the optics just as much as in politics. Indeed, paying attention to such distinctions can give us quite different perspectives on how we should think about inflation. Once we compare headline and core inflation in advanced economies, we can test the robustness of some inflation stories we read in the news.

According to one common story, prices are increasing everywhere because people started buying more stuff after the pandemic to make up for lost consumption during the pandemic. This was made possible because governments gave people too much money to spend during the pandemic, but given the breakdown in supply chains, there was nothing to spend the money on. As such, governments "overstimulated the economy" with such pandemic spending, and once the pandemic was over inflation was the inevitable result.

It's a good story, but what this story obscures is that despite a general increase in inflation across many countries, individual countries actually experienced very different types of inflation (good, bad, and ugly) and with different levels of coverage. While in July 2022 headline inflation was around 9 percent in both the United States and the eurozone, core inflation was higher in the United States (6 percent) than in the eurozone (5 percent). In the US, the prices of items other than food and energy explained half of the inflation. In Europe, in contrast, inflation initially derived mostly from energy costs due to the continent's dependence on Russian gas, which it was suddenly short of because of Russia's invasion of Ukraine.

Yet when we look at food inflation in isolation, which is arguably what most people care about, we get quite another story. In December 2022, food price inflation in the United States was 10 percent, in the UK it was 13.3 percent, and in Germany it rose to over 20 percent. Stripping out food from headline inflation clearly has a huge impact on what we are measuring, even if doing so tells us something materially useful about what is causing inflation. Germany, for example, unlike the US, didn't mail out checks to workers, and yet it had higher inflation than the US in that period, driven much more by food and fuel.

Different indexes of inflation also vary in the way they split so-called persistent components from volatile ones. Core inflation excludes food and energy prices due to their seasonal volatility. But other versions of these indexes exclude clothing and travel, which are also subject to changes, due to sales or holiday seasons. The idea behind all these approaches is to get a picture of the "true" trend of inflation. However, despite these efforts, none of these measures display the truth about inflation. Each is selective and subjective, and the predictive power of each measure varies over time. As such, the method used to slice and dice indexes can be a powerful political resource. What really matters with inflation is how broadly consumers and producers feel the change in prices, which is both inherently subjective and yet objectively determined by their position in the income distribution. Bluntly, when you are rich you care less about inflation's effects on your consumption.

Price rises can also be concentrated in a specific sector without affecting others. For example, in early 2022 the United States imposed an import ban on Mexican avocados following death threats (allegedly from members of a Mexican cartel) directed at an American plant safety inspector based in Michoacan, a Mexican state. The ban caused a shortage of avocados, pushing avocado prices up to a twenty-four-year high. While avocado prices spiked, this surge did not affect other products (with the probable exception of guacamole). Despite being styled the "avocado inflation" in much of the media, it was not an actual inflation, as the increase in prices was not sufficiently broad.

As the economic historian Adam Tooze put it, a "true inflation" occurs when "the price index increases and this is attributable to roughly proportional increases across a large number of subcomponents." This is why when people talk about an "asset price inflation" or "house price inflation," they are actually *not* talking about inflation. After all, house prices in the United States grew rapidly in the early 2000s despite the prices of many consumer goods (e.g. televisions) falling in the same period due to globalization's deflationary effects on the price of certain goods. How then should we think about such big-ticket items as housing or health care, which are not in our indexes, or are in there but in a weird way?

NUMBER 3: WHAT MATTERS IS WHAT IS MEASURED

If there is no true measure of inflation because we can construct that measure in different ways, how should we try to deal with it? And given this fact, how should we think about what causes inflation? This matters because if we go "under the hood" of the CPI, we see something important—that the contribution of each component of the basket to the index has become more dispersed over time. In plain English, this means that while in the past the prices of certain components had a tendency to rise and fall together, now they are more likely to move in different directions. This dispersion became particularly high in 2020 and 2021. Given this, it is important to figure out how *broad* an inflation is when the drivers of inflation might actually be concentrated into a few key sectors. For example, in the United States, housing rental costs in 2022 and transportation costs in 2023 were particularly strong drivers of inflation. Meanwhile in the EU, as noted above, almost half the index was reducible to energy cost increases.

Another element that matters but is seldom mentioned is that because inflation indexes focus on *changes* over time, the starting point we choose for an index clearly matters a lot. This became clear in 2021, when monthly inflation in the United States seemed particularly high. An analysis from the Roosevelt Institute warned that inflation numbers in April 2021 would look particularly high as a result of the *base effect* (on a 12-month change) of inflation measurement. This effect simply means that if we compare April 2020 with April 2021, inflation in April 2021 will look very high, but only because in 2020 the pandemic caused prices to fall abnormally. So inflation in 2021 will not reflect really higher prices in 2021, but rather falling prices in 2020.

Furthermore, when looking at the CPI we should take into account what it excludes. The baskets of goods and services that inflation indexes are built on may not always be representative of people's consumption over time. COVID-19 provides a clear example of how this happened. The pandemic changed people's lives, and their spending behaviors followed those life changes. Many folks had to work from home and didn't take public transport or drive so much. The price of a flight suddenly became irrelevant because most people were discouraged from traveling. The same goes for restaurant meals. Should we care if the price of a flight or a restaurant meal has increased or decreased if no one is buying it anyway? Indeed, we may want inflation indexes to weight more heavily the price of goods that weren't significant pre-pandemic, such as protective face masks or gym equipment. As a result of such concerns, economists and statisticians have begun to wonder if we should rethink inflation measurements. For instance, Harvard economist Alberto Cavallo has used data from credit and debit card transactions in the United States during the pandemic to propose an update of the official baskets. He indeed found that during the pandemic people spent more on groceries and less on transportation, restaurants, and hotels.

This problem is not new. It is just another version of the perennial dilemma of how to accurately weight prices. Basically, it all boils down to this—should the basket be held constant, or should it change to adapt to new patterns of consumption? If we keep it constant, it is easier to compare its values over time. Such an index is helpful insofar as it allows us to understand whether today's inflation is really going to be as bad as, for example, that of the 1970s. But our consumption today is also very different from that of the 1970s. Many products, such as smartphones, didn't even exist back then. So changing the weights in the index seems a reasonable idea. Indeed, some central banks do. However, once we do that, it's reasonable to ask if we're comparing apples to oranges. Can we really compare this inflation with that of the 1970s if we update the weights all the time and put very different items in the basket?

This may seem pedantic, but such factors do matter, a lot. Germany is a compelling example. During COVID-19, as lockdown measures were put in place, spending on transport crashed, causing a fall in transport prices. Other prices, such as the prices of food and beverages or the prices for furniture, went up. Yet the weight given to transport services in German inflation indexes adjusted slowly (more slowly than in the UK, for instance). The reason is that the weights of spending categories are updated based on surveys that are not taken frequently, since consumer habits are slow to change. COVID-19 was clearly an exception that quickly and profoundly changed the way people consume. All of a sudden, everyone stopped traveling and started buying groceries. However, the weights in official statistics did not adjust that quickly. As a result, while food prices were going up, forcing many to tighten their belt, official inflation figures were telling us that inflation was not that bad, because while food prices were rising, transport prices were falling. What these statistics clearly didn't take into account is that during COVID-19 no one was buying transport services. (We know this from research that used credit card data to show how consumption patterns changed with the pandemic.) So yes, inflation was worse than reported. German inflation was largely underestimated, simply because a category where no one was spending much anymore was still valued as a frequent spending category as much as the others. When in September 2021 the basket was fully adjusted, prices in travel-related services were given lower weight, because there was less spending in this category. As a result, inflation in Germany accelerated sharply and moved from 3.4 to 4.1 percent in one month.

Another example comes from living in a more digitized world, where some products we consume, such as internet searches or access to digital platforms are notionally free. They are not, of course, actually free insofar as we pay for them through being exposed to advertising, or by being the product in the case of, for example, Facebook data. But they are definitely consumed. How should we think about inflation in such items? And if they constitute a bigger slice of our consumption, how should we reflect that in our inflation weights and measures? It's far from clear how to do this. In short, what matters is not just what gets measured, but how it's updated; and what is missing from the basket in the first place is as important as what is in it. This is nowhere clearer than with housing.

NUMBER 4: WHY IS IT SO HARD TO MEASURE HOUSE PRICE INFLATION?

Questions about what's missing in inflation indexes predate the current moment. The biggest question, both before the current inflation and especially now, revolves around housing. Specifically, why are house prices not included in inflation measures, even though the price of a house is probably the biggest cost anyone faces, if not the most expensive thing a person will buy in their lifetime, and the item most likely to respond to interest rates? Moreover, given that house prices have been on a tear for a generation across many markets, and play a significant role in creating wealth, surely it must figure into our thinking about inflation in some way? For example, thinking in terms of "weights" again, a change in the cost of our housing rather obviously affects our consumption of other items way more than a change in the price of a loaf of bread ever will. So if the whole point of measuring inflation is to capture the impact of changes in prices on our standard of living, why aren't house prices included?

Well, the truth is they are included, but in a weird way. For example, in the US, the CPI includes so-called "sheltering costs." These are measured by rental costs, and more complicated-sounding measures such as "potential rents," and "owners' equivalent rent." The costs of shelter represent one third of the CPI basket (and around 15 percent of the PCE), which is 40 percent of core CPI. But to see how complex putting housing into an inflation index can get, put yourself in the shoes of a statistician who has to come up with a measure of how house prices impact overall inflation.

Do You Eat Houses?

You might start with rents and collect data on how much rent each tenant pays to the landlord. This is a fairly good measure, but it excludes the costs faced by owners rather than renters. You could check how much a house has gone up in value, but that is a measure of an owner's wealth, not of their consumption. Houses, you see, are assets. Buying one is seen as an investment. Assets are, by definition, not consumption goods, and as the name of the *Consumer* Price Index (CPI) suggests, this index measures the price of *consumption*. You don't eat houses. Even if you have a mortgage, you don't "consume" a house on a monthly or yearly basis, as you do with bread or vacations. With a mortgage, your monthly payment pays down a debt and generates equity, which adds to wealth. Sadly, there is no equity generated in eating a sandwich. Seen from this perspective, a rent payment is pure consumption, but a mortgage payment is not. But we still want to include housing in the CPI because houses provide a service—shelter—that has a cost, and if that cost changes, so does consumption. Annoying, isn't it? So how would we estimate that cost?

In the United States, the Bureau of Labor Statistics came up with a measure to address this issue, which is called owners' equivalent rent. Owners' equivalent (and potential) rents are measures designed to get around the problem that unlike a loaf of bread, a house is not obviously consumed even if its price is rising, and we pay more for it. To create this measure, statisticians compute the potential cost you, a homeowner, would face if you were renting an equivalent house to your actual house on the grounds that such spending would be consumption, and therefore should be included in the index of consumption.

However, finding equivalent accommodation to a single-family home with a mortgage is not easy. Rental and owner-occupied units tend to be very different from single-family homes. Some family homes are very large, and it is difficult to find a comparable place that is available to rent. In addition, rental units are more frequently found in city centers while owned houses are usually spread among the suburbs. This is a problem because rental costs strongly depend on their location and are often negatively related to equivalent mortgage costs. That is, rents in city centers may be high while they are cheaper in the suburbs, while in contrast, for owner-occupied housing, the reverse is often true. So while the owners' equivalent rent is included in the official CPI, its estimate has important limitations, which is why the CPI includes a proxy measure of shelter rather than house prices per se.

A final reason why housing is not (directly) included in the index is historical and once again relates to the issue of updating weights and baskets over time. Governments first started collecting information on inflation at the beginning of the twentieth century. Back then the (male) population had just acquired voting rights, access to education, and the ability to organize in trade unions and go on strike. Governments of the day were interested in knowing whether the wages workers were earning were sufficient for workers to afford food, because hunger can push people to organize unions and strike. Consequently, the first inflation measures were based solely on immediate consumption goods. Only later did they expand to include a wider range of goods and, more recently, services.

However, between 1953 and 1983, the US's CPI index *did include* house prices. In 1983 house prices were removed and replaced with the owners' equivalent rent estimates because house prices represented an investment rather than consumption. Another reason (allegedly) for this revision was that having actual house prices in the CPI was pushing up the rate of inflation and making pensions and other benefits indexed to inflation too expensive. Removing house prices from the official index was an effective way to bring the CPI down, and with that the inflation-

FIGURE 1.1:

CPI SHELTER, 1970–2024

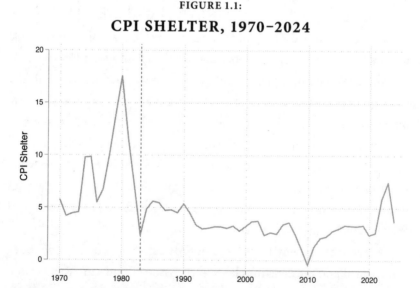

Source: Authors' elaboration based on US Bureau of Economic Analysis retrieved from FRED, Federal Reserve Bank of St. Louis data and inspired by the Council of Economic Advisers. Note: The chart plots the yearly percentage change in the Consumer Price Index for All Urban Consumers: Shelter in the US City Average, 1982–1984=100.

pegged burden of these social benefits. Consequently, the removal of house prices resulted in a decline of shelter inflation in the CPI, as shown in Figure 1.1.

Removing house prices from the CPI created a gap between the trend of house price growth, which was becoming explosive, at least in some areas, and the Consumer Price Index. This has obvious implications for how people experience inflation. Even if housing is a huge part of expenditures, and even if prices in that sector rise precipitously, this won't fully appear in official statistics on inflation. This is actually what happened at the eve of the global financial crisis of 2007–8. In 2005, while house prices were increasing at around 15 percent per year, urban consumers' inflation was measured at about 3 percent. Given public disquiet over this issue, central banks are trying to take so-called house-price inflation increasingly into account. But changes thus far seem to have unclear, if not troubling, implications.

What Happens When Housing Is Included?

In 2021, the government of New Zealand changed the central bank's mandate, forcing it to take house prices into account when making monetary policy decisions. According to the finance minister at the time, the reform aimed to further the government's effort to "support more sustainable house prices." However, the change in the mandate seemed to have almost no effect on either policy or house prices. After the reform, the governor of the Reserve Bank of New Zealand, the country's central bank, stressed that despite this change in mandate the bank's inflation targets remain unchanged. Between August 2020 and March 2022, average house prices in New Zealand increased by 41 percent.

Including housing in inflation indexes is still a matter of discussion among experts today. Following a major revision of its strategy, the European Central Bank decided that it should include the costs of homeownership in its inflation index. However, as of the time of writing, the ECB is still studying how to do so. The inflation index currently used by the ECB only includes the cost of actual rents (with a very low weight of 6.5 percent). Nor does the ECB impute the rent of homeowners through a figure like the US Federal Reserve's owners' equivalent rent. Were the ECB to include a similar estimate of owner-occupied housing cost, it has been estimated that measured inflation would be 0.3 percent higher.

In the UK, while inflation data includes the cost of home ownership, the Bank of England sets its target based on a different CPI index that does not include such costs. Meanwhile, back in New Zealand, house prices can rocket ever upward and yet the central bank sees no reason to change its inflation target once housing has been added to the index. Little wonder then that our own experience of inflation and the various measures offered of it can diverge so widely, and why, as we shall see shortly, what is measured (or not) offers a great resource for shifting the costs of inflation from one group in society onto another. Why, for example, tame housing prices by raising rates, which in theory would cool the housing market, if the index barely moves when house prices are included?

In sum, we often hear about house price inflation, but it is important to remember that there is no such thing. It's just the price of one item, an item that purchasers consider an asset, that has been bid up in price due to limited supply and the investment upside it offers. It can be an inflation driver and probably should be seen as one. But when measured by owners' equivalent rent and similar proxies, historically at least, it doesn't seem to make much of a difference. That point leads us to our last one in this chapter: Why you should care about all this?

NUMBER 5: WHY YOU SHOULD CARE ABOUT ALL THIS ARCANE STATISTICAL STUFF

This debate over "what's in, what's out" is no mere technical quarrel. Rather, it has important implications for who wins and who loses from

inflation. Some implications are direct, such as the inflation adjustment of
tax brackets. Every year, the IRS adjusts tax brackets to account for inflation since (nominal) wages go up with rising prices. In the United States,
until 2017, these brackets were adjusted using the standard CPI. However,
the CPI overestimated inflation as it didn't consider how quickly people
would substitute goods if prices rose.

In response to this problem, in 2017 the US Congress decided to use
a different index to adjust tax brackets. This index, called "chained" CPI,
was designed to take this substitution effect into account by capturing how
expenditures change when relative prices change and by adjusting the basket more quickly than CPI. Because a chained CPI tends to produce numbers lower than the standard CPI, this change had immediate consequences
for how people were taxed in the United States. As Michael Ng and David
Wessel from the Brookings Institution summarize, "Because the chained
CPI climbs more slowly than the primary CPI, the tax brackets will increase
by smaller amounts each year. More people will be pushed into higher tax
brackets than they would have under the old law." So taxpayers may end up
with a lower underlying rate of inflation, and yet end up paying more taxes.

Other aspects of inflation measurement can be less direct but just
as important in determining winners and losers. Suppose, for example,
that a certain weighting scheme suggests the surge in prices we see today
is very similar to the inflation of the 1970s. Given such a conclusion,
government officials may think that we should act in the same way their
predecessors did and raise interest rates to slow down the economy to the
point that it produces mass unemployment. In contrast, another type of
index that updated items more frequently might, like the chained CPI,
produce a lower number, which might encourage a less drastic approach
to inflation control. In the former scenario, wage earners lose as unemployment increases while renters and savers gain. In the latter case, the
redistribution from one group to the other is lessened.

These implications are even clearer when we think of the role of central banks in the economy. Most central banks are today "independent"

from elected officials insofar as they have a very specific legal mandate to preserve "price stability," the general definition of which is an inflation rate of around 2 percent. The way inflation is measured is crucial to assessing how to carry out that mandate, or whether the mandate has been fulfilled. Changing the reference index of inflation, or the weights inside the basket on which an index is built, can strongly influence the policy decisions of the central bank.

Think about how the Federal Reserve sees inflation. The Fed bases its decisions on the Personal Consumption Expenditures (PCE) index of inflation, which diverges from the CPI in ways we discussed earlier in this chapter. For instance, shelter inflation has more weight in the CPI than in the PCE, which means that if housing costs go up in the United States, the PCE will not grow as much as the CPI. The opposite happens if health care prices increase. Both the PCE and the CPI include consumers' out-of-pocket expenses, but the PCE also includes the costs covered by the employer or the government (through Medicare and Medicaid). Given such distributional shifts, the switch from one index of inflation to another is no mere technical issue. The example of the UK switching indexes in 2003 allows us to see what is at stake when we do so.

In 2003, the UK's chancellor of the exchequer, Gordon Brown, instructed the Bank of England to replace its Retail Price Index, the RPIX, with the Harmonized Index of Consumer Prices, the HICP, the commonly used index of the eurozone, which Brown considered more reliable and precise. The HICP also represented a political step toward closer integration with other European countries in view of the then potential accession of the UK to the eurozone. The main difference between the two indexes was that HICP did not include mortgage interest costs while the RPIX did, reflecting the fact that many more people in the UK own their homes than they do in some parts of continental Europe. Applying HICP to the UK would lower headline inflation rates, and indeed, the RPIX indicated higher inflation than the HICP (of around 0.8 percentage points), and the gap widened when house prices boomed. This was the case in November 2003, one month before Brown confirmed the switch of index. That month the RPIX was 1.2 percent higher than the HICP. As a consequence of the shift, the new HICP measure of inflation would provide a much more pleasing picture of the economy in which inflation was lower. And yet despite this upcoming change, the Bank of England's inflation target remained set at 2.5 percent. In other words, the target just got easier to hit.

This index switch also augured some important distributional implications. Since inflation was lower under the HICP, the Bank of England would need to lower interest rates to reach its target. Debtors would benefit from the change, as lower interest rates meant a lighter burden on the repayment of their debts, and the housing market, so integral to the UK economy, would continue to boom as mortgage costs fell. The opposite would hold for creditors, however, who would profit less from the interest rates on their loans.

Watching all this from the side were the financial markets, who reasoned that if the HICP estimated a lower rate of inflation, the Bank of England would then lower interest rates, making borrowing cheaper, and thereby sending house prices further upward. The markets bet that rates would fall but lost a ton of money doing so. When the bank officially changed its measure in June 2004, it surprised the markets by actually increasing the Official Bank Rate by 0.25 basis points to 4.75 percent. Basically, because the City was expecting this index-induced cut to happen, the Bank of England raised rates to offset the bet that was being placed.

Today, we witness similar considerations surrounding the future inclusion of housing in the European Central Bank's inflation index. Experts believe that including house prices will push the HICP inflation index up and prices in the eurozone will look higher than they used to. This may provide ammunition to the more "frugal" (inflation-averse) Northern European central bankers to adopt more hawkish stances, which generally translates into higher interest rates and a tighter monetary stance that benefits creditors over debtors.

In sum, how you count inflation counts toward how you see inflation. How you see inflation determines what you think you should do about it, and ultimately, who pays for it. Inflation is redistribution. That bit they might tell you. But how you measure inflation is redistribution too. That bit they don't tell you. As Mrs. Thatcher famously put it, she didn't lie. She was simply "economical with the truth."

2

═══

WHY DO WE DO WHAT WE DO WHEN WE HAVE INFLATION?

History is the same thing over and over again.
—Woody Allen

IF YOU ONLY HAVE A HAMMER: INTEREST RATES AND INFLATION

Why do central banks use interest rates to control inflation? Higher interest rates increase the cost of borrowing in the banking sector, making banks, in turn, more reluctant to lend money to everyone else. In theory, as banks make lending scarce, firms will cut back on investment and expansion, which in turn leads firms to reduce production, their number of employees, or both. As borrowing becomes more costly for individuals, consumption falls. So no matter whether you think inflation comes from higher price margins, or overstimulation of spending, or wage pressures, all of which we discuss in detail below, higher rates are the tool most often used to cool down an overheated economy. This time around was no exception.

In 2021, central banks responded to inflation with what we call "monetary austerity": very aggressive interest rates hikes. Figure 2.1 shows that interest rates in the US, eurozone, and the UK had hovered around zero since 2008, when the financial crisis of 2007–8 required expansionary

monetary interventions such as negative rates and fancy-sounding policies like quantitative easing (basically, buying bonds from the public and
hoping that the cash the public gets in return will find its way into the
economy) to revive the economy. Then, with the onset of the pandemic,
rates jumped up. The chart also makes it clear that while central banks'
reactions this time around have been dramatic, this set of rate hikes has
actually been quite muted when compared to those of the 1970s. To give
a sense of relative magnitudes, in the late 1970s and early '80s policy rates
peaked at 22 percent in the US in December 1980 and 17 percent in the
UK for most of 1980. In 2023, the interest rate set by the Federal Reserve
and the Bank of England was 5.25 percent, whereas that of the European
Central Bank was 4 percent.

FIGURE 2.1:

CENTRAL BANK INTEREST RATES
IN THE UNITED STATES, EUROZONE,
AND UNITED KINGDOM

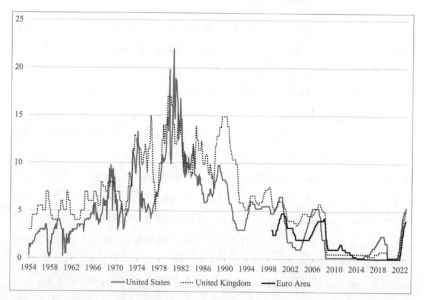

Source: Authors' elaboration on BIS data.

WHY DO WE DO WHAT WE DO WHEN WE HAVE INFLATION?   39

Since interest rates are the go-to tool to fight inflation, the obvious question we should ask is whether they work or not. To the extent that there is a debate in the mainstream, it generally focuses on *how much* of an interest rate increase is effective rather than the overall effectiveness of raising rates. In other words, the question is not really about whether the medicine works but how high the dosage should be. Raising rates too far risks creating a recession that is worse than the inflation it's trying to cure.

There are, however, other less mainstream views that see interest rates as the proverbial hammer. We use interest rates to regulate the economy, not because they are the ideal controls, but because in the 1980s we gave up on regulating the level of prices through fiscal means such as price controls, credit limits, and other such devices. Indeed, most industrialized economies really backpedaled on the use of fiscal policies in the 1990s because they were seen as inherently inflationary, as we'll discuss below. All that's left is the central bank and its monetary policy tools, of which there are mainly two.

Central banks can buy and sell assets to push cash into the economy, known as quantitative easing, which you do when you have a deflation (in Europe from 2011 to 2016, for example). And they can (crudely) raise the price of borrowing money—interest rates—via so-called open market operations, or paying interest on reserves to commercial banks, which you do when you have an inflation. In short, if all you have is a hammer, everything looks like a nail.

Unfortunately, everything that may seem nail-like may not in fact respond like a nail when it is whacked with the proverbial interest rate hammer. Economists quite opposed in their inflation logics, such as Larry Summers and Paul Krugman, for example, expected rate hikes in the United States to increase unemployment and slow the economy. Yet neither happened. Indeed, despite aggressive rate increases, the US economy boomed, and employment increased rather than decreased.

Rather than view these occurrences as disconfirming information and accept that there is something wrong with the underlying theory here, the mainstream response is to praise the Fed for achieving an immaculate disinflation. That is, hitting a supposed sweet spot, where we got a soft landing—disinflation without unemployment—*because of interest rate rises*. But if that is correct, then the trade-off between unemployment and inflation that we expect to exploit by tweaking rates is notable only by its absence. Why then do we think that rates are and should be the universal hammer? To answer that we need to go back, as we shall do a few times in this book, to the chief historical case for why interest rates are the go-to tool to bring down inflation: the inflationary experience of the 1970s and '80s.

THAT '70s SHOW: ACT 1—THE DISTRIBUTIONAL POLITICS OF VOLCKER'S HAMMER

In 1970, the United States faced a mild recession that the then Fed chairman, Arthur Burns, decided to fight with *lower* interest rates despite inflationary pressures building in the economy. Then, the common economic wisdom was that the US was generating inflation because of the combination of high government spending on social policy, the costs of the war in Vietnam, and the super-tight labor markets that resulted from both policies. That analysis also suggested that unemployment was a greater economic threat than inflation, and so the Fed decided to trade off a little less unemployment for a little more inflation by cutting rather than raising rates.

Burns believed that monetary policy could do very little to affect inflation anyway. At the time, both labor unions and large corporations were strong enough to push for wage and price rises regardless of the central bank's policy stance. Moreover, the Fed's expansionary monetary policy was aligned with the Nixon administration's plan to increase public spending. As Burns later admitted in a lecture titled "The Anguish of Central Banking," the "Federal Reserve was itself caught up in the philosophic and political current that were transforming American life and culture," preventing it from fighting inflation by, as he saw it later, restricting the growth of money supply.

Given this set of policy goals, the Fed relaxed its monetary stance despite rising inflation. In the first two years of the decade inflation fell slightly, then it rapidly accelerated for another two years. Inflation then fell for two years before accelerating further. And that's when President Carter, now in charge after Nixon resigned and his replacement Gerald Ford lost the 1976 election, turned to a banker named Paul Volcker to run the Fed. Volcker became chairman of the Fed in August 1979 and after a short delay began to rapidly raise rates from 10 percent in January 1979 to 19 percent in June 1981. Here's the key bit. Under his chairmanship inflation dropped from 13 percent in 1979 to around 4 percent in 1982. This is almost universally attributed to Volcker's insistence on driving rates up in order to drive employment down. That is the key lesson we take away from the 1970s. And driving up rates certainly seemed to drive down employment. Unemployment grew from 5.6 percent in 1979 to 10.8 percent at the end of 1982. Concomitantly, firms went bust in large numbers and the economy slowed considerably. The obvious question remains: Was the pain worth the cost?

Taken on its own terms raising rates may have been beneficial if the only policy goal was to tame inflation. But in reality there is never only one goal, and the interest rate hammer affects different constituencies, and even different countries, in a variety of ways. Volcker's hammer proved especially deadly for low-income individuals, as not only were their job prospects destroyed, they now faced higher rates of interest on their mortgages and loans. Unsurprisingly, the early 1980s recession spurred protests against the Fed. For all the insistence by the Fed (and other central banks then and today) that they "don't do" distributional politics, the Fed's monetary tightening brought about an important distributional shift. It rewarded lenders and punished borrowers, especially poor borrowers who already pay more for their credit and who are more likely to be made unemployed in a slowdown.

Moreover, by deliberately creating unemployment, the Fed lowered the bargaining power of workers and trade unions, which as we show later harmed long-term wage growth. It also made public debt more costly, pushing governments to moderate their social spending on such things as welfare expenditures and unemployment benefits. Social spending played a particularly important role in the 1970s, when many Western economies expanded their welfare states to compensate for these interest-rate induced shocks. Based on these considerations, Adam Tooze acidly observed that the reaction of the Fed and other central banks in Western economies in the 1970s to inflation effectively "delivered for the constituency of savers, business owners, and investors—none of whom liked inflation—as well as a swath of conservative political opinion that wanted stability restored." Central banks thus became "the extension of conservative politics by technocratic and nondemocratic means." In short, if you are supposed to be the neutral referee, and the partisan folks in the stadium figure that the cards are loaded against the visiting team, you may well influence who wins the game. But the costs of doing so will last long beyond game day, as we show next.

COLLATERAL DAMAGE: S&LS, LATIN AMERICANS, AND LONG-TERM GROWTH

Volcker's hammer actually claimed many more victims than is generally acknowledged. Domestically, the entire US savings and loan (S&L) sector effectively went bankrupt as a result of these rate hikes. S&Ls were financial institutions that were quite different from banks. Their specialization was to collect short-term savings deposits and then to issue long-term mortgages with those pooled deposits. The problem they faced was that the interest rate they could pay to their depositors was capped by a 1930s federal law known as Regulation Q. When the Fed increased interest rates past the Q rate, S&L depositors shifted their cash out of these institutions into more profitable destinations. Many S&Ls became insolvent, bankrupting savers while making mortgages more expensive and less available.

Internationally, given the global role of the dollar, Volcker's hammer also had massive negative repercussions abroad. Emerging markets such as Mexico, and Brazil and Argentina held huge loans denominated in dollars. They had been encouraged to borrow in dollars by US banks keen to recycle so-called petrodollars that they earned as a windfall when OPEC raised oil prices in 1973. Given an inflation rate of 9 percent in 1975, if you took out a loan at 5 percent the real rate on the loan was minus 4 percent. In such an environment, countries were being paid to borrow by the banks, and so they did, mightily.

And then Volcker's hammer descended. Raising rates in the United States made the dollar more attractive, because lending in dollars would yield higher returns, which meant that the value of the dollar increased against other currencies. Mexicans, Brazilians, and Argentines now needed to exchange much more of their local currency to repay the same amount of dollars. In August 1982, Mexico threatened to default, which would likely have blown up the US banks that lent them the money in the first place. Such an outcome—that US lenders might actually have to book their losses—could not be countenanced. Support packages funded by the IMF and the Fed prevented the default, on the condition that US banks would also extend additional loans to Mexico. But Mexico was not alone in this predicament, and soon the problem spread to Argentina and Brazil. The result was a debt crisis, a lost decade of growth for all of Latin America, and a pile of debt now so large that Latin America can never conceivably pay it back. Yes, US domestic inflation was tamed, possibly by raising rates, but at what price?

Furthermore, far from being a short and sharp shock that causes no long-term damage—a kind of emetic curative for the inflation hangover—monetary austerity actually leaves scars that take a very long time to heal. A recent study by the Federal Reserve of San Francisco of seventeen rich economies over the period 1900–2015 showed that higher interest rates slow the economy for much longer than has been commonly recognized. Economists tend to think that the impact of monetary policy is short-lived because "in the long run money is neutral." That is, dumping money into an economy can change the economy, but only for a very short period, after which it reverts to its long-term trend rate of growth, which is determined by the "fundamentals" of the economy. To the contrary, Fed researchers showed that a 1 percent increase in interest rates by the central bank lowers output by *5 percent*, even after twelve years, compared to what output would otherwise have been had the central bank left interest rates unchanged.

The study goes further and decomposes output to see why it falls. The authors argue that the drop is driven by sharp falls in capital investment and the knock-on effect of this on productivity. This suggests that by tightening money, central banks successfully manage to put a brake on investment. However, they do so not via unemployment, which happens more as a side effect, but by reducing investment, which slows long-term productivity growth. Cutting rates later provides no offset to these losses.

Given all this, why did central banks in 2021 so eagerly pursue monetary austerity? Well, to be fair, they actually hesitated for some months precisely because of these concerns. (They do read their own research output.) The crucial question was how long the inflation was going to last. If inflation was here to stay, then monetary tightening may be seen as the necessary medicine. Otherwise, central banks could have just waited for prices to wane. But if they had waited, if they had done nothing and inflation had accelerated, then they would have failed in their statutory mission. Given this, the urge to use the hammer rather than stay the blow was very strong indeed. So, to return to the opening question: Are we really sure that interest rates actually cool inflationary pressures, or do we just use them because the only thing we have is a hammer, and the temptation to use it is overwhelming? The answer seems to be that we know there is more to life than the hammer, but we are going to use it anyway.

For example, Isabel Schnabel, a member of the executive board of the

European Central Bank, has identified two key sources of uncertainty that prevent us from making a definitive judgment about the relationship between rates and inflation. First, economists at the ECB admit that they are not really sure about the effectiveness of rate hikes. The ECB has estimated the impact of its 2021 tightening up until 2025, what the central bank calls its medium-term effect. Using three different macroeconomic models, it reached the conclusion that the impact of its policy ranged between 0.9 and 3.9 percentage points. That is the equivalent of saying that, according to the model, monetary austerity could either have almost no effect on inflation or completely erase it.

Second, even if higher rates work, discounting their rather nasty side effects, we might expect higher inflation in the future coming from factors that are outside the central bank's control. Extreme weather linked to climate change will impact crops, likely keeping food prices high. Greater geopolitical conflict stemming from an unraveling of existing global trade agreements and demographic changes that will permanently tighten labor markets may also raise the rate of inflation going forward, a point we return to in the conclusion. In such a world, any monetary policy that uses interest rates as the go-to hammer of inflation is sure to miss many of its targets. After all, why would making the price of borrowing money more expensive do anything to address expensive intermediate inputs in global supply chains coming from foreign countries or the cost of imported food? Given this, are there any alternatives to interest rate hikes that should be considered? There are. And one in particular makes most economists foam at the mouth. Price controls.

THE POLICY THAT DARE NOT SPEAK ITS NAME: PRICE CONTROLS

Price controls are a straightforward way of containing inflation. For example, Nazi Germany had surprisingly low inflation during the Second World War because of price controls. If shopkeepers raised prices above those dictated by the Nazis, they could be shot. While perhaps extreme, this is a rather clear example of the principle underlying the policy. If you don't want prices to go up, simply forbid firms from increasing their prices and sanction them if they do so. Countries routinely do this during wartime. Keynes famously wrote a pamphlet called "How to Pay for the War" that highlighted the use of such controls. The US also used price controls extensively during the Second World War. But what about in periods that are less extreme? Are price controls a good policy in more normal times?

Economists tend to be extraordinarily skeptical about the effectiveness of price controls. They worry that capping prices can result in shortages, as firms become either unwilling or unable to produce the goods that are needed for a price that is lower than what they would charge or what they would cost to produce. If prices are capped below the marginal cost of production, firms will either cease production or find an alternative way of selling their products, encouraging black markets. If that happens, controls become self-defeating.

Another reason economists generally think that price controls will fail is a core belief of economics that markets are better at collecting information on consumers' preferences than the government. In theory, in a free-market economy, at least under "perfect competition," firms have to sell at the point between the price they would like to charge to profit from their product and the price that people are willing to pay to get that product. If a company tries to charge a price that is too high, people will not buy it and the firm will fail. Competitors can see this mispricing and reduce their prices to a point where they capture the sales of the failed firm, and the market, in the jargon, clears. Governments, instead, have to guess what the right price is. If they apply a price ceiling, there is no competitor out there able to spot that mistake and take that market share as feedback. As such, the risk is that when the government sets a price that is too low, consumers rush to buy that good and buy more than they would normally do, and as a result, we're left with a shortage of goods.

The situation is different, however, when we move away from a scenario with perfect competition among firms to one that is closer to a monopoly or an oligopoly situation, where a few, or even a single firm sells a specific product or service. This is the case in many sectors of rich economies, especially the United States, where there are just a few companies that dominate markets, such as the airline and grocery sectors. In such a world, firms with "market power"—the ability to set prices with less fear of competition—can already price above marginal cost simply because there is nowhere else to get the same good. In these instances, it is not only easier to deploy controls as the number of firms to be policed is smaller, they can work better insofar as the controlled price is less likely to lead to a shortage of the good in question if the firm already has higher than normal profit margins. This is why the temptation to deploy controls in certain markets is always there, and it sometimes, at least in wartime, works.

THAT '70s SHOW: ACT 2—NIXON EDITION

There are also historical reasons for why policymakers are careful about price controls. Similar to how our understanding of interest rates and inflation stems from Volcker's hammer, so our understanding of the utility of price controls stems from a particular reading of the events of the 1970s. President Nixon's attempt to use price controls to control inflation in the early '70s is often considered the crucial case for why price controls do not work and should never be used. They were tried. They failed. Period. But is the story really that clear-cut?

In 1971, President Nixon imposed price controls, announcing in a televised speech to the whole nation that he was "ordering a freeze on all prices and wages throughout the United States." This decision followed a period of persistently high unemployment and inflation that did not react to the Fed's (slightly) tighter monetary policy in that period, pushing the president to look for alternative solutions.

After the enactment of controls in 1971, inflation initially fell to 3.2

percent in 1972. However, it spiked again in 1974, when inflation reached 11 percent. In the same year, the Watergate scandal broke, which culminated in Nixon's resignation. The president failed, and price controls were considered to have failed alongside him. But when we look more closely at these events, history is a bit more forgiving than it first appears. Moreover, when we look closely at Nixon's price controls, it is really difficult to conclusively call them a failure.

Nixon's price control policy was divided into three phases. The first phase, which began in August 1971, was a general freeze on wages and prices alongside a 10 percent surcharge on imports. In a much more union-centered economy, with collective bargaining agreements that spanned whole industries, the administration was hoping that by imposing ceilings on wages and prices the cyclical pay rounds that were being negotiated would be revised downward. The import surcharge likewise aimed at avoiding inflation coming through imports. If you make imports more expensive, people buy fewer of them, therefore easing inflationary pressures through that channel.

In phase two, which began in October 1971, the administration moved away from a freeze and mandated that pay rises could be no larger than 5 percent and should tend toward an average of 3 percent. While this policy was combined with a limit on profit margins, the focus remained on wages, which were easier to control than profits because they are more transparent. The second phase also saw the establishment of a price commission, which was given a free hand in price setting, and a pay board to adjudicate fair wage increases. In 1972, headline inflation dropped, hovering around 2 and 3 percent, while core inflation fell to 1.8 percent. Nixon cheered his policy as "just right." In January 1973 the controls entered phase three, and that's when it all went wrong.

In phase three the regime became semivoluntary. That is, what were previously legally binding price controls became voluntary "guidelines" to orient firms and unions going forward. The assumption was that because the controls had taken core inflation down, the government could shift to a voluntary regime and get the same result. In short, businesses could go back to setting their own prices. And given that chance they decided to make up for all the profits and wages they had forgone in the prior two years and hiked prices well beyond the guideposts. Inflation came roaring back and settled much higher than before. For example, in the first half of 1973, meat prices grew at an annualized rate of 30.4 percent, which forced the government to reintroduce price caps on the prices of lamb, beef, and pork. But the damage was done, as was the credibility of price controls as a tool to fight inflation.

With hindsight, one could argue that the mistake Nixon made was to declare victory too early. Compounding this policy error were other factors that made the end of controls even worse. Instead of tightening monetary policy to support price controls, the Federal Reserve injected more money into the economy. The money stock (M2) shot up to 10.8 percent per annum during the period of mandatory controls, which gave consumers more money to spend than there were price-capped items to purchase. On top of this, the Arab-Israeli War of 1973 caused oil prices to rise 300 percent. As a result of this combination of missteps and supply shocks, by the time Nixon resigned wholesale prices were growing at an annual rate of 44 percent while unemployment sat at 7.6 percent. Perhaps, then, it is more reasonable to say that policy incoherence was mistaken for policy failure.

DID ANYONE TRY CONTROLS THIS TIME AROUND?

Perhaps you will be surprised to hear this, but yes, there were quite a few attempts. Three stand out: Hungary, Spain, and Scotland. The two EU economies that put price controls in place, Hungary and Spain, are today among the worst and best inflation performers in Europe respectively. Hungary was hit particularly hard by the 2022 inflation shock when its core inflation surpassed 17 percent in July 2022, the highest level recorded in the country in twenty-five years. In response, Prime Minister Viktor Orban imposed price caps on food, fuel, and energy bills.

FIGURE 2.2:

ANNUAL INFLATION RATE (%)
IN EUROPE IN JULY 2023

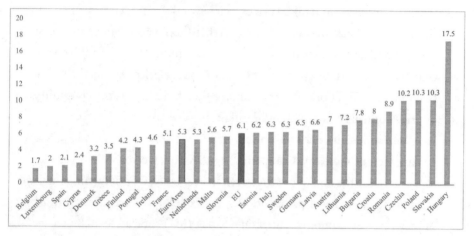

Source: Authors' elaboration based on Eurostat data.

President Orban's price controls proved a failure, however, and the government had to phase them out as they produced exactly the shortages that economists warn about. While Hungarian shoppers appreciated the lower prices, supermarkets started limiting purchases, forcing customers to shop in multiple stores each day to fill in their grocery list.

In Spain, in contrast, the government introduced price controls on rents and on the price of gas for heating. Specifically, rents could not be increased by more than 2 percent in 2022, while gas was capped in the wholesale electricity market. The government also lowered the cost of public transport, and most controversially, capped private sector profits. Unlike Hungary, controls in Spain seem to have worked, with Spain now having one of the lowest inflation rates in the eurozone. So does the Spanish experience vindicate controls? To answer that we need to figure out why Spain's and Hungary's experiences with controls were so different.

There are two main reasons. First, the two countries had different degrees of dependence on Russian gas, which had a huge impact on the energy component of inflation in each country since the start of the Ukraine-Russia war. Hungary gets most of its gas from Russia, whereas Spain imports it primarily from Algeria (even if in 2023 Spain began increasing its imports of Russian gas). The second important difference is that Hungary is poorer than Spain. Spain has a GDP per capita of 33,000 USD, whereas Hungary's was 21,000 USD. This strongly affects how inflation is measured in the two countries.

Poorer individuals spend a higher share of their incomes on food, which as we know from the last chapter is considered when measuring inflation. As such, food will have a higher weight in the inflation index in Hungary, which will translate into higher inflation. This is one of the reasons why food inflation appeared more strongly in Europe than in the United States. We also see this once we zoom in on the HICP and compare food inflation to headline inflation. In July 2023, food inflation was 12.4 percent in the European Union, 10.8 percent in Spain, and 21 percent in Hungary. In December 2022, Hungarians were dealing with food inflation of 49.6 percent (vis-à-vis 18 and 16 percent in the EU and Spain, respectively).

The same income effect applies to energy consumption, which takes a larger share of the income of a family in Hungary than in Spain, on top of the higher impact of the Russian energy shock in general. These factors made Hungary more vulnerable to the same energy and food inflation shocks that other countries experienced. Given this, it's not clear whether the differences in performance are wholly down to what we could call "smart controls" in Spain and "dumb controls" in Hungary. Rather, there are at best two lessons that we can take from these experiences with controls.

The first is that price controls are not always and everywhere bad. If implemented in the right way and in the appropriate markets, they can be effective tools. The second lesson is that it is really hard to figure out how to do that in advance, with the result that it's difficult to tell whether price controls will work or not, even after the fact, as their effectiveness is highly dependent on a country's macroeconomic policy mix, its level of income, the effectiveness of its state, and a host of other factors. In contrast, simply increasing interest rates has the advantage of affecting the economy as a whole, albeit with negative repercussions that we have discussed. Price controls, by contrast, can be targeted to specific sectors, but may be difficult to administer, especially if the economy is quite competitive.

A CAUTIONARY TALE?
PRICE CONTROLS IN SCOTLAND

Perhaps, then, the best we can say is that sometimes controls work when the stars, or the macroeconomic mix, align. But even when that is the case, you can still get it wrong if you don't focus on what the people who will have their prices controlled are likely to do in response to controls being announced. Scotland is an interesting case for controls because they are pretty much the only available tool the government there has, as its interest rates are set by the Bank of England. Consequently, if the Scottish government wants to impact a major component of inflation—rental costs spiraling due to higher interest rates pushing up mortgage costs on rental properties—they would have to act directly on those prices through controls. To that end, in September 2022 the Scottish government announced a freeze on rents and an end to evictions from rental properties. While there were some positive effects of the freeze, there were also some severe unintended consequences.

First, while existing rents were frozen, which protected sitting tenants, if a lease was broken or a new lease was negotiated, the landlord could charge whatever they like. Fearing a general extension of such controls, landlords increased rents across the board the moment they could in reaction to the controls. Second, while the controls targeted rents, they did not target what is in many cases the underlying determinant of those rents, which was rising mortgage costs. Scottish mortgages, like those in the UK in general, are mainly floating rate mortgages. As such, an increase of the mortgage rate from 2 percent to 6 or 7 percent can leave the mortgage holder unable to meet the payments on the property. As a result, many landlords sold their properties, thereby constricting the supply of rentals, which made the problem worse rather than better.

Third, behind that problem lay another that controls could not address: the underlying supply of the good in question, housing. Scotland, like many countries, effectively stopped building affordable housing at scale in the 1980s. As a result, private-sector landlords became responsible for what used to be a public-sector problem. Unfortunately, given the scale of operation of individual landlords, as demand increased, rental prices rose rather than supply rising to match demand. Controls only compounded this problem. While existing tenants were protected from rising rents, their protection came at the cost of reducing the number of available rentals and increasing the price of those remaining for anyone entering the market. Indeed, what has happened since the introduction of controls in the capital city of Edinburgh is a 15 percent year-on-year increase in rental costs and a shrinkage in tenancy periods so that landlords can regularly hike rents to take advantage of this shortage. In Scotland and Hungary, it seems that those old economists' warnings about price controls merely causing shortages came true. But there is another case where things worked out quite differently.

GERMANY AND PRICE CONTROLS: DIE GASPREISBREMSE (THE GAS PRICE BRAKE)

The first cause for the recent bout of inflation was the pandemic shutting down global supply chains; the second was the war in Ukraine. Countries supporting Ukraine embargoed Russian oil and gas, creating a massive (self-imposed) price shock for heavy users of gas, like Germany. Wholesale gas prices rocketed from 4.77 euro per megawatt hour in March 2021 to 150 euro per megawatt hour in July 2022. Desperate times call for desperate measures, and the German government set up a commission charged with developing a set of price controls for German gas. Given the scale of the price increases, the problem they tried to solve was nothing less than how to avoid the mass bankruptcy of German households and industry.

The commission eventually adopted a cap and subsidy model. For households, an average of past usage was calculated: the price of 80 percent of that usage was capped at the pre-pandemic rate, with the remainder being priced at the market rate. That would, it was hoped, incentivize households to save gas while government support covered the 80 percent that they really needed. For industrial users the design was similar, but with limits at 70 percent of pre-pandemic usage and a cash limit on total subsidies. The question is, did it work?

The Bundesbank, Germany's central bank, estimated that the cap reduced German inflation, then running at over 8 percent, by 1 percent. There were legitimate concerns about the ability of richer households to benefit more from the cap, given that it targeted average usage, but the cap and subsidy model prevented mass bankruptcies and poverty, while costing much less than envisaged. It was originally estimated to cost 40.3 billion euros over two years, but a fall in gas prices, a mild winter in 2022, and a general decrease in inflation 2023 all contributed to make it less expensive, at an estimated 13.1 billion. In other words, Germany bought social peace and industrial stability with a price cap that succeeded in bringing inflation down at the same time.

But even this story is contested. For example, is the "gas price break" really a price control measure? As economic commentator Noah Smith points out, producer prices are not being "controlled" in any direct sense here. Rather, the German state subsidizes the price. That is rather different. A subsidy is not a price control. When we talk about subsidies being given to the oil or gas sector, for example, we do not think about these as a form of limiting price increases. In fact, it suggests the opposite—it's a bung or a "bribe." But all that is, in turn, perhaps secondary to the fact that market prices are not being allowed to form. One way or another, the state is intervening to make sure that the price paid is not the price charged. In sum, semantics apart, interest rate increases may be easier to levy than controls for many reasons, and controls may have more potential to backfire or misidentify the target. But if you can control the right thing, no matter how you do it, especially when it's a huge component of your overall inflation rate, it's probably worth trying.

BEYOND INTEREST RATES AND PRICE CONTROLS: TAXES, SUBSIDIES, AND AGREEMENTS

To the extent that there was a debate in the mainstream of economic opinion over anti-inflation measures, it has mostly focused on how much, and for how long, central banks should have raised their rates. Price controls entered the scene outside the mainstream of economic opinion and immediately encountered strong resistance from many economists who see them as somewhere between a moral failure and a step toward socialism. This is no hyperbole. The fear that price controls represent a step torward a more interventionist economy created a lot of skepticism around these measures.

Yet despite all the hyperbole, governments actually control many prices. The US, for example, intervenes in the retail gasoline market by adding supply from its strategic buffer stock. China has historically used such quantitative buffers in many sectors of its economy. And the EU, despite all the talk about free and integrated markets, intervenes quite heavily in many markets. In the electricity market, for example, prior to the pandemic, fifteen countries out of twenty-eight intervened in some way in consumer electricity markets, and fourteen countries out of twenty-five did the same for gas.

As we've seen, some price controls were still implemented anyway during the pandemic, without too much fanfare, and with mixed results. The way this debate evolved, however, ignored quite a different set of possible anti-inflation policies. While the focus on central banks' monetary policy versus price controls captures a lot, it also misses how governments have put in place a set of policies that target inflation in specific sectors of the economy. Although they often go largely unnoticed, these policies are particularly interesting as they indirectly say a lot about a government's preferences over picking winners and losers in its battle against inflation. We can group these policies into three buckets: taxes, agreements, and buffers.

Windfall Taxes

The first is so-called windfall taxes on excess profits. The logic here is that rather than cap profits with price controls, why not just tax them after they are generated and use the funds to ease pressure on other sectors? Particularly if, reflecting the name, firms have not worked to earn higher profits? Governments can put these measures in place when they think firms are using inflation to charge higher prices. Needless to say, the targeted companies involved were none too fond of this idea.

Energy companies that quite clearly profited from these massive price spikes were obvious targets. The United Kingdom, for example, introduced an energy profit tax of 45 percent on abnormal profits. In Italy, the government also taxed the "extra profits" of energy companies. Companies were mandated to pay 10 percent of those profits above 5 million euros. Italy's prime minister Mario Draghi intended to use these funds to finance extraordinary measures in support of inflation's losers, such as low-income families and small enterprises that struggled with their utility bills. The Italian government managed to raise around 1.2 billion euros through the tax, which was significantly lower than the expected 3.98 billion euros they hoped to raise. This was not because the excess profits were not there. Rather, energy companies delayed paying tax, probably hoping that the judicial system would deem the measure unconstitutional, as it had in the past with a similar tax.

A variant of this windfall tax were taxes on the "excess" profits of banks that benefited from the high interest rates set by central banks. We go into how this happened in more detail in chapter 6, but in brief, bank reserves held at the central bank are treated as overnight deposits and get paid interest on those at the official interest rate. Higher interest rates thereby create a "windfall" for banks. While banks benefited from higher rates on their loans and their other holdings, they didn't share the wealth with a proportional increase in deposit rates, the interest paid to depositors on their savings. Banks benefited big-time from the spread or pass-through between deposit rates and loan rates.

The idea of taxing banks' windfall profits got the interest of governments of all stripes, from the right-wing Meloni government in Italy to the left-wing Sanchez government in Spain. Italy introduced a 40 percent tax on the "excess profits" that banks collected in 2022 or 2023 (depending on the year when the bank profited the most), relative to 2021. Hungary did something similar but gave banks the possibility of reducing their windfall tax payments by up to 50 percent, conditional on how many (new) Hungarian government bonds they purchased. There certainly were windfall profits to be had. Such taxes are not inflation-control devices as much as they are devices to transfer resources from inflation's winners to inflation's losers, but precisely this dynamic that makes windfall taxes politically appealing.

Unlike interest rate increases, windfall taxes don't hit society as a whole, but rather target a specific sector. In principle, windfall taxes are also easier to implement than price controls. You don't have to constantly monitor the market, checking whether products are being sold at the controlled price and sanctioning those who charge higher prices. With windfall taxes, in theory, all you have to do is compute how much profit the energy company or a bank collected over some past period (a), average that out, look at the "inflation-boosted" profits in the present (b), subtract (a) from (b), and set a tax rate on that difference.

But sadly, it's never quite that simple in practice. For example, Italy tried this in 2022 and 2023 when they introduced the 40 percent tax. There were good reasons for trying this. First of all, Italy's largest banks recorded profits 75 percent higher compared to the same period in the previous year, while being very slow in passing the benefits of higher interest rates to their depositors. Second, the Bank of Italy estimated that the weight of energy and food, the two sectors where prices grew the most in 2022, was double in the expenditure basket of the poorest compared to that of the richest. Given this, robbing Peter to pay Paul made both political and economic sense. The funds raised from the tax could be used to shift resources from inflation winners to losers to the tune of around 5 billion euros.

However, things didn't quite go as planned. To begin with, by taxing the interest margin, the tax penalized smaller banks that rely more on traditional lending activities rather than large banks that base their income on a wider set of sources. If you penalize small banks, you're effectively taxing the borrowers of those banks, who tend to be small and medium-size enterprises. These firms not only typically struggle to obtain credit but are also among inflation's worst losers as they can't push prices up to protect their margins. So taxing their smaller banks hits them with a double whammy.

Moreover, the surprise announcement of the policy rattled the Italian stock market. On the first trading day after the announcement, the Italian stock market lost 27 billion euros in capitalization as banks' share prices plummeted. In reaction to these losses, the government revised the policy by restricting the pool of taxed banks to those that profited the most and by fine-tuning the maximum impact of the tax based on a bank's size. As a result, the funds raised from the windfall were (possibly) less than the losses made by the big banks from the fall in their share price, while the small banks and their customers found themselves both double taxed and shortchanged. In short, windfall taxes may be easier to implement than price controls, but the outcomes they generate may be just as uncertain as those associated with controls themselves.

Price Control Agreements

An alternative approach consists of *agreeing* with firms to cap prices without really forcing them to do so. The logic here is that if lower prices result from an agreement, there should also be less conflict between the government and the most affected firms of the kind you get when you "surprise" firms with windfall taxes. The French government sought an agreement along these lines in July 2023, when seventy-five French food producers pledged to the French government that they would cut their prices on a basket of goods, accounting for 80 percent of French food products.

While it may look like firms are acting against their (profit) interests by joining such agreements, there are actually commercial reasons for them to do so. The supermarket chain Carrefour got on board and promptly advertised on its website that "to fight inflation" it "has frozen the prices on 100 everyday products in a bid to protect people's purchasing power in France." While doing so might lead to lower transitory profits, such firms may calculate that the long-term marketing goodwill earned by doing so is probably worth more. A second reason for firms to agree to lower their prices is the logic of a "cartel." Joining a price cartel helps them coordinate their expectations about their competitors' strategies. Once in the agreement, it would be hard for a competing firm to increase its prices without there being a negative impact on that firm's reputation.

Such agreements seem to be a win-win for both the government and the firms. The government manages to reduce prices quickly, without lengthy legislation, and the companies trade short-term volatile profit for long-term price stability, steady profit, and good PR. So, what could go wrong with price agreements? The short answer is that cartels are inherently unstable, because firms may not keep their promises to one another not to raise prices. Or better still, they may find ways around them.

It wasn't much of a surprise then when in August 2023 France's minister of finance criticized the parties to the food price agreement for not sticking to what they pledged to do. He stated that while some multinationals such as Nestle, Unilever, or PepsiCo did "a bit, but not too much" to reduce prices, many of the firms that boasted of cutting prices actually engaged in *shrinkflation*. That is, shrinking the volume or weight of a product while keeping the same price. This gives the impression that the company is keeping prices steady while it's actually increasing the price relative to the quantity sold. As a result, while food prices in August were lower than in June when the agreement was sealed, they were still 11 percent higher when compared to the previous year, and they were still rising at double the inflation rate.

Again, such voluntary agreements are good in theory, but as Nixon found out, it's very hard to make them work in practice. Interestingly, the politics around this agreement created conflicts between the companies that were part of it. In January 2024, the *Financial Times* reported that the food retailer Carrefour decided not to sell any more products from PepsiCo, such as Doritos and 7UP, because they have become too expensive.

Price Buffers

A final approach rests on the buildup of so-called buffer stocks. The logic here is that states can stockpile a specific resource that they expect to be susceptible to price volatility, such as oil, and release this buffer stock once prices go up in order to control prices. As we've noted above, the United States does this with its Strategic Petroleum Reserve, while China does this with a whole host of critical commodities ranging from cooking oil to medical supplies. Buffer stocks flip the inflation problem on its head. If prices are up because there is too much demand for a good and not enough supply, instead of capping those prices, you expand supply, bringing prices back to their normal level.

This is exactly what the Biden administration did with oil in the United States. In November 2021, Biden announced that the Department of Energy was to release 50 million oil barrels from the country's reserve "to lower prices for Americans and address the mismatch between demand exiting the pandemic and supply." This was followed by an injection of 180 million barrels in April 2022, the largest release of reserves ever recorded in history. A study by the US Treasury estimated that this strategy was effective in lowering the price of oil, which went down by a range of 17 to 42 cents per gallon.

Once again, this elegant solution is easier said than done. Identifying strategic resources to stockpile is not as straightforward as it seems. Remember the lack of masks and gloves in the pandemic? Even with "strategic" commodities that the economy runs on like oil, should building a longer-term buffer be a policy goal? After all, is oil going to be as useful in the future as it is today if we transit more and more toward renewable resources? Also, stockpiling oil is not costless. On top of the cost of storing it, holding oil without selling it means you're losing on what economists call its opportunity cost. That is, you could have done something else with the money you spent establishing the stockpile. Finally, the capacity to build a buffer stock matters. The US can produce more oil than most, but even other advanced economies would struggle to stockpile oil. The same applies to natural gas, which European countries mostly import from abroad. So while buffers can be effective in dragging energy prices down, they can be very expensive and difficult tools to acquire, maintain, and use.

WHO GETS WHAT WITH THESE OTHER TOOLS?

Each of these non-interest-rate-based anti-inflation tools has both benefits and drawbacks. These instruments are distributional in a different way from interest rates. Raising rates rewards savers and punishes borrowers, impacting low-income households with fewer assets the most. These alternative tools can be used to target specific sectors of the economy, taking from one group and giving it to another group. Such decisions are more obviously political than central bank rate hikes, and for this reason they are put in the hands of elected officials. If the majority of voters are unhappy about how those resources are distributed, they can vote for a different government in the next election.

But the voters don't get to vote on central banks' interest rate increases. To account for this lack of accountability, central banks are usually given the narrow mandate of maintaining price stability. But, as we saw already, tackling inflation with a single instrument that affects the economy as a whole disguises the quite different impacts inflation has on various segments of society. To be fair, central bankers know this. They have research staff who are well aware of the costs stemming from their policies. As we have already noted, this book often uses analyses from central banks' staff to prove the negative implications that central banks' policies may have. But knowing this fact does not mean that they are not engaging in distributional policies.

The second lesson that we learn from the response to the 2020s inflation is that these instruments work well when combined, rather than when applied separately. If we use only higher interest rates, for instance, the brunt of the costs are borne by the bottom end of the income distribution. Transferring some resources from the winners to the losers can instead compensate for these losses. Francesco Corsello and Marianna Riggi, two economists at the Bank of Italy, showed that fiscal measures that supported the most vulnerable households are important supplements for monetary policy, which would otherwise result in higher inequality. Similarly, in a 2023 study, Isabella Weber and Evan Wasner summarized how these policies can complement one another, forming an effective anti-inflationary arsenal. They argued that states holding buffer stocks in a wide range of commodities can stop firms profiting from inflation, while the threat of windfall taxes can further curtail such "sellers' inflation."

The policies we analyzed in this chapter should hence not be seen as competing options, but rather as a set of levers that gives governments options beyond the interest rate hammer. Fighting inflation may be crucial, but it should never be considered a battle that we have to fight only one way, no matter the costs it creates. The victims that the anti-inflation battle creates should be taken into account just as much as the victims inflation creates. Since interest rate hikes worsen the situation of many due to their broad impact on the economy, they should be used with care. Policies to alleviate such costs may be tricky to get right, but they are certainly worth the effort.

3

——

INFLATION STORIES AND THE POLITICS OF BLAME

The search for a scapegoat is the easiest of all hunting expeditions.
Attributed to Dwight Eisenhower

WHO CAUSES IT . . . PAYS FOR IT

So far we have discussed what inflation is and what it is not; how it is measured and what those measurements do and do not capture. We then discussed why interest rates are seen as the universal hammer for the inflation nail and noted what other policies might be used to address inflation. But there is actually a prior step to all that. Why did inflation happen in the first place? And perhaps just as important, who, or what, is to blame? When you identify who or what causes inflation, you focus the blame, and thus the responsibility, for fixing it. Consequently, while we are definitely interested in what "really" causes inflation—even if there is no one correct measure of it and the policies used to tame it may cause more harm than good—we are also interested in the way different commentators talk about it and how politicians use it to pass the costs of inflation around.

The most recent surge in inflation has been accompanied by an equally large surge in the number of different inflation stories that are out there vying to explain it. Each story identifies quite different causes and proposes quite different solutions to the problem. This is important because just like policies, different inflation stories have very different distributional consequences. For example, if you blame the rise in prices on a supply-side shock like COVID-19, it's not clear why raising the cost of someone's mortgage is the right response. While the authors of these stories may admit there are many factors involved in today's inflation, they have quite different perspectives on the *main* drivers of inflation, and consequently, on who, or what, is to blame for it.

In the United States, for example, the two most prominent stories since the start of the recent bout of inflation are those associated with Larry Summers and Paul Krugman, two prominent economists. Summers, a former Treasury official, Harvard president, and Obama adviser, argues that inflation today is like that of the 1970s and '80s, when wages and prices chased each other up in a spiral, and therefore should be fought in the same way it was fought in those years. That is, by generating a recession through high interest rates, which will produce a prolonged period of higher than normal unemployment. In this story, only downward pressure on demand that shows up as unemployment will cool the economy.

Economics Nobel Prize winner and *New York Times* columnist Paul Krugman disagrees vehemently with Summers. He maintains that today's rising prices resemble more the inflation of the late 1940s and early '50s, not the '70s. Inflation back then was generated by the problems of converting the World War II economy back to civilian use, combined with the unexpected demand and supply spikes caused by the Korean War. In the latter case, both sets of factors proved to be transitory. That is, they had specific causes that were time limited. The shocks hit, prices rose, and eventually, as the economy adjusted to higher prices by expanding the supply side (making more steel for the Korean War, for example), prices fell as the inflation impulse dissipated and eventually passed. If Krugman's inflation story is right, the correct policy response is not to cause a recession and throw people out of work, but to wait it out.

These are only two of the most prominent public heavyweights generating and propagating particular inflation stories during the recent inflation spike that each have different villains, heroes, winners, and losers. Broadly, these stories, both this time around and in prior inflationary episodes, can be grouped into four main genres. We'll examine these stories not as economic explanations, but as political rhetorics that enable agents to push the responsibility for, and thus the costs of inflation, onto someone else. Part of getting rid of inflation is policy. But a very large part of it is politics.

GENRE ONE: THE PROBLEM IS TOO MUCH MONEY

First up: the notion of the economy being afflicted by "too much demand." We have encountered this argument already, but here we examine it in detail. These stories generally attribute recent inflation to governments "overstimulating" the economy during the COVID-19 pandemic. The simplest form of this story claims that government spending to compensate for the closure of the economy during COVID-19 gave people too much money to spend, which ended up chasing too few goods, thus overstimulating the economy. Sometimes, the supply side is brought in to complement the "too much demand" story. In 2021, for example, the level of available goods was already lower than normal due to COVID-19 shutting down global supply chains. As such, excess-demand-driven inflation was compounded as "too much money" chased "far fewer goods than there normally would be." The result had to be a sharp rise in prices.

This story found particularly fertile ground in the United States, where the government engaged in a $5 trillion fiscal stimulus to offset the deflationary effects of the COVID-19 shutdown. Before inflation fully appeared in 2021, Larry Summers invoked this line of reasoning, claiming that the Biden stimulus "will set off inflationary pressures of a kind we have not seen in a generation." Despite Summers being a Democrat, or perhaps because of it, blaming a Democratic president for inflationary pressures quickly became a very appealing argument for US Republicans. As Senate minority leader Mitch McConnell argued when inflation appeared in 2021, "There's no relief in sight. It's a direct result of flooding the country with money." But guess what? It's not quite as simple as that.

Multiplier Problems and "Stimulus" Checks

The key economic idea underlying this story is that of the fiscal multiplier. The fiscal multiplier measures how much each dollar of government spending translates into a dollar (more or less) of private consumption. If the multiplier is positive, then one dollar spent produces more than one dollar in final consumption. Logically, then, if you have a positive multiplier and are short of the stuff you want to buy, the result must be rising prices. The problem with this story is that the multiplier is very difficult to estimate in the real world. Economists of different political persuasions tend to disagree on its size, which has both political and distributional implications. For example, during the Great Recession of 2009–13, conservatives in the EU and the US, and their attendant economists, consistently argued that the multiplier was negative in order to delegitimate any government spending as a way to alleviate the recession. Today similar voices estimate the multiplier as being positive so that they can blame left-leaning governments for generating excessive demand and ultimately inflation.

There is truth to this story—governments spent money to offset the COVID-19 lockdown and struggling supply chains caused shortages— but the fiscal stimulus story has many limitations. First, it does not explain why inflation was a global phenomenon. While fiscal stimulus was a common policy in reaction to COVID-19 in other countries outside the United States, it was neither universal nor uniform. Countries that stimulated less, such as Germany, had inflation as high or higher than the US, which suggests that something other than the local COVID-19 cash handouts may be at work.

Second, there is the question of timing and duration. If inflation is caused by the stimulus, then we should expect inflation to fade quite quickly as the short-term impact of fiscal expansion dissipates. This would require no specific policy action as the stimulus in the United States was inherently temporary and time limited. What went up must come down. And it seems to have come down quite a lot in 2023 and 2024, which is well after the much-blamed stimulus checks were mailed out and cashed in. Something else must be at work in keeping inflation up.

Third, irrespective of its size, we cannot confidently attribute an inflationary effect so large to government spending alone. While some estimates, for example from the Federal Reserve of San Francisco, suggest that in the United States the stimulus might have led to prices that are 3 percent higher than they would otherwise be, the authors of this study are careful to note that these estimates are too uncertain to be taken as an established fact. The confidence interval of estimates is large enough as to render them no better than darts thrown at a board.

Fourth, while the headline figure of US spending during the COVID-19 crisis sounds extremely large ($5 trillion or 25 percent of GDP), that needs to be put in perspective. The COVID-19 crisis shut down large parts of the world's largest economy—especially its service sector, which is 80 percent of the economy—for an indefinite period. As such, COVID-19 spending should properly be thought of as compensating for the loss of income and output generated during the shutdown, rather than as a stimulus that was added to an already fully employed economy.

For example, if one examines the bit of the stimulus program that gets the most blame in such analyses, the direct cash transfers component of US spending, you will find that $1.8 trillion of the $5 trillion went to individuals and families. Of that $1.8 trillion, $653 billion went to unemployment benefits, which were in many (but not all) cases, less than the wages they were replacing. As such, unemployment benefits, by definition, could not be stimulatory. Rather, they partially compensated for the spending that usually would have been there.

That leaves $817 billion, which was paid out in three waves of stimulus checks over an eleven-month period that ran from April 2020 to March 2021. Family households with an income of under $150,000 per year and individuals with an income of under $75,000 received three income replacement checks of $1,200, $600, and $1,400 respectively, for a total of $3,200 per household. When we consider that median family income in the United States in 2021 was just under $80,000, these combined stimulus checks added the equivalent of 4 percent to that median income. In fairness, those checks were larger as a percentage of lost income the further down the income scale one goes, and the further down one goes the likelihood that the cash will be spent now rather than later increases. Nonetheless, if those payments were less than the income lost by COVID-19, it's very hard to see how they could be stimulatory in any strong sense of the word. Surely there were supply constraints, perhaps driven by stimulus-enabled spending, that pushed prices up. But if we imagine a counterfactual where no checks were spent, would we have predicted a mild recession with 80 percent of the economy in lockdown?

It also matters what those check recipients spent their money on. Data on consumer credit from the New York Federal Reserve tells us that around 20 percent of those checks went toward paying down credit card debt. As the New York Fed noted in their 2020 Q1 Household Debt and Credit Developments quarterly report, which examined spending changes after the first stimulus check was sent out, "Credit card balances declined sharply in the second quarter, by $76 billion, the steepest decline in card balances seen in the history of the data." By Q2 of 2021, following the last of the checks, the NY Fed noted that "credit card balances are $157 billion lower than they had been at the end of 2019." In other words, around 20 percent of those checks were spent on credit card reduction, which as a debt repayment by definition cannot stimulate the economy. According to a Bureau of Labor Statistics survey of check recipients conducted in August 2020, "66 percent reported using at least a portion of it for food," which is hardly a sign of irrational exuberance.

NY Fed data further reveals that as well as paying down credit cards and buying food, many recipients used the cash to avoid mortgage delinquency. For example, in Q4 2019, 1.07 percent of all mortgages were delinquent 90 days plus. By Q2 2020, after the first checks were spent, that figure fell to 0.84 percent, and despite the COVID-19 shutdown, by Q2 2021, it had fallen by more than 50 percent from its peak to 0.47 percent.

Finally, the timing doesn't add up. The checks seem to have been spent in 2022 but also show up as so-called excess savings in late 2023 to explain why consumption in the United States remains robust despite high interest rates. But these are not Schrödinger's checks. They cannot simultaneously be spent in one period as stimulus and remain unspent in another future period as savings. That simply makes no sense. In sum, despite many sensational media stories about the checks being spent on bitcoins and gambling, most Americans seemed to buy financial peace of mind by paying back debt, or buying food, instead of increasing their consumption, all of which is inherently non-stimulatory.

In fairness one could legitimately point to the stimulatory effect of the other $1.7 trillion in spending, half of which went to the Paycheck Protection Program. However, it is telling that those pushing the "too much demand" line always focus on the checks to individuals and hardly ever on support to business. Business and its allies do not want to get the blame, and so at least in the United States, this story of too much money tends to focus on laid-off workers and their overly stimulatory checks as the cause of inflation.

GENRE TWO: THE PROBLEM IS TOO MUCH EMPLOYMENT

Stories in genre two focus on the labor market. Workers get the blame again, but this time it's not for spending checks. The basic idea here is that when there are too many employment vacancies relative to the supply of available workers, workers will bargain for higher wages than they would in a world with higher unemployment. If an employer refuses to pay workers the higher wage that they seek, they can walk away and look for alternative jobs, some of which will pay that higher wage. Average this out over the whole economy and you get higher wages pushing up prices.

One crucial difference from the excess demand story is the worry about the "expectations" of workers. That is, the storytellers of this genre extrapolate from the worker searching for a higher wage to all workers now expecting a higher wage due to inflation. In doing so those workers will anticipate future higher prices as a result of everyone chasing a higher wage and will ask for wage increases that are high enough to shield them against future anticipated price hikes. But, and here's the rub, by doing so, they become the driver of inflation, since wages are themselves a price.

Professor Phillips's Curve

The economic model underlying this story is the much-talked-about Phillips curve, named after a New Zealand professor of economics who back in 1957 first spotted an inverse relationship between unemployment and inflation in data from the UK. That is, when unemployment goes up, inflation goes down, and vice versa. This statistical relationship has informed most central banks' interest rate decisions, and most thinking about inflation, since the 1970s. The Phillips curve is why conventional wisdom holds that there is a trade-off between reducing inflation and unemployment that central banks can exploit by moving interest rates around. When central banks observe data on prices and unemployment and they don't like what they see, they can decide whether to sacrifice one variable to reduce the other.

This Phillips curve is also why Larry Summers, whom we quoted earlier, combines genre one and two in his pronouncements, and why he came to the conclusion that the only way to decrease inflation is to increase unemployment, which is handy because workers are to blame anyway because of their inflated wage expectations. And if we believe that today's inflation is basically the same as the inflation of the 1970s, then this policy becomes the only game in town, despite its social and economic costs. To see why we think this is the case, let's jump back to the late 1970s and early '80s for a moment.

THAT '70s SHOW (AGAIN)

As we've discussed, in the early 1980s, Federal Reserve Chair Paul Volcker aggressively hiked interest rates, reaching 19 percent in July 1981. This caused a dramatic increase in unemployment as thousands of businesses that had expected lower borrowing costs to continue went bankrupt. Unemployment more than doubled from around 5 percent in 1979 to just under 11 percent in early 1982, with inflation dropping from 13 percent to 4 percent over the same period. As the Phillips curve would predict, generating a massive recession was the necessary pain to win the war against inflation. But is today's inflation really the same as the one we experienced in the 1970s? And further, was the "Volcker Shock," as it has become known, really necessary to tame inflation?

For some, the answer is a resounding yes. The story goes: Just as we saw in the 1970s, inflation today surged after a period of low rates and easy money following the Great Recession of 2009–13, which combined with a supply-side shock in the form of a huge increase in energy prices pushed up other prices. In both the 1970s and during the pandemic, the reasoning was that had the Fed raised rates sooner, the rates shock needed to tame inflation would have been smaller, creating less unemployment. Thus, the argument goes, the Fed again waited too long, and so now we need to have higher rates for longer and endure a bigger recession to reset inflation.

There are, however, several very important differences between the 1970s and today that were highlighted in a recent paper by economists from the World Bank. First, the energy shocks of 1973–74 and 1979–80 were on the whole significantly higher than the ones we are experiencing today, and crucially they impacted economies that were much more oil dependent than they are today. For example, in the early 1970s, one in six jobs in the United States was in the auto sector and one in three was in the broader industrial economy. Because of this industrial structure, inflation in the 1970s was more broadly based than today, which meant that it affected the prices of almost every good. The inflation of the 2020s, as we saw in chapter 1, was more strongly concentrated among energy-intensive and pandemic-affected sectors. Gas and oil most obviously, but also travel and housing, especially rents.

That industrial structure has been utterly transformed since the 1970s. Manufacturing shrunk from being over 25 percent of value added in the late 1970s to 11 percent today. Meanwhile, services have grown to almost 80 percent of the economy. In such a transformed economy we would have to expect the impact of rate increases to be vastly different from what we experienced before, as the sectors and products and processes that they impact are vastly different, which indeed seems to have been the case as inflation has come down while *employment*, not unemployment, went up.

Furthermore, and again in contrast to the 1970s, the Fed certainly raised rates between 2021 and 2023, twenty-two times up from base, but for most of the period from 2021–23 real interest rates (the nominal rate the Fed sets rates at, minus the inflation rate) were still negative. That was not the case in the 1970s. Even when rates became positive as inflation fell further in 2023 it was still sixty-six times up—from a baseline of barely above zero. Indeed, seen over a twenty-five-year term, the current Fed funds rate of 5.33 percent is roughly the same as where it was in 2007, and as we write this in August 2024 rates are lower today than in June 2001. No one in either the 2000s or the 2020s was trying to cause a recession with "high" rates, as they were not seen even in those periods as being particularly high.

WHAT WORKERS EXPECT

The key to the idea that "necessary" unemployment will work deflation-ary magic is workers and, specifically, their inflationary expectations. As we noted above, this story rests on the idea of the Phillips curve and its trade-off between inflation and unemployment. A consequence of that model is that workers should be incentivized by already rising prices to bargain for higher wages. In doing so they will generate that wage-price spiral of tail-chasing inflationary forces, which is the fundamental rea-son why we need more unemployment to cool things down. We need to, in the language of central banks, "re-anchor inflation expectations." Yet this logic falls down on at least two levels when you start to pick at it.

The first is, as Keynes pointed out over eighty years ago, workers bargain over money (so-called nominal) wages, not real wages. That is, when they sit down to negotiate a contract they may target a wage that is trying to account for inflation, as they anticipate higher future prices. But according to Keynes, they can't actually do that. They can't really take into account how all the other prices in the economy are moving around because they simply don't have that information. They control one price, the price of their labor, which is the nominal, not inflation-adjusted, wage. As such, they cannot actually bargain over their "real" wage (that is, inflation-adjusted wage) since they do not know and cannot control all those other prices. Yet the Phillips curve story assumes that workers know what their real wage is and that they can bargain over it.

Second, on a deeper level, the Phillips curve story assumes that workers suffer a very odd form of what economists call "money illusion." A money illusion is the idea that people view their income in nominal rather than real terms: that is, they focus on the numbers written on their paycheck rather than what that paycheck can actually buy. As such, they are under some kind of illusion about their actual incomes. For example, imagine that your employer offers you a 2 percent wage increase. Inflation is 3 percent. In real terms you just took a 1 percent pay cut, but you have the illusion that your wages still went up, albeit by a depressingly small amount. Sound familiar?

A very odd but seldom commented upon thing about the Phillips curve story is that for it to work, workers must have no money illusion about wages—they seem to know and bargain for the real wage, which causes the wage-price spiral—but they must have a permanent money illusion about all other prices. After all, if they knew that all those other price increases were simply nominal adjustments, why would they ever get caught up in that wage-price spiral? Instead, the rational thing to do would be not to adjust to prices going up by asking for more, and, if the Phillips curve logic is right, prices would fall all by themselves. So, for this story to hold water, workers need to be able to bargain for their real wage while being quite schizophrenic regarding prices. That's really odd when you think about it.

What Workers Can Actually Demand

A further issue that complicates the "wages driving prices" story is how the balance of power between capital and labor has changed dramatically since the 1970s in favor of capital. Another of the unspoken assumptions of this genre is that workers automatically share in the productivity gains of their employers. This is also highly dubious and is not borne out by empirical evidence. A simple glance at the share of GDP that goes to capital and the share that goes to wages shows that despite consistent productivity increases there has been a massive swing of profits away from wages toward capital incomes over the past forty years, on the order of 10 percent of GDP. The result of this shift has been that the bottom 90 percent of the income distribution is $2.5 trillion poorer than they would have been without this shift taking place. So the question becomes, Why did this shift take place?

What historically enabled workers to share productivity gains with their employers was membership in trade unions and participation in collective bargaining agreements that had legal teeth. Gaining higher wages was not the result of some automatic mechanism where wages simply rise in tandem with productivity. Such increases needed to be negotiated by labor. Workers had the effective threat of the strike, which would increase employer costs, thereby encouraging them to share the profits.

Beginning in the 1980s, employers succeeded in undermining the power of labor unions, while outsourcing and then globalization effectively ended strikes as a bargaining tool for labor. The result was visible in the steep fall in trade union density (the number of folks in unions relative to the working population as a whole, Figure 3.1, second panel) and the number of strikes. As trade unions got weaker, workers simply lacked the platform and the strength to ask for higher wages, and if they did, they were either fired or the job moved elsewhere. Profits rose while wages rose much less or even stagnated. It is not surprising, then, that the decline of trade unions is associated with a decline in the correlation between wages and price inflation (Figure 3.1, first panel), further suggesting that the Phillips curve relationship is not at all what it's cracked up to be.

In line with this reasoning, Isabel Schnabel, the economist at the European Central Bank we encountered earlier, has argued that profits, not wages, are the main contributors to inflation, as firms pass on higher costs to consumers to increase their earnings, and not to pay more to their workers, a point we shall return to below. Given all this, it is difficult both to argue that and to find any evidence for the claim that the advanced economies are facing a wage-price spiral. A recent study by the International Monetary Fund looked at the historical experience of advanced economies since the 1960s and found that wage-price spirals are quite rare events, definitely the exception and not than the rule. Research from economists at the Bank for International Settlements and the European Central Bank supports this finding. As such, the veracity of this story, and the model that underlies it, must be called into question.

FIGURE 3.1:

THE DECLINE OF TRADE UNIONS

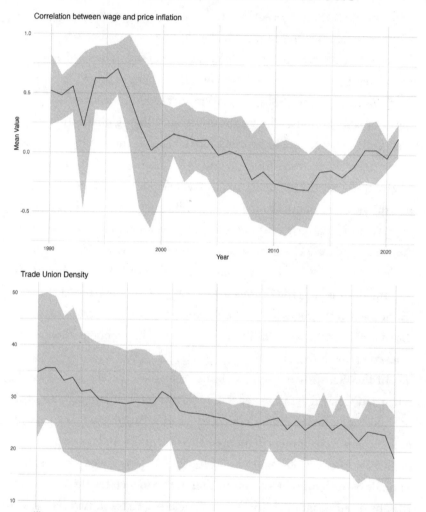

Source: Authors' elaboration based on Boissay et al.

THAT '70s SHOW—REDUX

Finally, was the Volcker shock really necessary to tame inflation as this genre assumes? There are reasons to be skeptical. Recall, as we noted in the introduction, that many analysts of the 1970s inflation writing in the 1980s saw the causes of inflation as due to "special factors," as Alan Blinder put it, that had more or less run their course by the time Volcker jacked up rates. Specifically, running the United States economy super-hot to finance the Vietnam war without raising taxes was inherently inflationary. Having a weak Federal Reserve chair in the form of Arthur Burns, who was basically "in the bag" for Nixon's reelection, was inflationary. Incorporating women and minorities into the US labor market at scale for the first time without enough capital deepening to increase productivity was inflationary. Coping with two failed major harvests in the USA and the USSR, plus two oil shocks in a single decade, plus the decision to put mortgage costs into the US CPI after rates started going up, all pushed inflation higher and higher. But all of these factors passed. In the end they were transitory—even if the transition took nearly a decade. So perhaps, far from being the necessary medicine, Volcker's decision was an overdose added after the fact. If so, repeating that same policy today, what we now call "higher for longer," is surely repeating an error rather than embracing the optimal policy. Thinking this way brings us nicely to genre three, where such transitory factors take center stage.

GENRE THREE: THE PROBLEM IS THE SUPPLY SIDE (AND IT WILL ADJUST)

This third genre argues that the current inflation is a transitory phenomenon, and it too shall pass. And writing in mid-2024 it looks like they may be right after all. Proponents of this story, including Paul Krugman, are often dubbed "team transitory," and they sometimes even identify as such. As we have noted before, according to this view, today's inflation is more like the inflation of late 1940s and early '50s, which was a sharp but very short blip, in contrast to the persistent and rising inflation of the 1970s and early '80s. In this version of events, the drivers of inflation are supply-side shocks brought about by COVID-19 and the war in Ukraine.

Once these disruptions have worked their way through the economy and the supply side has adjusted, team transitory argues, inflation will revert to its previous low rate. In this version of events neither workers nor their expectations are to blame for the inflationary shock, but they do feature in why it doesn't become persistent.

One of the most interesting contrasts between this genre and the prior two is that in the other two genres inflation has distinctly local causes. "Biden spent too much." "The (US) labor market is too tight." In contrast, in this third genre, the transitory claim follows from global rather than local causes. Namely, the disruptions that mattered affected the global production of commodities, critical inputs such as fertilizers, and finished products. But it's not just the shortfall in supply that matters. Rather, these disruptions, in turn, were amplified by unpredictable shifts in consumer demand throughout the various phases of the pandemic, and further in response to the unexpected Russian invasion of Ukraine and the effect that had on energy prices. These shocks in turn affected particular sectors of production, generating at different moments, for example, a shortage of shipping containers that stressed port capacity, a shortage of computer chips that had knock-on effects on car production, or by making natural gas much more costly. According to team transitory, these changes are very destabilizing but are temporary. They will work themselves out. And this is where workers come into this story. This genre implicitly assumes that people know all this, which keeps those so-called inflation expectations well anchored.

According to this genre, the 1970s differed from the late 1940s and early '50s because people began to think that inflation was persistent. As a consequence, so the story goes, they kept buying goods with the fear that in the future such goods would be more expensive, which (supposedly) led to a self-fulfilling inflation spiral. Or alternatively, as we discussed earlier, they kept asking for higher wages, which pushed up prices via shifts in expectations. In contrast, in the earlier period, so this story goes, people believed that inflation was temporary, so they didn't binge buy, which explains why inflation didn't last for long.

So for team transitory, while the causes of the inflation are global, what determines the inflation rate is local—do the locals expect prices to keep rising or not? It seems that they don't, at least so far. US inflation expectations are, as far as we can tell (more on that below), still well anchored. Despite rising headline inflation, medium-term inflation expectations measured by the surveys conducted by the University of Michigan and the Federal Reserve of New York have declined rather than increased.

Yet, the team transitory story has two main issues that are in many ways mirror images of the problems of the "too much demand" and labor market stories. The first is that if the "too much demand" and labor market stories place too much emphasis on local monetary factors, this alternative story may give too much emphasis to global supply-side factors, which raises a key issue. How much does a country depend upon imports? That is, what is an economy's degree of "openness"? If you are really open to imports and your imports cost more, you will get inflation through what economists call the "import channel," and if those imports are stuff you really need like food, then the price shock will be large and your exchange rate will likely fall at the same time as a result, thereby compounding the inflationary effect.

If you are the United States, for example, and are largely self-sufficient in food and fuel, your situation is quite different to the UK, where two thirds of food is imported. For the UK, if the price of basic foodstuffs rises, the inflationary impact in a more import-dependent economy will be that much greater. Given this variation in openness, overall supply factors may not be as dominant as this school might think. For example, the World Bank estimates that while supply factors account for a large share of inflation in general, they are not dominant when compared to demand and oil prices. This holds for both advanced and emerging economies.

Two other studies on US inflation presented similar results. Adam Shapiro from the Federal Reserve of San Francisco managed to decompose inflation into demand- and supply-driven contributors and found that both drivers had similar impact. The other study is from former Fed chairman Ben Bernanke and former IMF chief economist Olivier Blanchard. Bernanke and Blanchard decomposed US inflation to identify its main drivers and found that most of the inflation surge of 2021 was driven by external shocks to prices, such as an increase in the price of commodities and sectoral shortages, which is in line with the team transitory narrative. However, they also found that while the labor market was not the cause of inflation, the growth of (nominal) wages was proving to be a more persistent driver of inflation than the supply-side shocks. The supply-side genre is convincing, but it is difficult to claim that this is the only cause of inflation.

What to Expect When You Are Expecting (Inflation)

There is another, deeper limitation of this story: the overreliance on the idea of inflation expectations. Although there are many and varied technical understandings of how expectations work, the core idea is very simple. If consumers/workers think that prices will go up, they'll move their purchases/wages up, thereby bringing about the very price rises they fear. It's a classic "fallacy of composition" problem. What is individually rational is collectively disastrous.

Suppose, for example, that you've been planning for a while to replace your old car with a brand-new one. This is a big purchase, and you can delay it for some period of time until you find a good deal. But now suppose that you're convinced that car prices next year will increase dramatically. In that moment the rational thing to do is to rush out and buy any new car, as you fear higher prices for all cars in the future. And if you do, and others like you think the same thing, guess what happens? Car prices indeed go up as everyone rationally anticipates the same thing.

But does inflation really depend that much on what people think future prices will be? Conventional wisdom holds that what keeps inflation expectations anchored is the "credibility" of central bank policy announcements. In theory, if people believe that the central bank is serious about controlling inflation, then people will not even try to ask for a wage rise above the current rate of inflation, for they will know that the central bank will raise rates to keep the economy cool, which will rob their wage gains of any real value.

It's a clever argument that gives central banks a lot of power, but do people actually listen carefully to central bank policy announcements and then adjust their beliefs concerning the future price of bread, gas, cars, and other goods in response? While economists have for a long time relied on the concept of inflation expectations to explain inflation changes, there is very little evidence that shows that people act in this way at all, adjusting their expectations based on movements in, for example, short-term interest rates or central bank announcements.

As Fed researcher Jeremy Rudd noted in 2021, the view that expectations matter relies on "the inflationary experience of the 1960s and '70s, even though that period provides no actual evidence that workers or firms tried to boost their wages or raise their prices in anticipation of future price or cost changes." Indeed, the evidence we do have shows the contrary. Surveys that measure one-year inflation expectations really reflect movements in the price of gasoline, which is something that depends on external factors and that central banks cannot really control. That's what people actually track, because they buy it twice a week and the price is emblazoned on the pump. For this reason, economists generally focus on medium-term expectations to avoid this bias.

But the problem persists even when we focus on medium-term time horizons. When asked about their beliefs on inflation, people give answers that are quite inconsistent with what economists expect. For instance, while economists agree that higher interest rates will lower prices by reducing demand, the general population thinks the opposite, that higher rates will lead to higher prices. Their belief is grounded in the idea that firms will shift the higher costs of borrowing they face from higher rates on to consumers, who will then face even higher prices, which is not an unreasonable assumption (see genre four below). Indeed, when we turn to experts, we notice that even their expectations may not be completely "rational." A recent study showed that experts' inflation forecasts are strongly influenced by personal experience. For instance, experts who worked in a central bank are less pessimistic and are less likely to predict deflation in comparison to their market peers.

Indeed, inflation expectations are actually quite chaotic (if they exist at all in a systematic way), even if we focus on only those people who are forced by their profession to pay attention to economic policy announcements, such as the managers of firms that borrow money. A study based on survey data from New Zealand, and another in the United States, showed that such managers are poorly informed about inflation dynamics, differ widely in the way they predict inflation, and oftentimes do not even know the name of the head of the central bank. Indeed, one study finds that far from seeking out such information to shape pricing decisions, "online searches for macroeconomic variables like GDP, unemployment rate and inflation are consistently topped altogether by online searches for puppies."

In sum, the problems of the transitory genre are in some ways the mirror image of the others. For example, in the "too much demand" story, consumers "expect" prices to keep rising because their expectations become unanchored, which explains inflation. But how do we know that it is expectations doing the work? Because prices are rising, of course. But that reveals a suspiciously circular logic.

In the team transitory story, the problem is not that expectations become unanchored. Rather, it's that they actually stay anchored because consumers and workers somehow know that current upward movements in prices are "transitory." In this case, the fact that expectations are *not moving* proves that they are important, as opposed to the other story where their movement does all the work. Again, this is more than a bit circular. There is, however, one more genre that doesn't care a hoot about expectations, isn't in the least bit circular, and is the one that intuitively most people think is right, and yet economists hate it with a strange passion. Probably because it's linked to price controls and suggests that power, rather than rationality and efficiency, is doing the work here.

GENRE FOUR: THE PROBLEM IS GREEDY CORPORATIONS

Our fourth genre is that of "price gouging," which focuses on the ability of firms to set higher prices because prices are already moving upward, which then leads to higher prices in the aggregate. That is, price gouging may not be the fundamental cause of inflation, but once inflation gets going it's arguably a large part of what keeps it going. For storytellers in this genre, focusing on workers' expectations and worrying about interest rates is the equivalent of the proverbial drunk looking for their keys under the lamppost because that's where the light is. Understandable, but ultimately pointless. Instead, we should simply look for firms to do what firms do best, maximize their profits, and then look for "excess" or "outsize" profits as our indicators of what is driving inflation. The price-gouging story often goes by the inflammatory name of *greedflation* and sometimes by the more technical term of "sellers' inflation."

According to this story, companies take advantage of the general level of prices increasing to jack up their prices beyond their usual profit margins to gain higher than normal profits. Rather than a wage-price spiral, set in motion by workers reacting to price increases that push them to seek higher wages, which firms then "reluctantly" pass on to consumers (as in genre two), in this story the same elements are rearranged. The global supply shocks we saw as "temporary" in genre three are in this genre opportunistically leapt upon by firms in highly concentrated markets as a smokescreen to raise prices far beyond what they could normally do, reaping windfall profits in the process. Given constricted supply and few alternatives, their customers just have to deal with it. The firms reap all the profits, and the consumers pay all the costs. The key economic idea underpinning this story, as we mentioned in the last chapter, is that firms set prices based on their market power rather than on the costs they face.

Briefly, in economics, there are typically three ways of thinking about firms and the prices that they react to. We encountered the first in our discussion of price controls. This is a world called perfect competition, which consists only of small firms in competition with one another, where none of them can set prices. In such a world, prices are set by the market, and firms that try to charge above that market price will be beaten by the competition. Think take-out pizza shops in a college town. Charge twice what the other guy charges and you are going down, fast. You can find such markets in the real world, but they are far from the norm in many cases.

The second is its mirror opposite, a monopoly. Russia became the quasi monopoly supplier of gas to large chunks of Europe. As a monopolist, Russia has a clear incentive to charge as much as it can since it faces no competitors. But that incentive to price gouge may be tempered by, for example, long-term contracts that guarantee buyers. When those buyers got upset with Russia over the invasion of Ukraine and told the monopolist (Russia) that they were done buying gas from them, Russia raised the price by constricting supply to the point that in 2022 spot-market prices for gas were traded at ten times forward historical rates. That's what a monopolist can do with its market power. It can set prices, and there is no way to make them change them, at least in the short run.

There are more monopolies and quasi monopolies around than you think. Think, for example, of multiple firms that supply a good like oil, which has an inelastic demand. One firm leads the price increase, and the others follow. That is, they cooperate to reap more joint profits than they would get by competing. That, as we talked about above, is called a cartel, and in the oil market that cartel is official. It's called the Organization of Petroleum Exporting Countries (OPEC).

The really interesting and perhaps most relevant case is the third market structure of oligopoly, in which a handful of firms can set prices above marginal cost, but only if they cooperate with one another to set either prices or quantities. Such cartels are often quite unstable because there is always the incentive to charge less or supply more in order to grab market share or hurt the competition, as we saw in the case of the French supermarkets. But as Thomas Philippon has shown for the United States and Brett Christophers has shown for the UK, the "effective" number of firms across many sectors in both countries has fallen significantly, which makes oligopoly pricing more stable and more profitable. For example, take the US airline sector—battered by COVID-19, hideously indebted, reluctantly bailed out by taxpayers, and loathed by consumers. Its effective number of firms is four. American, Delta, Southwest, and United collectively control 66 percent of the market. In 2023, prices are higher than ever. So are they, and firms in other similar sectors, "price gouging"? And is this what is driving inflation? Or are they passive victims of a wider inflation caused by other factors?

Evidence in support of this perspective is actually quite plentiful but is always contested by mainstream economists. Isabella Weber was one of the first to propose the idea that inflation was driven by profits. In her study with Evan Wasner, they showed that in the United States, firms' profits accounted for 9.4 percent of the increase in inflation (measured with the GDP deflator) since the third quarter of 2020, while wages accounted only for 4.7 percent. Carsten Jung and Chris Hayes find similar results for Brazil, Germany, South Africa, the UK, and the US. Both studies argue that the concentration of market power among firms acted as an inflation amplifier. By one account, in 2022, the profits of the average US firm increased by 49 percent since the beginning of inflation in 2021. Matt Stoller, research director of the American Economic Liberties

Project, analyzed these margin changes in depth and observed something interesting. While corporate profits remained stable from 2012 to 2019, they saw incredible growth in 2020–21 (see Figure 3.2). Based on his estimates, increases in corporate profits have cost the average US citizen $2,126.

An even more striking piece of evidence is to be found in a survey conducted by Digital.com in November 2021. According to this study, 56 percent of retail business acknowledged during earnings calls (when corporate CFOs and CEO get on the phone to their investors before they announce their earnings to the markets) that inflation gave them the ability to raise prices far beyond what they would have needed to offset higher production costs. As a result, on average, firms increased their prices by around 20 percent. As the simple economics story would

FIGURE 3.2:

RISING CORPORATE PROFITS

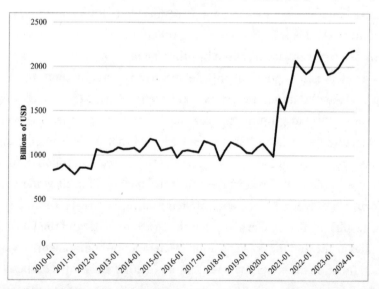

Source: US Bureau of Economic Analysis retrieved from FRED, Federal Reserve Bank of St. Louis.
Note: the line shows the evolution of profits after tax for the nonfinancial corporate business sector (without inventory valuation adjustment and capital consumption adjustment). The values are in billions of dollars, seasonally adjusted annual rate.

predict, this was particularly true for larger companies in concentrated sectors, with automobiles and e-commerce at the top of the list. This is hardly fringe opinion. The European Central Bank and the International Monetary Fund's own research has given us clear evidence that firms' growing profits fueled inflation in Europe.

However, size is not everything. Let's return to US airlines. Despite their super-concentrated positions and absurdly high prices, the sector as a whole was still making a loss through 2023. Nonetheless, estimates of how much price gouging matters for driving inflation suggests that corporate profits alone can account for 3.8 percent of the (at the time of measurement) 6.8 percent inflation in the United States in 2022. That is, corporate profit seeking is responsible for almost half (44.7 percent) of the current surge in prices.

According to this view, inflation is higher in the United States than in Europe not because of the higher fiscal stimulus (as the first genre maintains), or because of the peculiarities of the labor market (genre two), or global supply shocks (genre three), but simply because the American economy is more concentrated, and a handful of firms in critical sectors can set prices because they don't face significant competition and the government does not enforce antitrust laws. Why does this occur? Well, given that those firms are critical funders of those hugely expensive US elections that elect the folks who regulate these firms, one does not have to go far to see a conflict of interest at work here.

Unlike the first story, where blaming the government for "spending too much" sits well with the right, the price-gouging perspective is particularly appealing to US Democrats and the political left because it allows them to shift the blame for inflation to big companies, rather than to the mismanagement of the Biden administration or the machinations of greedy workers. But perhaps most important, this story finds traction among the general public, given their own lived experiences.

A survey conducted by the consultancy firm Deloitte showed that six in ten individuals believe that US companies are unfairly raising prices and are thereby eroding their purchasing power. Another recent survey confirmed what we proposed earlier, that in contrast to the opinions of economic experts, consumers believe that higher interest rates will generate higher inflation, as firms will shift their increased borrowing costs on to consumers, which it seems they actually do.

There are different ways to control inflation driven by price gouging, each of which is contentious. One way is to introduce price controls, which we talked about earlier. That is, to force firms not to push prices over a certain threshold. At the start of the recent burst of inflation, Isabella Weber compellingly described how price controls were part of the solution enacted by Roosevelt during the Second World War and its immediate aftermath. Her payoff for doing so, as we shall discuss in chapter 5, was to create a Twitter mob of angry economists who got really upset at the notion of price controls doing anything except causing communism.

A more long-term solution is to reduce firm concentration via antitrust policies. That is, break them into smaller units and force them to compete, which Lina Kahn, head of the US Federal Trade Commission, is keen to apply. A third solution is to tax away the price hike by introducing an excess profits tax, which would both discourage firms from charging higher prices and redistribute the gains from inflation from the users to the losers. As we noted in the previous chapter, the UK and a few other countries have done this to oil companies recently. When one considers that Saudi Aramco's net income increased 90 percent in the second quarter of 2022 to $48.4 billion, making it the most profitable company in the world, that only seems fair. Tellingly, raising interest rates would do little if anything to tame profit-driven inflation. Recent evidence shows that the more market power firms hold, the less effective monetary policy will be.

The Limits to Greed

Just like the other genres, however, the price-gouging story is not without its problems as a general explanation of inflation. One limitation is that it explains why inflation persists, but not why it happens in the first place. Supporters of the price-gouging story are quite open about this fact, however, seeing it not as a weakness but as a strength. They generally argue that companies saw prices going up during COVID-19 and weaponized the situation by raising prices. Consumers, meanwhile, had lost their benchmarks for what a fair price was because any product could have become more costly "because of COVID." This leads price gouging supporters to say that profiteering is "an accelerant of price increases" but not "the primary cause" of inflation. For this reason, some economists, like Jason Furman, a former director of the Council of Economic Advisers at the White House, believe that price gouging may not be the best explanation of inflation but will admit that it might explain some part of what is happening. In short, price gouging may be real, but it wouldn't exist without COVID-related supply-chain disruptions, higher energy prices due to the Russian invasion of Ukraine, or the stimulus bill. So the question is, How much of the recent inflation is attributable to it?

As noted above, advocates of this position see as much as half of US inflation being driven by this mechanism. However, others, such as German Lopez at *The New York Times*, argue that the link between profits and inflation, which is at the core of this story, is neither as strong nor as automatic as this genre's partisans would have it. For example, while inflation rose rapidly in 2021–22, stock markets plummeted just as rapidly over the same period, having their worst first-half-year performance in fifty years. This begs a very important question. If profits were up uniformly, and share prices reflect at least in some sense discounted cash flow, why would those share prices be falling? Second, some markets that are highly concentrated didn't set higher prices as inflation rose. This was the case with health care in the United States, which is nearly 20 percent of US GDP, where prices in that same period rose more slowly than overall inflation.

Nonetheless, there is something compelling and intuitive about the notion that firms in concentrated markets will try to resist a squeeze on their profit margins by raising prices, contingent on the other firms in that market doing the same. In the terms outlined by Weber and Wasner, such sellers' inflation occurs when "these cost increases are not unique to individual firms but experienced by all competitors, firms can safely increase prices since they have the mutual expectation that all market players will do the same." And we have seen US profits hit all-time highs in recent years. And what goes up (prices) does not necessarily come down.

But there is an observational equivalence problem buried deep within this genre. That is, the same things can be read in two different ways. US auto prices, for example, increased during the pandemic and have stayed high despite supply chain bottlenecks abating. So is this greedflation manifest in a new "lower-volume and higher-price" business model going forward, enabled by concentrated market structure? Maybe. Or maybe it's a result of higher input costs in general across the sector combined with demand destruction from those higher prices? After all, while profits are up, sales are well down. In short, this a compelling story, but it's probably the hardest one to pin down given that measuring prices is much easier than measuring profits. We return to this topic and stress its importance in chapter 6.

DEMOGRAPHY, GLOBALIZATION, AND INFLATION?

There is one minor genre worth talking about that focuses on the interaction of demography and globalization and is associated with ex–Bank of England economist Charles Goodhart. Goodhart, along with Summers, has been hailed as one of the "sages" who "saw inflation coming" before it happened. Yet while Goodhart and his coauthor, Manoj Pradhan, indeed predicted the return of inflation in their book published in 2020, the reasons they gave for its return focused on changes in long-term structural factors, rather than the conjunctural causes discussed in the prior four stories.

For Goodhart and Pradhan, the rise of China and the return of Eastern Europe led to the doubling of the potential and actual labor supply of the advanced economies between 1991 and 2018. When supply massively increases, prices go down. Unsurprisingly, then, core country wages fell or stagnated while prices of manufactured goods fell too. Deflation, not inflation, became normal. Those trends, he argued, are now in long-term reversal. The first is a function of a demographic shift across the rich countries and China where older people, often with chronic health conditions, will outnumber the younger workers who will have to pay for them. This will combine with deglobalization as both costs and reemerging geopolitical conflict leads to a decoupling of global supply chains. In such a world, wages will rise, growth will fall, and interest rates will rise, all leading to a sustained period of inflation, not deflation.

It's important to note that Goodhart and Pradhan thought this process would take many years to bear its bitter fruit, whereas the inflation we face today came all at once and came mainly from causes other than demography. And it now seems to be on the wane or is at least stabilizing at a higher than historically normal level. However, if Goodhart and Pradhan are correct, the transitory story we discussed above in genre three may have long-term structural forces lined up against it that will mean at least a higher baseline of costs as a new normal going forward, if not accelerating inflation like that of the 1970s. In contrast to the notion of transitory inflation, Goodhart and Pradhan might be the first members of what we could call "team structural." This is an important point we pick up on in the conclusion.

THE POLITICS OF INFLATIONARY STORYTELLING

So far, we have outlined four major and three minor genres, each of which contains a more or less compelling story about the causes and effects of inflation, who is to blame, and what should be done about it. Each story also contains significant weaknesses, and in many ways they contradict one another. For example, if you accept the "too much demand" story, then it's hard to square that with the "greedflation" story, which is probably why many economists resist the latter because they embrace the former. Similarly, if you think inflation is transitory, then demographic accounts should give pause for thought. But what if the point of all this is not really to diagnose causes but to shift the costs of inflation onto someone else? Seen this way, inflation stories are less scientific theories and more like political rhetorics.

In 1992, the economist Albert Hirschman published a brilliant book called *The Rhetoric of Reaction*, where he took two hundred years of arguments against changing various aspects of the status quo—the conservative response to the French Revolution, arguments against extending the franchise a century later, and arguments against building the welfare state later still—and showed that pretty much all these arguments can be reduced to one of three rhetorics, or theses, as he called them.

The first was the "perversity thesis," whereby attempts to push policy in one direction will inevitably push it in the opposite direction. How revolutions end up affirming the status quo or how attempts to push up taxation must lead to revenue losses are typical examples.

Hirschman's second thesis was the "futility thesis," whereby attempts to improve the lot of mankind will really not move the needle on the problem targeted. The war on poverty, for example, failed to solve poverty by entrenching a dependency culture. Progressive taxation failed to reduce inequality. That sort of thing.

The third was what he called the "jeopardy thesis," where, for example, extending the vote to the unpropertied will guarantee the end of private property, or taxing oil firms for unearned profits will jeopardize future investment, as then UK finance minister Kwasi Kwarteng recently argued. That is, striving for the new goal will jeopardize a prior, and perhaps more fundamentally important, set of goals.

These three theses can usefully be applied to each of our four genres.

Genre one, the "too much demand" school, is really just a jeopardy thesis. You might think that "stimulating" the economy to prevent a depression is a good idea, but no. If you do that, the result will be runaway inflation that is more dangerous than the recession you are trying to avoid. Beware.

Genre two, the "problem is the labor market" school, is effectively a perversity thesis. You might think that higher wages and increasing the wage share, especially when prices are rising, is a good thing. But no. Doing so will generate the very inflation you are trying to avoid, so above all, don't do it.

Genre three, "team transitory," combines the futility and jeopardy theses. Given that inflation is transitory, hiking rates will only cause more damage to an already stressed economy (jeopardy), especially when well-anchored expectations (if they exist) mean that doing so will not change inflation dynamics (futility). The demographic subvariant is really a futility thesis. You might think you can fight inflation through policy, but you can't. Demographics are destiny. Meanwhile, genre four, "price gouging," encompasses all three theses. When the cause of inflation is firms pushing up margins, it is futile to raise rates, perhaps even perverse, and doing so will jeopardize the economy by causing an overly strong contraction.

What this exercise of cribbing off Hirschman demonstrates is that inflation stories are political and distributional stories in that they contain, and indeed rely for their power on, their rhetorical form. This is the value of rhetorics. They compel us to accept an argument despite contrary evidence. And they give their partisans a convenient way to ignore contrary evidence and champion their preferred story. This is why we need to pay such close attention to different inflation stories and to whom is telling them to us. Those who get to attribute the blame don't have to pay the costs.

4

=====

WHEN INFLATION GOES HYPER

> There is a big logical jump between acknowledging the destructive nature of hyperinflation and arguing that the lower the rate of inflation, the better.
>
> —Ha-Joon Chang

WHY HYPERINFLATION IS NOT COMING TO A COUNTRY NEAR YOU

We argued earlier that are three types of inflation: the good, the bad, and the ugly. Let's get into that a bit more because it is important. To recap, inflation can be good if it's moderate and wages are growing in line with workers' productivity even if they (usually) don't get their fair share of it. Bad inflation stems from negative supply-side shocks that push up prices and depress the economy, which is what we have had recently due to post-COVID-19 supply-chain breakdowns and energy price spikes. But ugly inflation is the one that most people have in the back of their minds when they think about inflation. Ugly inflation can get *very ugly*. It occurs when inflation really gets out of hand and a country enters a state of *hyperinflation*. In this chapter we examine hyperinflation, mainly to demonstrate how rare it actually is, and to show how the conditions that make it possible really don't apply to most economies most of the time.

Despite the vehemence with which economists denounce hyperinflation, they actually have quite different views on when you have one. The most common view defines hyperinflation as a monthly change in prices that exceeds 50 percent. For example, the price of a gallon of milk moving from $5.00 to $7.50 in one month, and then from $7.50 to $11.25 the next month. Based on this definition, the IMF estimates that there were eight cases of hyperinflation in the interwar period (1920–46), none between 1947 and 1984, and fifteen cases between 1984 and 2007. While this definition seems very precise it has its drawbacks.

Phillip Cagan, the economist who came up with the 50 percent threshold, acknowledged that the definition he proposed was arbitrary, but served the purposes of his study. In a later work, Cagan argued that "there is no well-defined threshold" to identify hyperinflation. Indeed, a particular threshold doesn't say much about what is happening in an economy because of this inflation, or where such high inflation is coming from. It's a bit like saying a patient's fever is any temperature above 101 degrees Fahrenheit, but not focusing upon why the fever is there in the first place.

Economist Michał Kalecki proposed an alternative definition: "a very rapid rise in prices *and a general tendency to convert money into goods.*" This definition doesn't really focus on how large the change in prices is or is not. Rather, it focuses on what it means for behavior. Such a perspective assumes that the key problem with hyperinflation lies in people's beliefs that prices will always go up, rather than the matter of how much they go up. Again, as per the "expectations" story we have already encountered, if this psychological mechanism is in place, then people will buy goods now for fear that tomorrow those same goods will be more expensive. The problem this time is that in doing so they'll accelerate the *velocity of money*, the speed at which money is spent in an economy, and thereby trigger further inflation.

Kalecki's definition is especially helpful as a tool to help us understand hyperinflation when it is applied to open economies (countries that rely on exports and imports for growth) with a weak currency (it tends to fall in value relative to others, or at least be highly volatile). In such cases Kalecki's definition can be adapted to define hyperinflation as "a very rapid increase in prices *and a general tendency to convert units of domestic currency into foreign currency.*"

Why does this idea of "open to trade with a weak currency" matter? Because in an open economy where money can flow in and out of the economy quite freely, if prices go up a lot people can lose confidence in the ability of their domestic currency to buy the same amount of goods. One option they have to preserve their purchasing power is to "panic buy" the goods they need. But another option is to exchange that currency for a stronger, less volatile currency, such as the US dollar, which will help retain that purchasing power. Understanding this helps us understand why the most cases of hyperinflation occur in open economies with weak currencies.

GOING HYPER

But how do you generate a hyperinflation? There are basically two views on this, and they make for strongly contrasting stories about what went wrong and who is to blame. The first is the "fiscal" view, which is a derivative of the "too much money" story we already encountered. According to this view, in the words of Peter Bernholz, "hyperinflations are always caused by public deficits, which are largely financed by money creation." Hyperinflation is therefore a problem of excess demand created by excessive money creation by the government. Hyperinflation is then nothing more than a common or garden variety inflation that has simply gotten out of hand, as the result of irresponsible policies enacted by governments that printed money to either pay off their key constituencies or engage in projects that they could not afford.

The second view and contrasting view is the "balance of payments" view. According to this version of events, hyperinflation develops when countries have an exchange-rate crisis, which needs a bit of unpacking. The exchange rate of a currency is the value of one currency relative to another. For example, how many dollars do I need to buy one euro (or vice versa), and how that changes over time? If a country's currency depreciates, its domestic prices must go up as it gets more costly to buy imported goods. This affects the balance of payments, which is the difference between the amount of money that flows into a country (export earnings) and the money that flows out of that country (import payments). Following a currency depreciation, as foreign goods get more expensive, a country needs to print more money to buy the same goods. In the short term that helps pay the bills, but in the longer term that devalues the currency further, which makes the problem worse. Eventually, but for quite different reasons than you get in the "too much money" story, you still get "too much money" trying to pay for "too few goods," and the overall level of prices goes up. The result end is that both foreign and domestic goods get more expensive.

However, the problem really gets bad and becomes "hyper" if holders of the currency lose confidence in it, resulting in a rapid sell-off and a "crash." Then, in a panic-driven version of our inflation expectations story, as more and more people do panic sell rather than panic buy, the further the currency falls, and the less it buys. This mechanism, rather than profligate politicians, is key to how inflations go hyper in this story.

Starting with these two views of hyperinflation, in this chapter we examine four of the most famous cases in the historical record. Three are quite recent: Venezuela, Zimbabwe, and Argentina. We then examine one famous historical case, the Weimar Republic that preceded the Nazi regime in Germany. We note that in all these cases hyperinflation was preceded by an abnormal monetary expansion. This has convinced many observers that Milton Friedman was right when he claimed that "inflation is always and everywhere a monetary phenomenon." However, that which comes before does not (necessarily) explain that which comes after. Once one gets into the specifics of these cases we can see that the factors that led to such monetary expansions were not only very different, they were driven by quite unique and unusual prior causes. In short, hyperinflation is never the result of a single flawed macroeconomic policy, be it money printing or fiscal stimulus, nor is it reducible to a single irresponsible monetary expansion. The truth is far more interesting—and it shows us that generating a hyperinflation is actually quite unlikely. Once you accept this as plausible, these two things follow.

WHY A (PURELY) MONETARIST LENS DISTORTS OUR VIEW

First, the simple monetarist theory of inflation is too simple. A large amount of money being shoveled into the financial system is certainly a precondition for inflation, but that is not the same thing as a cause. After all, the United States and many other rich countries engaged in massive monetary expansions after the 2008 financial crisis and inflation failed to show up. Indeed, the EU fell into deflation by 2014, despite such a monetary expansion. Second, this theory also suggests that policies that are designed to fight inflation, based on a simple monetarist theory, may not actually work because they misidentify causes.

Let's take two examples, inflation targeting and central bank independence. Inflation targeting means that the central bank sets a target inflation rate, for instance, a 2 percent yearly change in the Consumer Price Index, and then pulls various policy levers to hit that target. Inflation targeting is supposed to be effective in reducing inflation as it "anchors expectations." That is, the public knows what to expect prices to be in the future because the central bank is "promising" to reach a certain inflation rate, and as a result of that (credible) "expectation," price changes converge to the target. In some countries this seemed to work insofar as countries with inflation targets tended to hit them. But the question of causality remained. Did they get low inflation because of the targets, or would they have gotten the low inflation anyway due to other developments, such as the effect of outsourcing and globalization on prices?

Evidence for this latter stance lies in the fact that inflation targeting seems to work best when inflation is already quite moderate and may already be falling. It also seems to be a lot harder to hit the target when the inflation rate is already high. For example, with inflation hovering around 40 percent in 2016, Argentina adopted an inflation-targeting regime. While the adoption of this new policy initially coincided with a period of falling inflation, in 2018 prices began to rise again, reaching almost 50 percent, despite the same target. As a result, the Argentinian central bank abandoned the target after only twenty-five months.

The other case that makes us question the centrality of money as "the" cause of hyperinflation is to see central bank independence as the cause of falling inflation. That is, it's not the belief in the target that matters (expectations) as much as the belief in the independence of the institution (credibility). As we discuss in detail in chapter 5, a consensus emerged in the 1980s and '90s around the idea that central banks should be independent from politicians in order to achieve lower inflation, because politicians could not be trusted to keep low-inflation promises due to the "time inconsistent" nature of their preferences. In plain English, you can't trust politicians to keep their promises with an election coming up. They say that they will not spend, but they will, and that will cause inflation.

It's a rather cynical view of politics and a rather saintly view of central bankers, but the available empirical evidence in the 1990s seemed to suggest that the higher the independence of the central bank, the lower the average inflation rate. However, not all cases of independence are equal. For example, when Zimbabwe reformed the Reserve Bank of Zimbabwe, its central bank, to make it more independent, things went a bit differently. As Figure 4.1 shows, following the reform, inflation in Zimbabwe didn't slow down. On the contrary, it skyrocketed.

In less extreme cases than Zimbabwe—pretty much every other

FIGURE 4.1:

CENTRAL BANK INDEPENDENCE
REFORM AND INFLATION IN ZIMBABWE

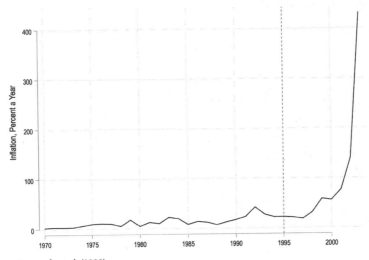

Source: Acemoglu et al. (2008).

case you can find—we encounter a problem that might be called the "bystander hypothesis." In the period 1980–99, among rich countries it is plausible to argue that if you had an independent central bank you did in fact disinflate faster than those that did not have such a central bank after the inflation of the 1970s. But countries that didn't make their central banks independent, or were less independent, disinflated too, albeit at a slower pace. After 2010 however, the difference in disinflation performance between the two groups disappeared. So what's driving what? Did the institutional fix help adjust expectations down in the first period but not in the second? If so, why? Or perhaps there are factors other than the quantity of money or people's supposed expectations of future price movements pushing prices around here? That is, far from being causal agents of lower inflation, central banks were more like bystanders at an accident scene. They record what happens and may have rendered some assistance, but they didn't cause the accident.

In short, while the symptoms are similar—leaving the impression that we can find common economic laws that apply to all cases—the origins of inflations, especially hyperinflations, are actually quite different from one another and crucially depend on their historically specific context. We demonstrate this by looking in depth at our four "hyper" cases.

CASE ONE—VENEZUELA: OIL PRICES, DUTCH DISEASE, AND CAFÉ CON LECHE

For many economists and policymakers, Venezuela is, along with Argentina, the poster child for hyperinflation in the twenty-first century. At the beginning of the so-called Bolivarian Revolution that brought the government of Hugo Chavez to power in 1999, inflation was already high, hitting 23.57 percent per year, compared to the average inflation in the rest of Latin America, which at that time was 9.28 percent. By the end of 2014, Venezuelan inflation had reached 63.4 percent, while the rest of Latin America's average remained at 9.30 percent. By 2017, Venezuelan inflation reached the jaw-dropping rate of 2,585.8 percent.

It's hard to think about what such an inflation rate means. To get a sense, imagine that you visit Caracas, the country's capital, once a year, around January. One morning in January 2021 you go out and order a café con leche. That coffee would cost you around 2 bolivars at the January 2021 inflation rate. One year later, you go back to the same bar, order the same coffee, and it now costs 8.74 bolivars. Now, fast-forward to January 2023, you go back to the same bar and order the same coffee. You may believe that the bartender is tricking you when the bill says 53 bolivars. But by October of the same year, the cost of the café con leche will nearly double to 90 bolivars. This is what an economy looks like with an annual inflation rate of 224 percent. Now, apply these changes to a wider basket of goods, and you can understand why inflation at this level is devastating for any country.

How did Venezuela get there? The standard story is "too much spending." In fairness, there was, by historical standards, a lot of spending under Chavez. From the moment Chavez took power up until his death in 2013, he engaged in a wide and costly set of social policies called "Bolivarian Missions," aiming to help the poorest individuals in the country, who were, perhaps unsurprisingly, his main supporters. These policies focused on providing income for poor families, houses for the inhabitants of the *ranchos* (urban slums), and jobs supported by government-financed training programs for the unemployed. On top of the policies targeted to the poor, pension rights were extended to all citizens regardless of their individual contributions to the national pension fund.

As taxes did not increase to pay for all this spending, the government's deficit necessarily increased. From 2010 to 2012, the deficit rose from 9 to 12 percent of GDP, and over the same period, the monetary base (M2) growth rate increased from 28.6 to 43.6 percent, which suggests that excessive monetary growth could be the culprit. There is just one wrinkle: despite all these classic inflation-boosting policies, Venezuelan inflation was actually quite stable, and even decreased from 27 to 20 percent over the same period. It took more than a year after this increase in the money supply for prices to boom and inflation to soar to 56.1 percent. Even allowing for a lag in cause and effect, the timing in the "too much money" story is a bit off.

That observation, in turn, brings us to the one factor that can't be overlooked in the story of Venezuela's hyperinflation, a factor that counters the fiscal view quite strongly: oil. Chavez financed his spending program through the export of oil, which is abundant in Venezuela. Indeed, it's so abundant that by some estimates over 90 percent of total exports were oil or oil related, which in turn produced 16 percent of GDP. This made Venezuela's balance of payments extremely vulnerable to global changes in the price of oil, which the government cannot control. It also meant that if its currency crashed as a result of a decline in the price of oil, the price of Venezuela's imports would go through the roof.

This is where the balance of payments view kicks in, because as well as the money supply expanding between 2010 and 2012, the difference between money inflows and outflows decreased, meaning that there was less and less money flowing into Venezuela compared to the money flowing out of it. That meant the exchange rate was about to go down rapidly, which it did, and which fueled inflation through the import channel. Venezuela's heavy reliance on oil income is a typical case of what's called "Dutch disease." This is what you get when an abundance of natural resources ends up hurting rather than helping a country's economic development.

FROM DUTCH DISEASE TO HYPERINFLATION

When the global price of oil goes up, Venezuela gets more money for each barrel it sells, which adds to the government's coffers. However, since Venezuela sells oil in its local currency, the bolivar, foreign investors will start exchanging their US dollars for bolivars, so that as the bolivar strengthens they are not caught on the wrong side of the appreciation. As the demand for the bolivar increases, its value increases too. This in turn means that *every* good sold by Venezuela, not just oil, gets more expensive. As a result, foreign investors would be less likely to buy other domestically produced goods, as they can get them more cheaply in other countries. Oil, however, is a scarce resource that can be found only in a few places. For this reason, oil became a large component of total exports and GDP, and the dependence on oil posed problems for Venezuelan producers in other sectors that struggle to compete with exporters from other countries. The long-term consequence of this situation was that Venezuela became extremely dependent on imports as its own industries were priced out of the market and replaced by imports, thanks to this Dutch disease.

So far, so oil-dependency making. But how does this lead to hyperinflation? As we saw, proponents of the fiscal view see the origins of inflation as being caused by the expansion in public spending in 2010–12.

However, during that same period Venezuela was already dealing with an oil price crisis that began in 2008, when prices plummeted from $129 to $31 per barrel in six months. As public revenues collapsed, the government tightened its spending to stop the balance of payments (and hence the bolivar) from spinning out of control.

However, instead of letting the exchange rate float (it was fixed against the US dollar), which would have resulted in a devaluation that would have made exports cheaper and imports dearer, thereby encouraging domestic consumption, the government decided to maintain fixed parity so that the bolivar would not lose value relative to other currencies. To do so, it reduced the amount of bolivars that could be exchanged by the public to buy imported goods. Imports fell by 20 percent, which helped the balance of payments, but Venezuelan producers that relied on intermediate imported goods for their own goods struggled to keep their production at normal levels due to cost increases.

While this strategy was initially effective in containing inflation—as we noted earlier, it fluctuated around 20 and 27 percent—this situation couldn't last for long, as the government would have to keep spending precious foreign exchange reserves to keep it at that level. And those foreign exchange reserves were made possible by a high oil price, which had now collapsed. Eventually, in 2010, the government abandoned the fixed parity and the bolivar rapidly depreciated.

As the currency devalued, exports picked up and the government received more bolivars from abroad than usual. This allowed the government to increase public spending, which grew between 2010 and 2012. That is what showed up in spending programs and in the money supply increase in this period. Imports, however, became much more expensive. Since the country was heavily dependent on imports given its acute case of Dutch disease, then and only then did inflation shoot up markedly. So what is the take-home here? That the expansion of the money supply came *after* the collapse in oil revenues in the attempt to maintain parity. It was these prior factors that drove inflation through the import channel and the collapse in exports. The expansion of the money supply was more an economic effect than a political cause of inflation.

In 2012 the bolivar's depreciation accelerated. As the currency depreciated, workers became less able to buy already expensive imported goods, which was compounded by the restrictions in place on obtaining foreign exchange, noted above. And the firms that employed those workers, that faced higher costs trying to buy intermediate goods from abroad? They produced sellers' inflation by passing their costs on to consumers, further reducing workers' purchasing power and stoking inflation higher.

Thanks to those high oil prices and the government's redistributive reforms, at the start of the crisis unemployment was low and unemployment benefits were high, placing workers in a particularly powerful position to bargain for higher wages. Given accelerating inflation, labor disputes increased. By using strikes and other measures to bargain for restorative wage increases, workers managed to partially offset the costs of those depreciations by increasing their wage share of GDP from 32.4 percent in 2010 to 39.1 percent in 2014. But these pressures from workers to increase their wages combined with the desire of firms to maintain their profits to drive prices ever upward. Venezuela did indeed enter a classic wage-price spiral.

The situation worsened in 2015, when oil prices fell by another 50 percent. President Maduro, Chavez's successor, tried to control inflation by imposing price controls, which as economists would predict, seemed to result only in a sharp reduction in production and investment from both domestic and foreign firms. After all, if prices are capped while input costs are rising, profits have to fall, so you either make less or quit production altogether. As a consequence, Venezuelans lost faith in the bolivar, and in the country. They began to prefer holding dollars to holding bolivars.

This preference for dollars, given the state of the economy and the shortage of dollars in non-oil sectors, became a chronic problem in the country that persists still today. Remember our modification of Kalecki's notion that we should define hyperinflation as a situation where there's "a general tendency to convert units of domestic currency into foreign currency"? Having experienced uncontrolled fluctuations of the value of the bolivar, Venezuelans indeed looked for a more stable alternative currency, US dollars, in order to purchase foreign goods. And when President Maduro tried to restrict the exchange of bolivars into dollars, another form of price control, Venezuelans developed an extensive black market for dollars. Eventually, economic conditions became so bad that by some estimates seven million Venezuelans fled the country.

The case of Venezuela tells us a lot about inflation and the various stories that seek to explain it. All four of the inflation stories that we outlined earlier are at play here. Chavez's social spending program created too much money, which is a fiscal story, even if it's undermined by the exchange-rate view. Thanks to better social protections, workers' bargaining power strengthened, allowing them to ask for higher wages. This eventually led to higher prices, as we learned from the labor market story. Supply-side shocks affecting the price of oil, and therefore the value of the bolivar and the prices of imported goods, were crucial to Venezuela's descent into hyperinflation. This matches with the supply-side story that team transitory is telling us today. Finally, when the currency depreciated and prices of imported goods went up, local firms had an excuse to charge higher prices on their products, as the price-gouging narrative compellingly describes. However, none of these narratives alone, or even in combination, can fully explain how Venezuela ended up with hyperinflation. Hyperinflation in Venezuela was highly contextual. It was the result of a political revolution; the increasing dependence of the country on a single sector, oil; as well as of the roller coaster in oil prices that the country had to suffer, which had huge implications for its exchange rate and domestic prices. Money was certainly involved, but it's too much to claim that it was the sole, or even primary, cause of the disorder.

CASE TWO—ZIMBABWE'S INAUSPICIOUS ORIGINS

If you think it's impossible to hold a trillion dollars in your hand, you probably haven't been to Zimbabwe. In 2009, the value of the Zimbabwean dollar declined so much that the central bank had to print a banknote worth 100 trillion Zimbabwean dollars. It was worth about thirty US dollars. And if you think that the four-digit inflation in Venezuela was scary, inflation in Zimbabwe was estimated to have reached 79.6 *billion* percent in mid-November 2008. We say "estimated" because inflation was so high that in July the Zimbabwean government simply stopped reporting official inflation statistics. This astonishing number gives Zimbabwe second place in the highest monthly inflation rate that was ever recorded, second only to Hungary's hyperinflation in 1946. How did Zimbabwe get there? Zimbabwe is another of those cases that show us that inflation cannot be reduced to a single policy error, such as excessive money creation. It is rather the result of a combination of different and sometimes seemingly unrelated policies that together push the exchange rate down, which then pushes inflation up.

Before independence in 1980, Zimbabwe was ruled by a very narrow, violent, and oppressive white minority regime. Although run for the benefit of this white minority, Zimbabwe was nonetheless seen by the international community as a reasonably well-performing low-income economy and an important agricultural exporter in Sub-Saharan Africa. But in reality, Zimbabwe started its postcolonial period with huge socioeconomic problems, such as extreme inequality of both income and wealth between the white and black communities, especially among farmers.

As a result of the colonial and then postcolonial apartheid-type regime, at independence the income of black workers was one tenth that of whites, and this wage differential was twenty-four times higher in the agricultural sector. In terms of wealth-producing assets, the majority of the land was concentrated in the hands of about four thousand white farmers, while the much larger black population engaged in subsistence farming. It is therefore not surprising that in 1980 the newly elected government of Robert Mugabe focused its first actions on a land reform aimed at redistributing the land from white minorities to black farmers. And there was precedent in doing so for reasons that lay beyond issues of historic justice.

THE LAND REFORMS WITH A WEAK STATE

Land reform has a long pedigree as the backbone of redistributive reforms that led to economic growth. In Japan, South Korea, and Taiwan, large-scale land redistribution from traditional elites to peasant farmers in the early and mid-twentieth century massively reduced inequality, increased output, and laid the foundations for later industrial transformation. In these so-called East-Asian "developmental states," postcolonial relations between the colony and the former colonist were much weaker, and the state in these countries had developed both policy autonomy and capacity vis-à-vis its private sector over prior decades, which allowed them to increase productivity on the back of these reforms.

In Zimbabwe, however, these reforms were implemented abruptly by a weak postcolonial state in a divided and highly unequal economy without much consultation or compensation. Some farmers were given a one-day ultimatum to evacuate their farms. Sometimes the land that was taken was redistributed as much among politically connected local officials as among local farmers. This lack of effective state capacity in implementing such a massive reform, undertaken without seeking even the partial cooperation of the white landowners in the transition, meant that the knowledge and skills needed to farm at scale evaporated as the white farmers left the country after independence. In addition, the dispersed and fragmented nature of the land distribution itself increased farming costs that would have been previously dampened by economies of scale.

But perhaps most important, the fragmented nature of the land reform made it impossible for farmers to use land as a collateral for bank loans and thus develop their new farms. The banks' traditional customers had fled, while the prospective new customers had land in small pockets with little or no capital to farm it. As a result, banks stopped lending to farmers, and the government had to step in to supply credit and equipment using public spending. Of course, this was all new for the government too. The result was a sharp decline in agricultural production, the country's main export, which was compounded by severe and consecutive droughts throughout the 1980s and '90s, which in turn further undercut agricultural production and exports. The agricultural sector, which was the crucial source of the foreign currency that paid for postcolonial Zimbabwe's imports, was effectively on the ropes from the moment of independence.

EXPORT CREDITS, UNFUNDED PENSIONS, AND WAR WITHOUT TAXES

By the middle of the 1990s, Zimbabwe was a combustible cocktail of contested land reforms, declining agricultural productivity, falling foreign exchange earnings, and a population that would rather hold foreign currencies than their own domestic currency. All that was needed to make this worse was an asset price collapse, which duly arrived in 1997 in the form of a stock exchange crash. The result was a massive flight of foreign capital out of the country.

The crash, as usual, had several causes. It was partly endogenous, stemming from investor concerns over unbudgeted fiscal expansions to finance further land reforms, and the desire of the government to pay pension benefits to war veterans. Both of these moves would have been inflationary, which would have devalued financial assets further still. But war veterans were a particularly important protest group due to their role in the newly independent states' liberation. Initially, the government sought to finance these pensions with a war veteran levy, but that faced opposition from the rest of the labor force. Eventually, lacking other options, in 1997 the government borrowed money to finance these expenses, which amounted to around 3 percent of GDP. The stock market collapse was also partly exogenous, stemming both from the contagion effects of the East Asian financial crisis of that year, and from the social unrest that followed when the government faced more than two hundred strikes.

Capping all this off, the very next year, Zimbabwe's leader Robert Mugabe declared war on the Democratic Republic of Congo. Fighting this war required the mobilization of huge economic resources, which further ballooned the fiscal deficit to the tune of around an extra six billion Zimbabwe dollars. Pumping the deficit to this level was not going to sit well with international creditors, so Zimbabwe duly hid these costs from the official accounts. When their creditors eventually found out, they suspended their lending to the country.

Given this inauspicious context, the Reserve Bank of Zimbabwe tried to boost exports by permitting local banks to use a part of their reserves to subsidize strategic exports. In simple terms, this meant that the central bank lowered the cost of lending to exporters via the banks, on the condition that the banks would issue loans to exporters at subsidized rates. As a result, central bank money was released as export credits at an interest rate of 30 percent, which was cheap when compared to the bank rate of 56 percent and the inflation rate of 54 percent. As a result, borrowers took advantage of these cheap credits under the guise of boosting "exports," and credit growth accelerated from 30 percent to 60 percent from 1999 to 2000.

As a further measure to boost exports, the central bank devalued the currency by 24 percent. Despite this, the currency was still overvalued as the unofficial "street" market was 25 percent less than the now devalued official rate. This mattered because it signaled that people preferred to hold a foreign currency, such as US dollars, at a lower rate than the central bank would offer. Once again we see Kalecki's "swapping currencies" problem. This suggested to Zimbabweans that the spread between the official and street rates would fall further in the future, creating an incentive for them to spend their money more rapidly, which they did, adding further to inflation.

All these factors combined led the government to finance public debt by repeatedly borrowing from the banking sector. While Zimbabwe's central bank tried to contain inflation by limiting the amount of commercial bank reserves in order to limit further credit expansion, it failed to do so because government spending kept exceeding the spending target. In the early 2000s, the situation worsened further when under pressure of economic collapse, the Reserve Bank of Zimbabwe started lending money at very low rates to sectors—those most favored by the government—that were unlikely to repay their debt.

IT'S A LONG ROAD TO GET THERE

In short, while money printing was again certainly involved, Zimbabwe's problem was never as simple as "too much money printing led to hyperinflation." This situation developed over a thirty-year period and went exponential at the end. Inflation went from a very high 386 percent in 2003 to a staggering 231 million percent in 2008. The currency was "redenominated" three times within two years, meaning that the government literally removed three zeros from its currency in 2006 and ten zeros in 2008, so that the use of the Zimbabwe dollar was physically manageable. But by that time, Zimbabweans clearly understood that their currency was worthless and had begun to use foreign currency to conduct almost all transactions.

This, as economists would predict, and as we also saw in Venezuela, led to the development of an "informal sector," where Zimbabweans would cross the border to buy goods cheaply and sell them at home for higher prices while accepting payment only in dollars. In response, the government tried different ways to fight inflation. In 2007, the government introduced price controls on basic goods. However, this policy didn't take into account the ability of firms to sustain production at the controlled prices, and so shortages arose as production fell, which provided a further incentive for the development of the informal sector and the continuing use of foreign currency. By 2009, the central bank had pretty much lost control as the public used mostly US dollars, South African rands, and Botswana pulas in preference to the national currency.

However, since you don't get to print someone else's currency, and because the economy was a shambles, by 2016 Zimbabwe faced a chronic and continuing shortage of foreign currency to pay for imports. To deal with this, the government encouraged the use of different forms of money that were theoretically backed by US dollars. The government went as far as to pay its employees in a digital currency called EcoCash, a form of mobile money widely used in the country. But the public didn't trust the peg between EcoCash and the US dollar and preferred to hold the real dollars still in circulation.

Ultimately, given the lack of alternatives, in 2019 the government simply banned the use of foreign currencies in Zimbabwe as payments and introduced the Zim dollar (or RTGS) as the sole means of payment. The Zim's value was pegged at twenty-five Zim dollars for one US dollar. But given the state of the economy, Zim dollars soon lost value outside the official exchanges. While officially one US dollar was theoretically worth twenty-five Zim dollars, for the people trading it unofficially it was worth one hundred Zim dollars. Though it has declined from its early 2000s highs, hyperinflation is still a problem for Zimbabwe today. Before the pandemic hit, estimated inflation was around 300 percent.

Zimbabwe's situation defies any simple explanation. Yes, money was involved, and in certain moments it was causal. But so was the collapse of agricultural exports. So was fighting a war without raising taxes. So was buying off-key clients and constituencies to retain political power. So was the collapse in asset prices and the huge increase in import prices as the currency collapsed. And the whole process took thirty years to manifest itself. The role of the central bank in monetizing the debt and expanding credit cannot be ignored as a crucial piece of this inflation story. Nor can the fiscal incontinence of the government. But when you have a hyperinflation like this, an out-of-control central bank running the presses hot is once again as much a symptom of a crisis as it is a cause. These multiple causes lie much deeper in an economic model that no longer works and where no clear alternative presents itself. But the case of Zimbabwe also strongly suggests that these are not cases of transitory inflation disappearing after temporary supply shocks. And that insight in turn has an upside. It suggests that such cases are remarkably rare, infrequent, hard to generate, and depend upon external as well as internal factors. To see why, we now turn to the poster child for chronic inflation that sometimes tips into hyperinflation: Argentina.

CASE THREE—ARGENTINA:
FROM BOOM TO BUST TO BUSTED

Argentina is different from our prior cases. While it produces oil, like Venezuela, it is far more economically diversified. It's also quite dissimilar to Zimbabwe in almost every respect. Indeed, in the latter half of the nineteenth century, Argentina was seen as the next US and had truly impressive growth rates. But since the downturn of the 1930s, when the Great Depression engulfed Latin America, Argentina has never quite recovered its luster. Indeed, Argentina has the distinction of having defaulted on its public debts nine times and having had several hyperinflations in the four-digit range since World War II.

Argentina has waged a continual war against inflation since the 1950s, often based on very different plans. More often than not, those plans produced the very inflation the economic generals were trying to crush. Today, plans to fight inflation remain the focus of politicians in their run to the Casa Rosada, Argentina's presidential palace. The current president, Javier Milei, got elected with a radical plan that includes abolishing the country's central bank, fully dollarizing the economy, and slashing public expenditure. This evergreen fight against rising prices makes Argentina a very interesting, as well as unfortunate, quasi laboratory to study inflation.

In 2016, Zimbabwe and Venezuela were the only two countries with a higher inflation rate than Argentina. But perhaps more telling, also in 2016, every other Latin American country except Venezuela had managed to leave their inflationary histories behind them and produce relatively stable prices. But not Argentina. Argentina's average inflation rate between 1945 and 2019 was 143 percent. In October 2022, the annual inflation rate hovered around 90 percent. At the time of writing it hovers around 254 percent. Out of seeming exhaustion the Argentines just elected a radical libertarian president determined to crush inflation once and for all. Will he succeed? The answer depends on the answer to another question: Why is Argentina so continually "inflated"?

The answer is not obvious. Simon Kuznets, an early Nobel Prize laureate and one of the most prominent growth economists, once allegedly said that there exist "four sorts of countries: developed, underdeveloped, Japan, and Argentina." Indeed, the peculiarity of Argentina—it should be rich and stable, but it never is—has led many economists to disagree on the causes of Argentina's inflation. The core of this debate focuses on whether these causes are once again domestic (monetary) or external (balance of payments). We think both are true but argue that there is a prior set of factors apparent in the Argentine case that makes both views possible, and indeed causal.

THE PROBLEM IS TOO MUCH (POPULIST) MONEY

The domestic/fiscal view sees the roots of inflation in the populist macroeconomic policies implemented by successive Argentine governments since the 1950s. This version of events argues that the causes of inflation are purely political and stem from the nature of these policies rather than being driven by external factors. Argentinean economic historian Emilio Ocampo, recently tapped by President Milei to join his government, directly channeled this view when he argued that "the intensity of Argentina's hyperinflationary episodes was closely correlated to the magnitude of the structural imbalances generated by populist policies." This domestic/fiscal view makes Argentina the best case for the monetarist economists' understanding of inflation. Monetarist economists conclude that the causes of Argentina's inflation were to be found in the excessive growth of the money supply, and not in other factors, such as the exchange rate. This observation leads to a particular history of Argentina that sees a clear and causal link between the populist policies that led to monetary expansion and perpetual inflation as the inevitable outcome.

According to this interpretation, the roots of Argentina's chronic inflation problem date back to 1945, when the newly elected president Juan Peron implemented three major policies: more public spending; increases in effective protection on imports, which broke the link between domestic and international prices; and corporatism, collective bargaining with strong unions, which to some degree detached wages from productivity. This inherently unstable regime reached a crisis point in 1976 when the military intervened and suppressed the unions to restore profits and discipline.

Unfortunately, so this version of events goes, after the military regime ended in 1983, Argentina's new democratically elected government engaged in further fiscal profligacy. The military may have suppressed the unions, but they didn't do much for the economy's overall fiscal imbalances that made inflation rise above 600 percent by 1984. Inflation decelerated temporarily with the introduction of the so-called Austral plan in 1985, which combined fiscal austerity with wage and price controls, and introduced a new currency, the Austral. But that stabilization, in turn, failed by 1988.

That government resigned and was replaced in 1989 by one led by Peronist politician Carlos Menem. In due course, inflation reached the historic high of 3,046 percent, pushing Menem's new government to firmly commit to fiscal and monetary austerity alongside economic liberalization. Menem's minister of economy, Domingo Cavallo, led the charge through the Convertibility Plan of 1991. The plan set a fully convertible one-to-one peg between the Argentine peso and the US dollar, stipulating that the central bank must back 100 percent of the money it issues with foreign reserves. This necessarily limited public expenditures to what was earned in exports and opened up the economy to privatization and liberalization in order to secure new forms of inward investment. The plan was a tremendous success; one year after its introduction, inflation fell to below 20 percent. This led observers to conclude that such restrictive policies were the only way to finally defeat Argentina's embedded inflation.

This is indeed a persuasive story. But as we saw in Venezuela, a purely monetary history provides an incomplete version of events. The alternative and yet in this case complementary *external view* sees Argentina's inflation problem as generated from exogenous factors that regularly push the country into a balance of payment crisis.

THE PROBLEM IS (STILL) THE BALANCE OF PAYMENTS

According to this view, exchange-rate crises, not domestic policies, are the chief drivers of Argentine inflation. The rationale is simple. Suppose that an external shock such as a drought increases the cost of servicing foreign debt (of which Argentina has a ton, more on this below) due to agricultural exports, and hence agricultural tax revenues, going down. This pushes the central bank to lower its exchange-rate target so that the reduced flow of exports still generates a sufficient surplus to repay foreign debt. For instance, if the exchange rate is low, buying Argentinean products becomes cheaper, because one dollar can buy more Argentinean wheat, and thus pesos. But while depreciation translates into more exports, it also means that imports get more expensive.

As we saw with Venezuela, Argentina's imports not only include final goods that the country does not make, such as aircraft and computers, but also intermediate goods that are imported by Argentinean firms to help them build their final products. As these firms face higher prices due to the lower exchange rate, they will have to overcome these losses by increasing the domestic prices of their goods. As such, you get inflation through the import channel in both intermediate and final goods. For an open economy that is heavily dependent on the export of a few key commodities, even if the economy overall is quite diversified, this creates a structural bias toward inflation.

This view fits an Argentinean economy that since the 1970s and '80s has been increasingly open and therefore more vulnerable to external shocks. As described by Adam Tooze, in 2001 around 80 percent of Argentina's debt was denominated in US dollars. This made the actual cost of debt dependent on the exchange rate between the peso and the dollar. This dependence extended to the private sector, as Argentinean savers stashed their money in dollar-denominated deposits, and banks issued dollar-denominated credits to hedge against the volatility of the peso's exchange rate. In this context, Argentina's decision to peg its currency to the dollar at a fixed exchange rate through the Convertibility Plan aimed to reassure investors. Under such a peg, the government cannot manipulate the value of the currency to lower the cost of debt through inflation.

However, if that was the benefit, the cost of the fixed exchange rate was that it put the Argentinean economy in what Harvard economist Dani Rodrik called a "golden straitjacket." In this situation, monetary policy is on autopilot as it is fully dependent on the amount of capital that flows freely in and out of the country. If cash flows in, the central bank accumulates foreign reserves and automatically expands the money supply, which means more credit, and if it is used well, produces more growth. If cash flows out, foreign reserves drain out, shrinking the monetary base and credit, leading to a recession. Inflows tend to be welcomed.

The problem occurs if outflows trigger a mass exodus of funding, and the economy has a heart attack, called a sudden stop. Such a sudden stop is exactly what Argentina experienced in 2001, putting an end to the fixed exchange rate with the US dollar and driving the country into one of the harshest crises it ever experienced.

According to this view, money is a bystander once again as fiscal deficits necessarily *follow* the exchange-rate depreciation, which is the actual cause of higher inflation. For example, a late 1980s study by the International Monetary Fund compared the domestic and external views, which they call respectively "fiscal" and "balance of payments" views, for the high- inflation episodes in Argentina, Brazil, and Israel. Their empirical results support the external view. However, they acknowledge that in the case of Argentina (and Brazil), it was both the growth of base money and movements in the nominal exchange rate that continually drove inflation upward.

INFLATION BEYOND IMPORTS AND MONEY?

At the end of the day, which view is right? Both perspectives have their strengths. Both seem to be in play. And both have their limitations. A clear limitation of the domestic view emerges from an in-depth analysis of the anti-inflationary plans that scatter Argentina's history. If domestic economic policy was the root of the problem, then strong anti-inflationary domestic policies should represent a direct solution to rising prices. Argentina has had more than a few of those, like the Austral plan, but they never seemed to quite work, even if they successfully choked off growth in the money supply, suggesting once again that reality is more complex than the domestic/fiscal story suggests.

For example, Emilio Ocampo analyzed the effectiveness of ten Argentine anti-inflationary plans for the period 1952–2015. He considered a plan successful when it managed to bring inflation down to 15 percent for a sustainable period of time. While his study finds only half

of these plans to be successful, the most striking aspect is that it is difficult to determine what aspect of these plans really made a difference, or
even if it was the plan itself that made the difference. For instance, while
the Convertibility Plan proved to be the most successful plan in the sample, its success ended quite spectacularly in 2001 with a financial crisis
ignited by a mix of external and internal factors. While Ocampo's data
shows that, on average, plans based on monetary and fiscal tightening
were more successful than "heterodox" plans that were mostly focused
on price and wage controls, it also shows that "failure [of the latter] was
always associated with declining terms of trade," that is, with a decline
of export prices relative to the price of imported goods, suggesting that
external factors played a prominent role in determining the effectiveness
of any plan.

The external view, however, also has limits. For instance, Argentina does not look uniquely vulnerable to external shocks when compared to other countries. Empirical evidence shows that the so-called
exchange-rate pass-through for Argentina, that is, the degree to which
exchange-rate moves are mirrored in domestic prices, is not particularly high compared to other Latin American economies. As such,
the reason why Argentina remains so "inflated" cannot be simply
attributed to abrupt shifts in the exchange rate and relative prices.
Likewise, in 2001—the year of the crisis that killed the anti-inflation
peg—only 25 percent of the Argentinean economy was export oriented. While this amount is enough to play a role in generating a large
trade deficit, it is not so large as to explain chronic and persistent high
inflation over longer periods.

Against this backdrop, to find the truth about Argentinean hyperinflation, we need to look beyond just monetary or exchange-rate factors.
While particular crises can be reduced to particular causes, one cannot
generate a general theory of Argentina's near constant and always high
inflation from these factors alone. To get there we need a more encom-

passing political and economic explanation. Luckily, a political economist called Jazmin Sierra has provided us with one.

GLOBAL CAUSES AND LOCAL INFLATIONS

According to Sierra two things need to be acknowledged in any discussion of Argentina. The first is the timing of and the terms upon which
a country is incorporated into the global economy. The second is the
politics of such incorporation. Turning to the first point, Argentina is a
part of Latin America, and like the rest of Latin America, was incorporated three hundred years ago into the global economy as a commodity producer for northern countries, and it still is one today. Indeed,
some 70 percent of jobs in Latin America are in one way or another
tied into commodity production and exports. That matters because it
gives Latin American economies a particular economic structure that
is dominated by a small number of commodity-producing families and
firms and is vulnerable to persistent exchange-rate crises and so-called
commodity cycles.

Commodity cycles occur when demand for a commodity increases
and suppliers increase supplies to match demand. That drops prices
further, which increases demand further, which then increases supply.
This virtuous circle eventually becomes a vicious circle when demand
reaches its peak while supply is still being added. Eventually that leads
to the characteristic "busts" we see in commodity markets when prices
collapse. This in turn depresses the exchange rate and makes imports
more expensive, eventually causing the exchange rate to collapse. This
is not a bug unique to Argentina. It's a feature built into the wider Latin
American export and commodity-led growth model. But if this is a general feature, why then is Argentina so (hyper)inflated so much of the
time in comparison to its neighbors? Having acknowledged that point
we can now turn to Sierra's second point that not only does the timing

of incorporation into the world economy matter, the politics of doing so
matters too.

WHY ARGENTINA INFLATED WHILE
EAST ASIA GREW

The successful East Asian NICs (newly industrialized countries) provide
a useful comparison. When Japan copied Germany in its drive to industrialize in the late nineteenth century, it suppressed labor and domestic
consumption to fund a high rate of investment by the state. When Japan
exported that model to Korea in the 1920s via colonization, South Korea
was able to use the same "low-consumption/high-investment" playbook
in its postcolonial moment and grow rapidly. Taiwan did more or less the
same. Essentially, labor and peasant farmers were squeezed to fund the
investment needed for industrialization. In all these countries, behind
these industrialization drives were massive land reforms with a strong
state behind them that disabled the power of the landed elites to oppose
the state while increasing agricultural productivity.

In Argentina that road was closed before it opened. Strong unions
and a robust prewar democracy meant that unions were necessarily a
part of the postwar growth coalition that brought populist "Peronism"
to power in 1946. As it was a core part of the winning coalition, the state
could not squeeze labor to fund its investment plans. Similarly, lacking
a peasantry and lacking the strength to dispossess the landed elites who
controlled and thrived by commodity exports, the Latin American state
had to look elsewhere for investment. Given the dislocations of the 1950s
and '60s, in the '70s and '80s that "elsewhere" became foreign borrowing.

Remember the Volcker shock that raised interest rates in the early
1980s? That came on the back of US banks trying to recycle the dollars
they were receiving from OPEC countries who had just quadrupled the
price of oil in 1973. Flush with these so-called petrodollars, Citibank's
chairman Walter Wriston famously said that US banks should lend these

dollars on to governments "because they never go bust." And indeed, between 1946 and 1974 no state of any stature ever did. And strictly speaking no state borrowing in its own currency can go bust. But what if they borrow in a foreign currency like the dollar? And what if they borrow at a negative real rate where the inflation rate is higher than the loan's interest rate, which was Latin America's situation in the mid-1970s? In such a situation you'd be mad not to load up on loans because it's free money—until it's not.

When Volcker's hammer descended in 1980, the free money suddenly became expensive, and by 1982 Latin American countries were spending, in some cases, nearly their entire export earnings on interest payments on their foreign debts. The result of this was a so-called lost decade of growth. Moreover, a structural dependence on highly volatile foreign capital to fund investment became embedded, which compounded the exchange-rate swings already inherent in a commodity-driven economy.

This is the mechanism that makes Argentine inflation both persistent and intractable. Persistent because it is generated not just through the exports and volatile exchange-rate mechanism discussed already, but because it is amplified by the equally volatile effects of foreign capital dependence. Intractable because just as labor could not be squeezed to pay for the surplus for investment, as governments in East Asia could, so labor in the Peronist coalition, the dominant political coalition in Argentina for decades, was and is unable to push the costs of deflation onto their own constituents.

The result has been persistent and high inflation occasionally relieved by the earnings from commodity booms. Such a model suits those inside the growth coalition with dollar accounts who can protect themselves from the inflationary effects of a rapidly depreciating local currency. But those outside that group, especially the 40 percent of Argentines who find themselves below the poverty line, have no such protection. This is why some 53 percent of Argentines have just voted for radical libertarian President Milei. Whether Milei, a maverick libertarian economist wedded to a purely monetary theory of inflation, can solve such a thorny set of problems remains to be seen.

The main inflation stories in the Argentine case are similar to those in our prior cases, with a "too much money/domestic" faction arguing against a "current account/exchange rate/external" faction. Greedy capitalists and transitory factors are not at all prominent. But even here that is not enough to exhaust the set of possible causes. Argentina reminds us that global factors such as the timing of a country's incorporation into the world economy and placement in its value chains, what it produces, and who the government can squeeze in its own society to fund investment, all matters. Telling the story of Argentine inflation without also telling these stories is both incomplete and misleading, and once again shows us why these cases are quite unique. All of which bring us to our last hyperinflation case, which is probably the most famous and the most misunderstood: Germany in the 1920s.

CASE FOUR—GERMANY: FISCAL INCONTINENCE OR FIGHTING THE FRENCH BY OTHER MEANS?

The "facts" of the German hyperinflation of the 1920s are well known and are still eyepopping even today. In 1914, the exchange rate between the German mark and the US dollar was 4.2 marks to one dollar. In 1919, after Germany had lost World War I, the exchange rate fell to 48 to 1. By November 1923, one US dollar was equal to 4,210,500,000,000 German marks. What caused this is quite another matter. The German case stands out in many analyses as the quintessential example of a "too much money" inflation caused by excessive government spending. This is not wrong, but it is seriously incomplete. What is often missing in this version of the German story is how this turn to hyperinflation was no accident. It was instead government policy. To see why any government would want hyperinflation, first consider why Germany's exchange rate against the dollar had depreciated tenfold by 1919. The short answer is: losing the war.

Germany did little to keep inflation and demand in check during World War I, in contrast to the UK and France, which imposed income and consumption taxes as well as rationing and other controls. The Germans gambled that in winning the war they could do to the French what the French had done to them in 1871. That is, demand an indemnity, a cash or material payment, to cover the costs of waging war. By not winning the war, not only did that strategy fail, but the Treaty of Versailles that ended the war also loaded Germany's now much smaller and more indebted economy down with 132 billion marks (33 billion USD) in reparations.

Given ongoing inflation through the balance of payments channel due to the already significant devaluation of the mark that had taken place since 1918, when these reparation payments came due in 1921, those demanding payments didn't want the freshly printed papiermarks that were the new currency of the postwar Weimar Republic. They wanted goldmarks, the old imperial currency at the 1914 fixed exchange rate, or the equivalent in US dollars or another "hard currency." The two ways that Germany could acquire such hard currency were to issue new bonds, which investors would only accept at very high rates, thereby indebting the country still further, or by simply printing more money to cover their debts, which is what they ended up doing. Keep doing this—print to cover imports and as the exchange rate falls print more, which pushes down the exchange rate further, so you print more—and you will end up in a hyperinflation. So far this explanation for Germany's hyperinflation is very monetarist. But was that all that was going on? Indeed, why do this at all? Why not just default and walk away from the debts?

BEYOND A MONETARIST READING (AGAIN)

The monetarist reading of this episode shows the folly of government spending to avoid a recession. But that's not what was actually driving policy. First of all, the German inflation of the 1920s didn't just happen to Germany. Other countries such as Austria, Hungary, and Poland all experienced hyperinflationary episodes around the same time. Their common origins lay, as noted above, in how World War I had been financed, through running up debt rather than through taxes, which lowered postwar exchange rates and made imports more expensive, which in turn fostered inflation through the import channel. This is a standard version of the exchange-rate story we have seen several times already. It wasn't just "too much money chasing too few goods." It was simultaneously driven by the current account.

What is missing from the standard story is that the German hyperinflation was intimately bound up with the desire of the German government to break the stranglehold that the war reparations owed to France had on the German economy. Basically, if you went to work every day and for every mark of value that you generated forty pfennigs went straight to the French treasury, you might look for a way out of this dilemma. Anticipating that this "tax" on future German growth was likely to be resisted by the Germans was why France wanted Germany to pay off its war reparations in either gold or foreign currencies. But to earn foreign currency when its own exchange rate was falling required either selling more and more exports to earn them, which was hard for a war-ravaged and unstable economy to produce, or printing more and more marks to buy foreign currency, which depreciated the exchange rate still further.

WHEN HYPERINFLATION BECOMES POLICY

German resistance to paying reparations, plus the torrid state of the German economy in the early 1920s, led the French to occupy the Ruhr Valley area of Germany, its industrial heartland. In response, the German government decided to continue to pay the wages of workers in the occupied zone rather than pay reparations. The only way to pay those wages was simply to print the cash, which of course turned the inflation hyper. But why would Germany, in a sense, choose hyperinflation? Perhaps knowing that putting one's fiscal house in order—keeping up with the reparations payments—would be rewarded by giving the French ever more money meant that Germany decided to pull its fiscal house down.

As historian Albrecht Ritschl argues, "Inflation proved to be a formidable weapon against reparations creditors [as] it paralyzed the financial system that would have been needed to organize an orderly transfer of reparations." Specifically, the domestic consequence of hyperinflation as policy was that as the exchange rate plummeted ever more steeply, producers would increasingly only accept payment in a hard currency. The papiermark went into free fall as its holders sold the currency, which exploded the deficit. This in turn required the central bank to either raise interest rates to pull in capital or to monetize the problem. As such, the inflationary genie was being deliberately pulled out of the bottle to scuttle reparations.

In sum, the hyperinflation episode that is taken as the prime example of "what not to do" in policy was not actually promoted by simple monetary profligacy. Rather, it was part accident due to bad war financing, and part deliberate policy to make the payment of reparations, especially after the French occupation of the Ruhr, all but impossible. Indeed, the hyperinflation had the effect of wiping out large amounts of government debt, and therefore, future reparations payments to France. It also ended very abruptly with a currency reform in late 1923. That is, the government printed new money, the Rentenmark, which was tied to real estate assets, which almost immediately stopped the inflation in its tracks. Why this monetary reform succeeded while others failed remains a bit of a mystery. Nonetheless it worked, and on the back of this a new stable Reichsmark succeeded it within a year.

Defaulting on the French via inflation also got Germany a reduction in reparations (which became a de facto stop), as well as a "seniority swap" in the debt renegotiations (in the so-called Dawes Plan of 1924) that gave commercial credits (US capital imports) seniority in bankruptcy over war credits (to the French), which quickly powered the German economy out of crisis and away from inflation. The next four years saw the German economy perform rather well, as long as US capital flows kept flowing in. Those flows unfortunately turned off in 1929, when the Fed raised interest rates to cool the US stock market bubble, and in response the Reichsbank raised interest rates to encourage capital inflows. But the flows failed to return, generating a classic sudden stop in funding that turned the stability that followed the hyperinflation into a sustained deflation.

DOES INFLATION OR DEFLATION LEAD TO DISASTER?

Seen in this light, what happens next to Germany also deserves a second look. Building on the standard "money plus bad policy" rendition of the German hyperinflation, a line is commonly drawn from the hyperinflation to the Nazi period. The argument generally made is that the destruction of middle-class savings by the inflation left fertile ground for the Nazis to build political power. There are three flaws with this argument. The first is that middle-class savings were largely destroyed before the hyperinflation due to the massive currency devaluations that had taken place in the prior two years. The second is that the timing is off. Hyperinflation ended in 1923, and as we noted already, the German economy not only stabilized between 1924 and 1929, it boomed due to large, short-term capital inflows.

Third, when those flows ended in 1929 and the German government raised rates and slashed spending to balance the books, the bottom fell out of the economy as demand crashed and unemployment shot up. It was on the back of this deflation, not inflation, that the Nazis picked up support in the 1930 election, winning 18.3 percent of the vote and becoming the second largest party in the process. They were, after all, the only party actively arguing against deflation and cuts. Building on this success, the July 1932 elections saw the majority party SPD vote collapse and the Nazis receive 37.3 percent of the vote. In 1933 they took 43.9 percent of the total vote. Hyperinflation did not bring the Nazis to power. Excessive disinflation a decade later did.

Even within the class of hyperinflations, one of these cases is not like the others, and that case is Germany. It's certainly a prominent example of the monetarist "too much money" school; no one can deny that the Weimar Republic generated an absolute shedload of cash to paper over the cracks of Germany's postwar economy. But it was also a case of the long-term effects of bad policy stemming from World War I, and inflation through the import channel via the current account.

The German example also teaches us something new. It shows us that hyperinflation can become a policy. Hyperinflation has terrible costs, especially for anyone without the ability to hedge exposure by holding real assets or hard currency. Venezuela didn't set out to get it, but its Dutch disease plus US sanctions pushed them into it. Zimbabwe excelled at it, but from the postcolonial moment onward they were set up to fall into the inflationary trap. Argentina built it up over decades, allowed it to explode in the 1980s, controlled it in the 1990s, and saw it rise again in the 2010s.

Germany shares in all the standard sins of monetization and import dependence with a weak currency, but it's the only case where hyperinflation was weaponized as policy. It lasted at its peak nine months. Thereafter it stabilized and was never seen again. In its aftermath Germany negotiated debt reduction and attracted massive capital imports from the United States. Only when it began to embrace deflation as a policy goal in and of itself did it succumb to the Nazis and the eventual destruction of the state.

WHY HYPERINFLATION IS NOT COMING TO YOU ANYTIME SOON

All our cases of hyperinflation stand apart from more general cases of inflation for several reasons. First, unlike the general inflations of the 1950s, the 1970s, and the 2020s, they were not due to supply shocks, and they did not burn themselves out. Rather, they were decades in the making and required extremely specific circumstances to come to fruition. From monocrop dependence on oil exports (Venezuela), to failed land reforms (Zimbabwe), to a political coalition unable to pass the costs of inflation on to others (Argentina), to the desire to stop paying reparations (Germany), the causes of hyperinflation are not generalizable. Hyperinflation arises in moments of deep crisis, against a backdrop of an essentially dysfunctional economy, in which inflationary pressures have been building for years. Most importantly, they are incredibly rare. Given all this, when inflation hawks start their warnings that "we can all end up like Argentina" or opining that "inflation brought the Nazis to power," remember that we do not have the structural weaknesses or the politics of Argentina, and that deflation, not inflation, brought the Nazis to power.

Hyperinflation is the result of long-standing structural problems. In that sense, it's not a surprise. That's different from our recent experience with inflation. Despite the spread of independent central banks around the world, all armed with anti-inflation mandates, whose job is to watch out for inflation, we were actually quite surprised by the return of inflation in 2021. In fact, much academic work on inflation in the prior decade focused on why deflation rather than inflation was the new normal state of affairs. Why were we so blindsided? To answer that we need to go back to 2009 and ask the same question Queen Elizabeth asked the economists at the London School of Economics: Why didn't we see this coming?

5

WHY DIDN'T WE SEE
THIS ONE COMING?

> The task of the historian is to understand the peoples of the past
> better than they understand themselves.
> —Herbert Butterfield

THE QUEEN'S QUESTION STILL STANDS

One of the enduring images of the global financial crisis of 2008–12 was
the visit of Queen Elizabeth II to the London School of Economics in
November 2008. She asked the assembled LSE's economists, "Why didn't
you see this coming?" A year later, at a conference at the British Academy,
the Queen finally got her response. It's worth quoting in full:

> So in summary, Your Majesty, the failure to foresee the timing,
> extent and severity of the crisis and to head it off, while it had many
> causes, was principally a failure of the collective imagination of
> many bright people, both in this country and internationally, to
> understand the risks to the system as a whole.

One might legitimately wonder if the same charge could be lev-
eled today about the inflation of the past few years. Just as the collective

"bright people" of 2008 failed to see a massive financial crisis brewing in plain sight, why did this cohort of "bright people" remain so blind to the possibility of a return to a world of inflation? While, as we have noted already, a few folks like Larry Summers and Charles Goodhart did see it coming, what they saw turned out to be quite different from the actual drivers of inflation in most cases. Moreover, our central banks were supposed to guard us from exactly this eventuality, and in that regard they singularly failed. So, the Queen's question still stands, though in reference to a different crisis. Why didn't we see it coming? The answer to that question takes us back to someone we have met before, a young economist called Isabella Weber.

TWITTER STORMS AND OFFICIAL HISTORIES

In the spring of 2022, in the midst of the rising debate about rising inflation, Isabella Weber published an op-ed in *The Guardian* that set off a Twitter storm. Weber was attacked on Twitter by all and sundry, from professional luminaries down to bog-standard Twitter trolls. What had she done to earn such opprobrium? She had dared to suggest that price controls might be a part of the solution to inflation. In her brief op-ed she drew upon the historical experience of the United States during the Second World War, in the immediate postwar period, and in the 1970s, to make the case that while such controls might not be *the* solution, they were at least *a* solution worth looking at. The entire field disagreed vehemently, and with an unanimity that seldom characterizes economics. Examining this episode reveals something worth investigating if we want to know why we didn't see inflation coming this time around.

That is, as well as being a theory of the world that tells you how it works, economics is also a language of power. To see this in action imagine two politicians vying for office in a public debate. One accuses the other of "economic illiteracy" and is able to use the economic language of "costs, markets, efficiency," etc. to make the other politician look uninformed and unauthoritative. Now imagine the same debate, only replace "economic illiteracy" with "anthropological illiteracy" and imagine the outcome. The speaker would seem weird, and the opponent could easily parry. As sociologist Elizabeth Berman has recently demonstrated in her study of how economics became the language of US public policy teaching, economics is a language of power in a way that the other social sciences are not. Whoever gets to define what is "efficient" or what is a "cost" sets the field of play for everyone else. It is a political intervention as well as an analytic tool, which leads us to the second item of interest.

For economics to have that power it must have some special leverage over other ways of thinking. It makes those claims in terms of its predictive powers. But recent events, ranging from the failure to foresee the 2008 financial crisis; to support for austerity policies after the financial crisis; to the current debates over inflation, where the mainstream response has been to dust off the 1970s playbook and go from there, suggests otherwise. So where, then, does such surety come from? We argue that it comes from an "official history" of that period upon which the field as a whole not only agrees, despite differences among various schools of economics, but upon which it bases many of its core concepts and hence its authority claims. This is the history that Weber unintentionally disturbed and that sheds light on the Queen's (standing) question.

According to the official history, price controls, whether in the form of crude price caps or more sophisticated prices and incomes policies, or even buffer stocks in China, cannot be rehabilitated. As Fed economist Christopher Neely put it, "Price controls have had a very long but not very successful history." By suggesting otherwise, Weber inadvertently called into question the field's self-understanding of what happened in the 1970s, what inflation actually is, and how to cure it. By upsetting that history, Weber challenged both the field and its members' claims to authority. The result was a Twitter storm whereby the respondents to the op-ed rendered visible the authority claims upon which this particular field of knowledge rests. It also gives us a window into why the dominance of one version of history over another can leave us very blind as to what is coming next.

BUILDING THE "OFFICIAL" HISTORY OF THE 1970s: ECONOMICS AFTER THE WAR

Histories are written, as they say, by the victors. The victors in this case were those economists who successfully challenged the "Keynesian consensus" that characterized economic policymaking in the Western world from the 1940s until the 1970s. The postwar Keynesian consensus in economics rested upon a set of ideas concerning markets. Namely, that they were inherently unstable (prone to booms and slumps) and contained no natural tendency to operate at full employment, with the level of employment being determined by the level of output and not the level of income. As such, the job of the government was to push output to the full employment level via fiscal policy, and to keep it there by ensuring sufficient aggregate demand. By the 1960s, it seemed that this task had largely been accomplished. Full employment had become self-sustaining throughout the Western world.

But that accomplishment came at a price, which was inflation. The UK, for example, had an annual rate of inflation of around 4 percent from the 1960s onward. The US rate hovered around 3 percent. If growth was 3 percent and inflation was 4 percent, then in real terms the economy was gradually shrinking people's purchasing power. Trying to get out of this trap while sustaining full employment became the focus of policy. The policy responses took two forms. The first was to try to get ahead of inflation by improving productivity. That was a hard economic problem. The second was to try to control inflation directly through the imposition of controls on prices (which really means profits) and wages. This was thought to be easier, but it turned out to be an even harder political problem.

WHY NOT JUST RAISE INTEREST RATES?

The reason policymakers didn't simply raise interest rates to reduce inflation, the common-sense solution of today, was because they thought about the problem of inflation in a very different way. Rather than inflation being "always and everywhere a monetary phenomenon," per Friedman, Keynesian economists tended to see inflation as the result of so-called "cost-push" (labor and product market forces) factors rather than "demand-pull" (monetary) factors. This also suggested a political problem that lay at the heart of the Keynesian order, a problem that an economist named Mikhał Kalecki, whom we have already met when we discussed hyperinflation, diagnosed as far back as 1944.

Basically, if a government is committed to maintaining full employment and they achieve that goal, it opens itself up to a situation where workers can strike for higher wages while employers can pass consequently higher prices on to consumers because their rivals face the same labor market conditions. In such a world, "cooling" the economy by raising interest rates would directly conflict with the government's full-employment target, so using interest rates as a primary anti-inflationary weapon was largely kept off the table. Instead, governments would have to make both labor and business keep wages and prices in line with productivity in order to generate both full employment and low inflation. In other words, they wanted to control price increases "just enough" while hoping that the supply side of the economy would expand to bring prices back down. Inflation, in such an understanding, should therefore be controlled by what was known back then as an "incomes policy."

The problem with implementing an incomes policy is that doing so not only leads to the microeconomic problem of distorting prices. And it also allows governments a much larger say in private capitalist decisions, which is a political problem. As such, economics had to step up to protect private markets from state encroachment. To successfully challenge this "interference" in this most central of capitalist freedoms, the right to set prices, non-Keynesian economists began to attack the then dominant Keynesian understanding of how the economy worked. After all, if you wanted to get government out of the price-setting business, you had to undermine its rationale for doing so, and that meant going after the full-employment target as the basic objective of economic policy. If you could delegitimate that target by using controls to get there, controls would lose their legitimacy too.

DEBUNKING KEYNES BY ATTACKING CONTROLS

The attack came first in Milton Friedman's 1968 AEA Presidential Address on the assumed stability of trade-off between inflation and unemployment embodied in the Phillips curve. Demoing what became known as his "expectations augmented" Phillips curve, Friedman created an alternative model of the macroeconomy where attempts by the government to maintain an employment level beyond what he posited as the "natural rate" that the economy could sustain must show up in inflation. In contrast to Keynes, who saw unemployment as "involuntary" and due to a collapse in demand, Friedman made unemployment an entirely voluntary choice, and he gave workers, as we noted in chapter 2, the power to distinguish their real wage from their money wage.

As a consequence of making these two assumptions, agents' individual decisions to work or not to work based upon their real wage became the driving force in the economy, rather than the overall level of effective demand. In such a model of the world, full employment pursued by fiscal tools ceased to be a plausible target of government policy. After all, if a target rate of employment cannot be hit because agents actively anticipate price and wage changes, then the notion of an incomes policy that would help deliver such a target becomes, at best, dubious.

Next, the so-called rational expectations economists entered the fray. Rather than viewing expectations as "augmented" by experience, as Friedman had argued, these economists argued that any attempt by the government to boost the level of employment through boosting demand would be immediately discounted by such agents who would rationally anticipate it. They would know that current spending would have to be paid by future taxes and would therefore save more in the present. By saving, they would end up offsetting the stimulating impact of government's spending. The same would hold true for an incomes policy. If they saw it coming they would discount it and so it would not work.

Combine these two ideas and you enter a world where anti-inflationary policy operates through managing expectations of future inflation by central bank signaling rather than through incomes policies. Meanwhile, policymaking authority should be moved to the autonomous central bank rather than the Treasury, the institution tasked with implementing an incomes policy. In this world, you do not cure inflation by establishing pay and profit norms, let alone by putting ceilings on prices. Rather, you take the policymaking levers away from democratically elected officials who are mistakenly committed to producing more employment than is possible. You give these responsibilities to "conservative" central bankers, who are insulated from political pressure and can use monetary policy (interest rates) to "dominate" fiscal policy to a level that they independently determine is fiscally sustainable.

It was on the back of these new ideas that a new and quite particular history of the 1970s was constructed. One where shortsighted politicians generated too much demand by spending too much money and/or by generating inflationary cycles and/or by accommodating greedy unions. Given that the economy now has a speed limit defined as its "natural" rate of unemployment—that is, the rate of unemployment at which inflation, theoretically at least, does not accelerate—attempts to go faster than the speed limit can only lead to rising prices. And because agents either adapted to, or rationally saw through attempts by government to boost the economy past the speed limit, such interventions could only be desta-bilizing. Governments, rather than being a part of the solution, became, as President Reagan famously observed, the problem.

The official history thus concludes that the inflation of the 1970s spurred a new generation of economists to reimagine how the world works, and together with some heroic central bankers and a handful of rogue politicians they raised rates, cut taxes, deregulated, privatized, integrated, and eventually globalized Western economies over the next two decades. It's a nice story. And it's not even wholly wrong. Rather, as usual, it's what that story misses out that is most telling.

THAT '70s SHOW (FINAL EPISODE)

All academic fields rest upon official histories that tell them how they got to where they are today and why they think the way they do. Economics is not exceptional in that respect. But the story of how this particular his-tory was constructed is exceptional insofar as it wholly ignores causes of the inflation of the 1960s and '70s that are not agents' expectations and choices—the key ideas used to undermine the old Keynesian order and its policy goals. When we detail these other factors, it becomes apparent that not only was there room for other causes, there was also room for solutions other than raising rates to "re-anchor expectations" and dele-gating policy to central bankers. Keynesian economists had pretty good ideas about what caused inflation and how to cure it. They were simply unable to do so for political reasons.

According to this alternative view, the core problem of the inflation of the 1960s and '70s lay in the inability of the Johnson administration to raise taxes to pay for the Vietnam war. Knowing that doing so would cause Congress to choose between guns—the war in Vietnam—and butter—the war on poverty at home—and that Congress would choose to fund the former by cutting the latter, Johnson chose to fight the war "off the books." As a result, the administration's economic projections of a slowdown in inflation in the mid-1960s failed to happen as actual war expenditure far exceeded what was being admitted. As then Council of Economic Advisers chief economist Arthur Okun put it at the time, "Everything depends upon Vietnam spending, but we can't get a goddamned word out of [defense secretary] McNamara."

The Johnson administration's inflation control policy consisted of a set of wage and price guideposts for business and labor, inherited from the Kennedy administration, to coordinate their bargaining. As these guideposts were voluntary and lacked statutory authority, they were worthless as an anti-inflationary tool. Vietnam drove inflation from the demand side. There really was too much (war) money chasing too few goods.

The Nixon administration inherited the same policy framework and the same inflationary problems. With five hundred thousand potential workers directly tied up in Vietnam and millions at home supporting this off-the-books war economy, and with women and minorities being increasingly incorporated into the labor markets, which gave the economy a further consumption push, inflation was still being propelled by excessive demand. That demand-pull inflation (too much money) inevitably spilled into cost-push inflation (prices and wages pushing each other upward). In an economy where one third of the labor market was unionized, a spiral of labor militancy, wage increases, and price increases was ignited, exactly as a Keynesian would predict.

The weakness in the Keynesian response was the assumption that when inflation appeared the solution was to raise taxes. In an economically reasonable world, tax increases are a functional substitute for interest rate increases as both reduce economic activity by constraining consumption. But in our very political world, raising taxes is seen as electoral suicide by elected politicians. As a consequence, raising taxes as the control valve for inflation was out of the question, even if it wasn't already compromised by the prior full-employment target.

By the early 1970s, the United States had convinced itself that interest rate rises didn't work because they couldn't really raise them enough without making unemployment the inflationary control valve. Tax increases were also off the table. All roads then led to price controls and incomes policies. We already touched on Nixon's price controls in chapter 2, but it's worth going back to them to uncover something deeper: why the lesson of this episode was that controls do not work, and that the only way to deal with inflation is to raise rates and cause a recession.

THE OTHER LESSONS OF NIXON'S PRICE CONTROLS

When Nixon embraced price controls and incomes policies, the economist John Kenneth Galbraith, a longtime advocate of controls, remarked that he felt like "a street-walker who has just learned . . . that the profession was not only legal, but the highest form of municipal service." His irony was justified. Here was Nixon, a Republican president, imposing price controls in peacetime. This was not only unprecedented, but also for many sections of US capital and the Republican Party, unacceptable. As we noted earlier, Nixon's price controls and incomes policy came in three phases. Phase one was a ninety-day freeze of wages and prices with a 10 percent surcharge on imports. Phase two created a statutory price commission and pay board that mandated pay increases of no more than 5 percent and set a limit on profit margins.

What's missing in the official history is that the phase two controls actually worked. Core inflation rapidly fell from over 6 percent in late 1970 to 2.8 percent in the summer of 1972, and that's when Nixon made a *political* mistake by trying to get angry Republicans off his back. As we noted before, given this success in controlling inflation by *mandatory* controls, Nixon made the third phase of controls *voluntary*. As we saw with the Kennedy and Johnson administrations' earlier experiences with voluntary "guidelines," both business and labor blew right through them. Again, as we noted in chapter 2, this was the policy failure that both delegitimated controls and enhanced the views of the anti-Keynesian econ-omists. Making controls voluntary meant that by the summer of 1973, meat prices had risen by one third while the stock market fell. Mandatory ceilings were reimposed on meat prices. There were no controls for stock prices. Serious people were losing real money and controls in toto were now seen as the problem.

But stepping back a moment, perhaps what this episode really showed us was that controls could work if they were mandatory, but not if they were voluntary. But to make them mandatory created a political problem, which was to bring state control into the heart of capitalism by directly regulating prices, and thus profits. Mandating prices was what communists did, and even if that was done for the purpose of fighting communists in Vietnam, this was a step too far normatively for many US economists and policymakers.

Official histories are written by the victors, and the victors of the struggle to redefine inflation got to write the official history of the 1970s. A history in which price controls could actually work to control infla-tion could not exist inside a new policy framework where inflation is wholly the product of anticipatory or rational expectations. To maintain the integrity of the new expectations-based framework, something had to be expelled from the temple, and that something was the legitimacy and effectiveness of controls. In the official history of the 1970s, inflation cannot be controlled with controls, even if it actually was, but it can be controlled by giving up on the misguided goal of full employment. And if the pursuit of full employment inevitably leads to inflation, then inflation had to take precedence over full employment as the state's primary policy goal. These new ideas were the cement that glued the "official history" of the 1970s together and laid the foundations for a world governed by free markets, independent central bankers, and interest rates. It's the world that we built. And it's also a world where once inflation was defeated it should not come back.

A DIFFERENT HISTORY: SPECIAL FACTORS
AND SEQUENTIAL SHOCKS

However, an official history that places money, agents' expectations, and heroic central bankers front and center in the fight against inflation really only makes sense if a slew of other factors, especially what former U.S. central banker Alan Blinder has called "special factors," are left out of the equation. If these special factors are admitted as the alternative fundamental causes of the inflation of the 1970s, two things occur. First, price controls reemerge as viable polices. Second, and much more important, it allows us to figure out why we keep getting blindsided by events. What then were these special factors? They were a series of one-off price shocks that were both correlated and not normally distributed. That is, they amplified each other, and they all came along at more or less the same time, and then dissipated over time. Just like the inflation we see today.

Blinder blames the inflation of the 1970s on three shocks, each of which was transitory but collectively lasted a decade: "rising food prices, rising energy prices *and the end of the Nixon wage-price controls program.*" Blinder is emphatic on the effect of moving from mandatory to voluntary controls in producing inflation, arguing that "the end of controls then lifted inflation in 1974 some 1.7 to 3.1 percentage points higher than it would have been without controls."

Examining the later period of 1977–80, Blinder further argued that "once again, three factors led the way, *and none of them was money.*" Food and energy price spikes explain most of the variation in inflation rates in this period with "the CPI energy component [rising] . . . 56 percent between December 1978 and March 1980." Furthermore, the decision to put mortgage interest rates into the CPI in the late 1970s helped push the inflation rate up still further.

So important were these transitory factors that Blinder concludes that by the time they reversed, "the deceleration of mortgage costs and energy prices was so extreme that they alone were to bring the inflation rate down about 8 percentage points from the first half of 1980 to the second half." Indeed, Blinder goes as far as to argue that "many people continue to this day to give credit to the recession for breaking the back of the double-digit inflation, whereas, in fact, it was the waning of special factors that did the trick."

Blinder reexamined this thesis in 2013 with updated data and alternative methods and found that his "'old fashioned' supply-shock explanation holds up quite well." In this new analysis he found that the "special factors" still explained "*more than 100 percent* of the rise (and subsequent fall) of headline inflation—that is, the supply-shock explanation . . . actually overexplains the Great Inflation." Blinder further emphasizes once again that "anyone who tries to explain the rise and fall of *core* inflation over the 1972 to 1975 period *without* paying careful attention to price controls is missing something very important."

You can see how such an account of inflation places price controls in a more positive light and how accounts based upon money and expectations become suspicious. If the great inflation was really just an agglomeration of transient factors that wilted under their own weight, then the heroic central bankers, the farsighted politicians, the truth-telling role of economists, and the authority and prestige of their ideas and the idea that expectations are everything all fall into question. And along with that so does the contemporary understanding of inflation and how to respond to it. Pointing this out is what got Weber into trouble and started a Twitter storm. Indeed, for the prior thirty years no one wanted to hear this alternate history. After all, once the economy disinflated in the 1980s, things seemed to be going quite well.

THE NEW RELIGION: INFLATION TARGETING AND CENTRAL BANK INDEPENDENCE, 1980s–2000s

The period from the mid-1980s to the beginning of the global financial crisis of 2007–2008 marked a new era of economic policy, known as the

"Great Moderation." In this period, the volatility of everything from GDP growth and unemployment to inflation declined markedly. Remarking on this phenomenon in 2004, then Federal Reserve chair Ben Bernanke stressed the role that "better monetary policy" had played in providing steady low-volatility growth and low inflation. Then UK chancellor Gordon Brown drew from this lower-volatility world that there would be no more boom and bust in our economies. Perhaps most triumphantly of all, one of the godfathers of rational expectations macroeconomics, Robert Lucas, opined in his 2003 American Economic Association Presidential Address that as far as policy was concerned, the "central problem of depression prevention has been solved for all practical purposes." Of course, this all fell apart quite spectacularly when volatility returned with a vengeance as the global financial crisis hit in 2007–2008. But what is of more interest here in our quest to find out why we didn't see inflation returning in the early 2020s is how the ideas of the 1970s and the institutions that they spawned in the '80s that were supposed to safeguard us against inflation instead made us more vulnerable to its return.

INFLATION TARGETING: THE FRUIT OF THE KIWIS

There were two major policy innovations in the 1980s designed to fight inflation: inflation targeting and central bank independence. Inflation targeting, which we briefly touched upon in the prior chapter, consists of establishing a specific target inflation rate that the central bank aims to reach through its policies. For instance, if the central bank has an inflation target of 2 percent, but inflation is at 4 percent, we should expect the central bank to tighten its policy in order to lower inflation to its target level. Central bank independence means that the central bank is autonomous from political pressures, especially from the pressures of the government of the day. Although they had their theoretical antecedents in the ideas of the 1970s, both strategies were first deployed in New Zealand in the 1970s and '80s.

From the 1970s to the 1990s New Zealand had experienced several bouts of double-digit inflation. The governor the Reserve Bank of New Zealand, Don Brash, delivered a speech in 2001 in which he warned against the distributional impacts of inflation. He told the story of how he bought a house in 1971 for $43,000 by paying a small deposit and borrowing the rest from a bank back when inflation was around 10 percent. Fifteen years later, inflation spiked, so he paid back less for the house in real terms than he borrowed. Meanwhile, property had become an inflation hedge, so the house now had a market value of ten times its original price.

He then juxtaposed his experience of inflation—making out like the proverbial bandit—to the story of his uncle, an apple farmer who had sold his orchard, also in 1971. With the proceeds, he buys long-term government bonds that will provide him with some moderate but safe income in the years to come. Enter inflation. Rising prices wiped out 90 percent of his savings and his income in retirement collapsed. The farmer is left destitute. Brash concluded, "I, and people like me, benefited enormously at the expense of my uncle and people like him, and all because of inflation."

Brash made the fight against inflation the central bank's number one priority. From the year before his appointment in 1987 to the end of his term in 2002, inflation fell from 15 percent to 2 percent. New Zealand's inflation story became the poster child for other countries trying to cope with high prices. What made the difference? The first factor, according to this part of the official history, was inflation targeting. Originally, central banks targeted indicators over which they had a loose degree of direct control, such as the quantity of money or the amount of credit in an economy. While inflation was likely affected by these factors, the central bank's ability to directly influence inflation was thought to be limited. Inflation targeting, at least in theory, changed that. The 1989 Reserve Bank Act formalized inflation targeting in New Zealand. Price stability became the main objective of the central bank's monetary policy. The new policy required the central bank and the government to agree on a specific inflation target, and monetary policy had to be oriented only toward the achievement of such a target. But how could they ensure the achievement of that target?

This is where, again in theory at least, the second key reform, central bank independence, kicks in. Previously, it was normal practice for the finance minister to instruct the central bank around its policy priorities, including inflation. Such considerations were both highly political and inherently distributional. For example, reducing inflation meant, at least in theory and in much experience, higher unemployment (yes, the usual Phillips curve). As such, how much prices should come down was then a political decision that should be made by the elected government and not the central bank. Under the Reserve Bank Act, and with its greater independence, the only role of the government was to agree, together with the central bank, on the specific inflation target in what was called the "policy target agreement." It was up to the bank how to make that happen. The channel to make that happen was our old friend "inflationary expectations."

SPREADING THE NEW GOSPEL

To those promoting these new ideas and institutions, this combination of a precise inflation target and monetary policy independence strengthened the authorities' anti-inflationary commitment in the eyes of the public and worked its disinflationary magic via expectations. The short version of this story is that due to this joint public commitment of the government and the central bank, which puts the central bank in charge, businesses, trade unions, and households now find the new inflation target "credible" (they know that the bank will raise rates if it needs to but believe that it doesn't need to) and as such they will revise their own inflation expectations downward. This affects the public's future decisions to invest, consume, and save. Lending money to businesses looks better to banks if future inflation is not going to erode the value of their loans. Wage bargaining likewise does not have to consider rising future inflation. Working on expectations in this way meant that just four years out from the reform, annual inflation dropped from 6 to 1 percent, marking the success of the new institutional setup.

The case of New Zealand quickly inspired others, who followed suit. As did the example of the German Bundesbank's inflation performance vis-à-vis its European peers in the 1970s. In the 1990s, central banks around the world set inflation targets (often around 2 percent) and acquired statutory independence from political pressures. Canada was the first after New Zealand to adopt inflation targeting. Then came the United Kingdom in 1992 and Sweden in 1993. Swedish central banker Lars Svensson devoted much of his time to showcasing the success of inflation targeting and persuading other central banks to do the same.

The central bankers designing a new central bank for Europe were heavily influenced by these new ideas. The European Central Bank was created in 1998 as almost entirely independent from any sort of political input and was given a statutory price stability mandate and a target of below but close to 2 percent over the medium term. Over the next twenty years, twenty-six countries adopted these institutions, rules, and policies, including eleven advanced economies and fifteen emerging market economies. Simultaneously, central banks gained more political independence, taking away monetary policy decision-making from their governments.

The postcommunist revolutions of the early 1990s in Eastern Europe spread these ideas and institutions further still. Lacking even a basic banking infrastructure and having largely inconvertible currencies, the new democracies of the former Warsaw Pact needed both commercial and central banks, and the leading Western central banks duly dispatched training manuals and trainers to bring them up to speed with the latest thinking. They often became the most zealous in pursuit of their anti-inflation objectives and their pro-market stances. The gospel spread, found converts, and proclaimed success over the trials and tribulations documented in the official history of the 1970s and beyond. Things did

INFLATION IN SELECTED ECONOMIES, 1970–2000

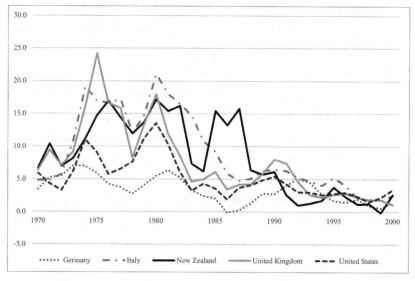

Source: World Bank Global Database of Inflation. Note: the figure displays the annual headline consumer price inflation rates.

look pretty good. Inflation fell pretty much everywhere. But the question was, if it fell pretty much everywhere, was it really central bank independence and inflation targeting that made the difference? Or was it perhaps, as we have suggested above, the eventual dissipation of those "special factors" we discussed earlier?

THE PROOF OF THE GOSPEL? REVISITING THE GREAT MODERATION

Let's go back to that coincidence of rising central bank independence, inflation targeting, and that period of extraordinary macroeconomic stability called the Great Moderation. This new era combined low and stable inflation with low output volatility and economic growth stabilized at levels moderately above previous trends in most developed countries. These changes were considered a sort of economic nirvana. Lower output volatility implied more stable employment and less frequent recessions, while lower inflation volatility meant reduced uncertainty and therefore easier economic and investment planning. But what provoked the transition from the turbulent economic volatility of the 1970s to the stability of the Great Moderation? The central banker's new gospel, or something else?

Some were tempted to attribute all this to the newly reformed central banks and their powers of expectation management. Former Federal Reserve chair Ben Bernanke and his coauthors captured what many economists believed when he stated that countries adopting inflation targeting regimes managed to lower "inflation and inflation expectations beyond that which would likely have occurred in the absence of inflation targets." But this view was not bulletproof, even if the central banking community rather liked it. In fact, scholars have identified three sets of reasons for the economic stability that characterized the Great Moderation: structural change, good luck, and good policy.

DEFLATION BY DIGITIZATION? INVENTORY CONTROL AND GLOBALIZATION

Supporters of the *structural change* view argued that the economy has changed its structure in a way that delivered greater stability and lower prices. The structural change view centers on business's improved ability to cope with shocks through improvements in inventory practices. Inventories are crucial buffers that stabilize the complicated interactions between a firm's production and sales. Businesses stock up inventories when production is higher than demand can absorb, and they sell them when demand exceeds production. New information technologies and globalization made it much easier for businesses to reduce their reliance on inventories. Firms could now more easily engage with intermediate goods producers to quickly expand or contract production. This increased production flexibility and reduced the likelihood that an unexpected shortage of inventories in one industry would disrupt sales or production in another industry. Supporters of this view attribute to monetary policy reforms only a small part of the overall effect on macroeconomic stability. Trade and financial deregulation and globalization certainly helped, but the structural adaptation of the economy that followed from the actions of private enterprises is seen as key.

A variant of the structural change view puts more weight on the role of globalization. The entry of labor from China, East Asia, and Eastern Europe into the global market exerted a downward pressure on prices, as workers from these places demanded lower wages. Economic historian Robert Skidelsky argues that central banks wrongly attributed the success of the Great Moderation to their own policies given the statistical link between interest rates and prices observed in that period. By contrast, he argues that "a better explanation of the correlation is the massive entry of cheap Chinese goods into the world market, which subdued inflation and enabled central banks to keep the cost of credit very low." Banker Stephen D. King shares a similar view, as he explains that the incorporation of low-cost producers, such as China and India, into the global trading system resulted in manufactured goods prices falling relative to Western incomes during the Great Moderation. In this period, central banks could choose between two options. One was to tighten their policy and allow prices to keep falling. The other was to follow the inflation target. This implied fighting the deflationary push by loosening interest rates to push prices up closer to the central bank target. They mostly opted for the second strategy, particularly around the end of the Great Moderation era. Between 2004 and 2007, central banks in the United States and Europe increased their policy rate, pushing asset prices upward. This context set the conditions for the financial bubble that put an end to the Great Moderation.

MAYBE IT WAS JUST "GOOD LUCK"?

The *good luck* view implies that the Great Moderation happened simply because no major shock occurred of the type we saw in the 1970s. As we've discussed, the 1970s were dominated by frequent interlinked crises that provoked major shifts in output and inflation. These shocks were not generated out of thin air but were the consequence of major conflicts in the Middle East, such as the Arab oil embargo of 1973–74 and the Iranian Revolution of 1979–78 that affected oil production, as well as Blinder's "special factors" that we discussed above. In the period from the 1980s through the 2000s, such shocks simply didn't happen or were of smaller scale. Political and economic systems reduced output volatility in the 1990s to the extent that serious scholars considered this epoch to be the "end of history," as Francis Fukuyama famously said.

James Stock and Mark Watson created a sophisticated statistical model to identify the occurrence of macroeconomic shocks. Importantly, their model allowed them to estimate how much each factor—the absence of shocks, structural changes, and monetary policy—contributed to lowering volatility during a chosen period of time. They concluded that the Great Moderation was simply a period where these shocks were more muted, and that most of the lower volatility could be explained by the lack of these shocks. They concluded that good luck appears to be much more important than good policy, while structural changes played a minor role.

This view is not bulletproof either. Critics of the good luck view argued that this perspective is based only on shocks that have actually occurred, and do not consider those shocks that may have occurred but never did. In other words, the new policy framework itself reduced the number and magnitude of potential shocks. As former Bank of England deputy governor Charles Bean put it, "Shocks are not measured directly, only their consequences." Another version of this critique is that large shocks actually did occur during the Great Moderation, but their impact was more contained. As noted by Banker Stephen D. King, these shocks include, among others, the failure of Continental Illinois Bank in 1984, the stock market crash of 1987, the Asian financial crisis in 1997, the dot. com bubble in 2000, and the 9/11 terrorist attack in 2001.

NO REALLY—IT WAS "GOOD POLICY"

Finally, the *good policy* view argues that much improved monetary policy that works on expectations, as promoted by Don Brash and his peers, explains the macroeconomic stability of the Great Moderation. Because of the shift to targeting inflation, central banks started to base their interest-rate decisions on shifts in inflation and output, and thanks to their increased political independence, they were now more able to move interest rates in reaction to such changes.

Empirical evidence emerged in the 1990s supporting this view. In the late 1980s and early '90s, Harvard economist Alberto Alesina published a series of papers that showed that higher degrees of central bank independence were associated with lower inflation rates. The most influential of these papers was coauthored with Larry Summers, which provided comparative evidence in favor of this claim. Figure 5.2 from their paper shows that countries where central banks enjoyed higher degrees of independence in the 1980s experienced lower average levels of inflation from 1955 to 1988.

The work of Alesina and Summers seemed to have finally found proof in the data for the claim that low inflation and low economic volatility in general stemmed from good policy. Importantly, Alesina and Summers showed that this result was specific to inflation, whereas central bank independence did not show any significant association with growth, unemployment, and real interest rates. This finding was not a limitation. Rather, it suggested an important policy lesson, that central banks should focus on inflation as their primary objective. As ECB president Mario Draghi put it, "Central bank independence was seen as a key

FIGURE 5.2:

CENTRAL BANK INDEPENDENCE WAS ASSOCIATED WITH LOWER INFLATION

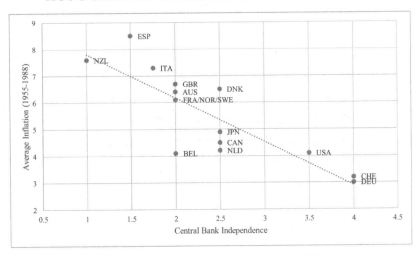

Source: Authors' elaboration based on data from Alesina and Summers, 1993.

factor in the lower volatility of output and inflation observed over this period—the phenomenon identified as the 'great moderation.'"

Chief economist of the Bank of England, Andy Haldane, recently stressed the relevance of these ideas, arguing that "cross-country correlations strongly suggested central independence was an important contributor to reduced inflation bias. . . . And this evidence, in turn, helped spur moves toward central bank independence in the latter part of the 20th century." And as we noted already, the head of the Fed sung from the same hymn sheet when he said that "monetary policy has likely made an important contribution not only to the reduced volatility of inflation (which is not particularly controversial) but to the reduced volatility of output as well." Tellingly Bernanke added, "[I am] optimistic for the future because I am confident that monetary policymakers *will not forget the lessons of the 1970s.*"

HOW THE GLOBAL FINANCIAL CRISIS (ALMOST)
MADE US THINK DIFFERENTLY ABOUT INFLATION

With Bernanke's optimism we come full circle. The ideas of the 1970s, that inflation may be "always and everywhere monetary" was really a claim about people's price and wage expectations becoming unanchored. Once that becomes the main lesson of the 1970s, it's a short step to viewing institutions that manage such expectations—central banks and their all-important "credibility" to raise rates—as the most important tools of economic management. But as we noted in chapter 3, these institutions have a very narrow set of operational tools—raise and lower rates, buy and sell assets. When things are going well we attribute the good outcomes to the institutions we have built to assure those outcomes. The fact that things were going well (low inflation) proved that inflation expectations must be anchored by those institutions. And what does the main lesson of the 1970s teach us? That such anchoring cannot happen without those institutions, which is rather circular, to say the least.

Two years after Bernanke made those remarks he would become the chair of the Federal Reserve. Three years later, the developed world would face the deepest economic and financial crisis since 1929. The Great Moderation ended abruptly in 2007. When the crisis hit, output dropped, unemployment soared, but importantly, inflation did not spike. To the contrary, prices began to fall in a deflationary spiral. Falling production led firms to curtail their investment and cut the wages of their employees. Lower wages cut consumption. Lower consumption meant lower demand, pushing firms to slash their prices to desperately attract more consumers. But as consumers saw prices falling day by day, they preferred to delay their less urgent purchases, which often involved durable goods, such as buying a car or a house. The deflationary spiral fed on itself.

Consumer price inflation in the US fell sharply from 3.8 percent in 2008 to −0.35 percent in 2009. In the euro area, inflation fell from 4 percent to 0.4 percent in the same years. The symmetric price stability mandate of central banks that requires them to fight deflation as much as inflation now forced monetary policy to do something it hadn't done in decades—use their policy tools to revive consumption. To do that they cut rates to zero and turned to the only other tool they had left—to buy financial assets and flood the markets with cash. In other words, they tried to create inflation, and in that regard they failed too. The US Federal Reserve formally adopted inflation targeting in 2012 and seldom hit its target. The ECB consistently undershot its target for the next decade as deflation rather than inflation took hold.

RETHINKING THE OFFICIAL HISTORY

What happened in the financial crisis suggests that the lessons of the 1970s may be flawed on multiple levels. Research during that lost decade after the financial crisis began to suggest that the modern version of Friedman's natural rate of unemployment, the so-called NAIRU (the Non-Accelerating Inflation Rate of Unemployment), was actually a statistical chimera insofar as individual countries' NAIRUs jumped around far too much and over too short a period to be considered either "real" or an actual "speed limit" for the economy. Likewise, research on the Phillips curve suggested that it had either vanished or had become horizontal over the prior twenty years as countries seemed to experience wildly different rates of employment with more or less the same very low rates of inflation, independent of their monetary policy stances and central bank constitutions.

Rising wage inequality and a concurrent shift in the capital-labor share across countries (the share of GDP going to labor and capital, respectively) further suggested that underemployment and weak labor power leading to deflation was more likely than "too much employment" leading to inflation. Research on very long-term interest rates by the Bank of England suggested that long-term real rates had been falling consistently since the fourteenth century. The 1970s spike in rates were therefore an outlier, not a trend in the data to which the economy naturally gravitates unless central banks stand in the way. Likewise, the theoretical and empirical underpinning of expectations was attacked from within the very organizations whose existence depended upon them.

Finally, R* (known as "R star") is the so-called "equilibrium real interest rate," which is an "ideal" rate that could be targeted by policy to bring all markets into balance. R* was suddenly seen as either far below zero (the secular stagnation thesis) and was thus impossible to hit, or it was seen to be just another artifact of overfancy models, since R* is the product of complex models and not a measure that can actually be seen in the world, like nominal interest rates. Given all this, were we really fighting an inflation at all in the 1980s and '90s and beyond? Did inflation targeting and central bank independence actually work to keep inflation low or was it just a blip that passed regardless of all that effort, and then came back because we still misunderstood it?

FIGURE 5.3:

LONG-RUN TRENDS IN REAL RATES

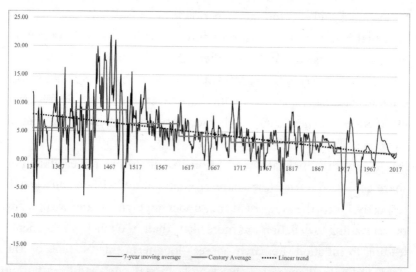

Source: Paul Schmelzing, Bank of England Staff Working Paper No. 686, "Eight Centuries of the Risk-Free Rate: Bond Market Reversals from the Venetians to the 'VaR Shock,'" October 2017.

REVISITING GOOD POLICY:
DID IT REALLY DO WHAT IT SAID ON THE TIN?

Let's begin with inflation targeting. A 2023 study by economists at the International Monetary Fund showed that inflation targeting did indeed reduce inflation among those countries that adopted it before 2000. However, when you look at countries that adopted inflation targeting after that date, only half of the cases succeed in reducing inflation. As we saw for the case of Argentina, adopting inflation targeting did not result in lower inflation and was quickly abandoned. The study concludes that "it is not easy to sort out what role [inflation targeting] has played in ensuring good outcomes" and that the "belief that [inflation targeting] adoption will be sufficient to achieve this goal cannot be taken for granted."

What about central bank independence? The idea that independence reduces inflation was long-lasting and still inspires central bankers today. In 2010, Bernanke stated that "undue political influence on monetary policy decisions can also impair the inflation-fighting credibility of the central bank, resulting in higher average inflation and, consequently, a less-productive economy." Or, in the words of Mario Draghi, "For much of the 1990s and early 2000s, the monetary policy framework went unquestioned. There was a broad consensus that granting independence to central banks had been successful in bringing inflation under control."

However, data-based evidence on this relationship is mixed, largely because measuring an abstract concept like independence is not easy. Originally, researchers measured it on the basis of how much the law protects the central bank from political pressures. For instance, if by law the government has the power to appoint or remove the head of the central bank, then the central bank of that country would have a low independence score. By looking at criteria similar to this, scholars can put together an index of independence, which allows them to compare different degrees of independence with different inflation rates.

This law-based measure (or de jure index, as academics call it) is the same one used by Alberto Alesina and his coauthors in the 1990s (and the one plotted in Figure 5.2), and it is still the most used indicator to compute the "effect" of central bank independence. Using the same index, decades after Alesina's work, Christopher Crowe and Ellen Meade confirmed that more independent central banks are associated with lower inflation. However, this was far from confirming that central bank independence had *caused* lower inflation. The two things may have simply happened at the same time, but for entirely different reasons, as we have suggested in this chapter.

Shedding further doubts on the claims of the good policy view, a number of authors have found that the link between independence and low inflation is not as strong as has been maintained and actually varies depending on how democratic a country is, or on the strength of its constitutional checks and balances. In other words, law-based central bank independence is useless if you apply it in an autocratic country where the government can undermine independence by other means. Indeed, the link between central bank independence and inflation can get even more intriguing. A seminal paper by Adam Posen showed that central bank independence is associated with lower inflation only in those countries where the financial sector has a strong vested interest in opposing inflation. In countries where the financial sector lacks this vested interest, the relationship between central bank independence and low inflation vanishes.

More recent work developed alternative indicators of independence delinked from the legal indexes, suggesting that a central bank's legal independence may not be enough to guarantee its actual autonomy. For instance, research has shown that despite their high level of independence, today central banks are still subject to pressures from governments or parliaments. Even more striking is the finding that the appointments of central bank governors has become more politically motivated over time, despite reforms that strengthened the legal independence of central banks. Even if politicians have increased the independence of central banks in the law, they tend to appoint governors who are politically close to them to guarantee their indirect control over monetary policy. This corpus of research casts more doubt on the negative relationship identified in the 1990s between independence and inflation, which nevertheless inspired monetary policy reforms and convinced governments that independence and targeting were the necessary means to guard against the ever present threat of inflation.

BACK TO THE QUEEN'S QUESTION: WHY WERE WE SO BLIND TO THE RETURN OF INFLATION?

We have covered a lot of ground in this chapter. Let's try to pull it all together to answer the question with which it began. Why didn't we see it coming? First, we didn't see it coming because of the single-minded fixation on the inflation of the 1970s as being caused by the de-anchoring of agents' expectations, which gave rise to the policy solution of constructing institutions that directly address expectations and keep them anchored. That is, independent central banks with inflation targets. But if the understanding of the 1970s embedded in those policies is flawed, as the work we have detailed throughout this book strongly suggests—ranging from business owners being more likely to click on a puppy video than a central bank policy announcement to sophisticated statistical work on expectations—and we misidentify the causes of inflation in that period, then we are likely to misidentify them in the present. Which is what seems to have occurred this time around.

Second, such understandings become embedded in the "official histories" we construct in academic disciplines and in policy. Once one understanding of a problem becomes dominant, the policy apparatus designed to respond to it can respond only in that same way. The performance of the European Central Bank under its then chair Jean-Claude Trichet in the early part of the financial crisis is emblematic. Despite evidence of deflation all around, Trichet was convinced that inflation remained the underlying problem facing Europe, even in the middle of a massive banking crisis, and he actually raised interest rates twice in 2011, making the situation worse rather than better. A popular joke at the time suggested that the ECB was ruthlessly focused on defeating an inflation that died thirty years previously. The joke was both accurate and not funny.

Third, we get a clue as to how fragile our understandings of phenomena such as inflation are when we see them being hauled into the open. We saw this in the Twitter response to Isabella Weber's *Guardian* op-ed on price controls, and in the resistance of those invested in the expectations-based theory of inflation to incorporate into their accounts factors such as price gouging by corporations and price controls by governments, even when they actually work and are supported by empirical research. Admitting that such policies may be useful undermines the case for recession and unemployment being the only way out of an inflation that stems from such ideas.

Add all this together and we end up with a classic "drunks looking for keys under the lamppost because that's where the light is" problem. We see inflation as having multiple channels, which we detailed in our inflation stories chapter. But our policy responses are skewed to seeing only one channel, the expectations channel, as being how inflation appears. In doing so we are in effect betting that inflation can come about only that way. Given such a bet, if we have built the "right" institutions around the "right" ideas, then inflation cannot return. That, after all, was the claim embedded in the institutions we built in the 1980s and '90s to control inflation. But if those premises are wrong, then not only can inflation happen, but the standard policy playbook for fighting inflation will not work. Indeed, it will actively do harm, at least to the many. And this is why it is to the topic of who wins and who loses under inflation that we turn to in our final chapter.

6

===

ARE INFLATION WARS
CLASS WARS?

A change in the value of money, that is to say in the level of prices,
is important to society only in so far as its incidence is unequal.
Such changes have produced in the past, and are producing now,
the vastest social consequences, because, as we all know, when
the value of money changes, it does not change equally for all
persons or for all purposes.

—John Maynard Keynes

There's class warfare all right. But it's my class, the rich class,
that's making war, and we're winning.

—Warren Buffett

ARE INFLATION WARS CLASS WARS?

In 2020, Matthew Klein and Michael Pettis wrote an important book that
asked a disarmingly simple question: "Are trade wars class wars?" Their
answer was yes. They note that the winners in trade wars—the exporting
countries—are actually losers in that keeping their costs down in order to
keep their exports and exchange rate competitive lowers their own workers' wages. Meanwhile, the true cost to the importing countries lies in

hollowing out their economies as imports replace their domestic industries. So, who wins if both sides lose? The owners of firms on both sides
and no one else. So when we get vexed about trade and have a "trade war,"
what we are really doing is doubling down on an ongoing international
class war of firms against labor. It's a superinteresting book, but now you
should ask what does any of this have to do with inflation?

Klein and Pettis don't actually say this, but we think it's fair to infer
from their argument that this class war is not "by design." Rather, it is "by
default." The structure of the global economy selects for certain behaviors, rewards them, and the side effect is that workers get stuffed. We
think something similar goes on in the fight against inflation. That is,
inflation wars are also class wars, but that outcome occurs by default as
much as it is by design. To see why, let's think about what central banks
can actually do when an inflation occurs.

As discussed when we encountered Volcker's hammer in chapter 2,
interest rates are the ever-ready tool that central banks use to tame inflation. But as we also noted in chapter 2, that comes at a considerable cost
to the economy involved and causes a lot of collateral damage. In chapter 5, we noted how central banks basically have only two tools. Interest
rates are one of them. Buying and selling financial assets to regulate the
amount of liquidity in the economy is the other, with various programs
of quantitative easing and the like. That's not much. And as we also discussed in chapter 5, we expect central banks to do an awful lot with those
two tools, which is a big ask.

Governments could use other tools to tame inflation, as we also
noted in chapter 3. They could use taxes, subsidies, pricing agreements,
and even controls. But they always seem reluctant to do so, delegating the
problem back to the central banks. Given that central banks tend to use
asset purchases to fight deflation and interest rates to fight inflation for
the reasons that we just detailed, we seem to be stuck, once again, with
Volcker's hammer as the only tool. So with that in mind, let's take a tour
of who wins and who loses from inflation and our default reaction to it—

raising rates—and then come back to our question at the end. If inflation wars are class wars, do they have to be?

WINNERS, LOSERS, USERS: INCOME, FISHER, AND CONSUMPTION EFFECTS

Okay, let's get to the heart of it. Everyone loses from inflation. Right? As former Fed chair Ben Bernanke famously put it, "The difference between inflation and unemployment is that inflation affects just everybody. . . . Inflation has a social-wide kind of impact." But is that true? Consumers are the first obvious victim when prices start rising, and we are all consumers. But not all consumers are the same. Logically, poorer consumers are going to suffer more. This is because of the *income effect* of inflation that affects how they spend their money when prices go up.

As we noted already, people with low incomes spend a greater share of their earnings on rent, food, and other basic consumption goods. As inflation erodes the real value of their income, they can purchase less than before with the same money, which will lower their living standard. In other words, when prices go up, everyone tightens their belt, but the poorer have to tighten their belts much more than the rich, while their pants have much less to give in the first place. This claim, however, needs to be qualified with another important distributional consequence of inflation, that inflation favors debtors and punishes creditors. This mechanism is known as the *Fisher effect*, after the economist Irving Fisher.

Suppose that someone lent you $100 last year, and you have to pay back $105 this year. You are effectively paying a 5 percent interest rate. If inflation is zero, then the $105 you pay back this year has as much value as the $100 you borrowed last year, plus $5. If, instead, inflation grew by 2 percent, the $105 you will pay back this year will buy only as much as $103 would have bought the year before. Or if inflation grew by 10 percent, then the $105 you will pay back this year will equal $95 in terms of what it buys. If so, debtors must benefit from inflation as the *real* value of their debts would erode over time as prices rose. This mechanism led the famous nineteenth-century economist David Ricardo to argue that inflation "enriches . . . the idle and profligate debtor at the expense of the industrious and frugal creditor." Basically, what people really care about is how much stuff they can buy with their present money in the future. And if the money you're paying back in the future buys less than the money you borrowed in the past, you are indeed benefiting from inflation. You are a winner.

Now let's think about this as a business model. Think like a "user" of inflation. If you know inflation is coming you would try to take on debt, knowing that the money you will pay back in the future will be worth less than it is in the present. In a way, you would be "short selling" the future, and that would be very profitable. But for that trade to work you would need to find creditors willing to lend. Assuming that they also see inflation coming, they would either curtail lending or raise their own lending rates to cover those anticipated losses. Add these two forces together and what you get is a collapse in credit that is both by design—that is what higher rates are supposed to do, slow the economy—and by default—it's going to hurt everyone, but some more than others.

CLASS-SPECIFIC INFLATION?

If this is true, the pain is still going to be unevenly distributed, and often not in the ways we expect. For example, when we talk about the poor "winning" by having their debts whittled away by inflation (Fisher effect), we need to qualify that by pointing out that the poor pay more for their credit in the first place (income effect), so rate increases hit them disproportionately hard. And when we switch the focus from income to wealth, things get even more complicated.

In investigating who wins and who loses from inflation in terms of wealth rather than income, NBER and Fed economists Matthias Doepke and Martin Schneider concluded that the poor were not the main losers because they don't have much wealth to start with. Rather, when it comes to wealth, "the main losers of inflation are rich old households," whereas the main winners are "young, middle-class households with fixed-rate mortgage debt." Or, as Mark put it in prior work, inflation is a class-specific tax.

Basically, if inflation benefits debtors over creditors, and there are many more debtors than creditors, attempts to safeguard the real value of money may "benefit us all," but they disproportionately benefit the creditor class for the simple reason that they have much more to lose and much more at risk. The rich have wealth. That is, they have assets that generate income. The poor can and will shift their consumption down to preserve the purchasing power of their income. The rich instead want compensation for their wealth losses, which is what they get through higher rates.

Thinking along these lines led Paul Krugman to wonder why we still believe that inflation hits lower-income individuals especially hard. Krugman ventured an answer by examining the inflation of the 1970s. He noted that when inflation began to fall in the early 1980s, income inequality started growing. This suggests that creditors were compensated by higher rates, covering the losses they experienced through inflation's effects on their assets in the prior decade, more than the consumption gains that poorer people got through lower inflation.

That compensation of the rich does not just happen through higher rates, it also happens through who gets to share in those excess profits. University of Massachusetts researchers recently estimated that the United States generated $301 billion in fossil fuel profits in 2022. Analyzing the U.S. distribution of those profits revealed that 51 percent of those profits went to the wealthiest 1 percent of the population, predominantly through direct shareholdings and private company ownership. In contrast the bottom 50 percent only received 1 percent. As the researchers put it, "The incremental fossil-fuel profits in 2022 over those in 2021 were enough to increase the disposable income of the wealthiest Americans by

6 percent and compensate all their purchasing power loss from inflation that year, thereby exacerbating inflation inequality."

But even restricting the focus to income throws up complications. As *The Economist* recently noted, "The sorry old truth that inflation hits the poor hardest still applies—just not always." They argued, based upon work by Xavier Jaravel at the London School of Economics, that the income group in the United States that has experienced the largest hit to their real income was actually the middle class. Jaravel showed this by teasing out the relationship between the income percentile (where you stand in the income distribution) and inflation in the US. This takes the shape of an inverted U curve, which means that those in the middle— those at the top of the inverted U—suffer the most. Meanwhile, those at the tails—the very poor and the ultra-rich—experienced inflation's welfare-reducing effects to a much lesser extent.

To make sense of this seeming "randomness" in who wins and who loses from inflation, you can simplify by looking at a third channel for inflation, the so-called *consumption channel*, whose effects depend on what type of goods we consume. If the price of meat goes up, vegans won't suffer that much. But consumption rather obviously varies across a more complex range of dimensions than veganism, including age, gender, years of education, etc. In reality, then, there are multiple inflations experienced by different classes across the income and wealth distribution, depending on the basket of goods we consume.

Taking this as their cue, a group of economists from the Bank of Spain and from Spanish bank BBVA investigated which of the three channels— the income, Fisher, and consumption channels—mattered the most across classes in Spain during the 2021 inflation. Looking at granular data on Spanish consumers' credit card transactions, they found that the income and Fisher channels drove wealth inequality, while the consumption channel had a smaller impact on income, which allowed them to better identify the winners and losers of inflation. In this study, the losers were low-income people over sixty-five years old who saw their income fall by almost 13 percent. The winners were thirty-six- to forty-five-year-old low-income individuals *who also tend to be debtors.* That class of folks experienced a very marginal fall in their income (less than 1 percent) compared to their older peers, and they also benefited from the lessening of their debts.

But does this mean that the consumption channel doesn't matter that much? This is, after all, how we generally think about inflation "hurting the poor," through what they consume. While in the Spanish case it seemed to matter less than the other two channels, it still played a prominent role in the United States. So why was the American consumer impacted through the income channel much more than their Spanish compadres? One of the main reasons was American's extreme dependence on cars for transportation.

When Jaravel examined how the individuals forming that inverted U-curve spent their money, he found that Americans spent much more than consumers in other countries on cars and gasoline. Middle-class Americans are not average consumers. They were also the world's greatest commuters, who between 2020 and 2022 bore the brunt of the rise in gas prices (which doubled) and used vehicles (whose prices increased by about 50 percent). This is not to say that rich Americans don't spend money on cars. Clearly they do, and on the more expensive models. It's just that they spend so much more on other goods, and therefore spend proportionately less on cars than the middle classes, that their share of spending on these categories is lower, so they were less affected.

That difference was also geographically and racially skewed in the United States. Rural Americans were inflation losers as they used cars more than their urban peers, while Black and Hispanic Americans suffered the most from rising prices in 2021 and 2022, according to estimates by economists at the New York Federal Reserve. Again, the reason is that these groups tended to spend more on gas and used cars than other groups. In short, who you are, where you live, what race you are, and how much you drive determines what you need to buy, and hence whether you will be an inflation winner or loser. We do not all suffer equally together.

The situation is similar in Europe, where inflation hit the poorest the hardest, albeit in their homes via the cost of gas for heating rather than, in their cars. Economists at the European Central Bank estimated that the 2022 inflation mostly hit lower-income households, which were only partially shielded by the fiscal measures put in place in some countries to compensate for higher prices. Building on this insight, in a different study published in 2022, ECB economists observed that inflation inequality in the euro area, defined as the gap in the inflation rate effectively experienced by the lowest- and highest-income people, rose to its highest peak since 2006. The source of this disparity lay in the fact that inflation in Europe mostly came from higher energy and food prices. These sectors have a strong distributional impact precisely because low-income households spend a higher proportion of their income on such goods. Similarly, in Italy, inflation led to higher income inequality. As prices went up most for food and energy, inflation widened the gap between the higher- and lowest-income households' purchasing power, again because of the pattern of poorer people's consumption spending.

INFLATION INEQUALITY ACROSS COUNTRIES

Inflation's inequality effects varied by country as well as by class. European countries experienced widely different inflation rates and different levels of inflation inequality, despite suffering largely the same energy and supply-chain shocks. Figure 6.1 shows the relationship between the inflation rate (on the horizontal axis) and inflation inequality (on the vertical axis) in October 2022. Inflation inequality here is computed as the difference between the inflation rates faced by the lowest- and highest-income households, defined in terms of bottom and top quantiles of a country's income distribution. The further to the right-hand side of the chart a country is, the higher inflation it experienced. Meanwhile, a country that is in a higher position in the chart experienced higher inflation inequality.

FIGURE 6.1:

INFLATION AND INFLATION INEQUALITY
IN EUROPE IN OCTOBER 2022

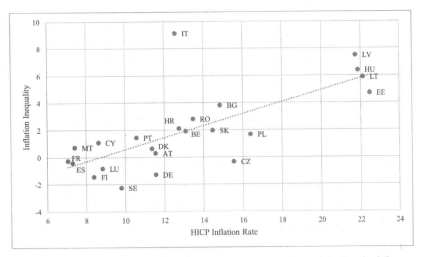

Source: Authors' elaboration on Bruegel, 2022. Notes: Inflation inequality is defined as the difference between inflation rates of the bottom and top income quantiles. The countries displayed in the charts are Austria (AT), Belgium (BE), Bulgaria (BG), Cyprus (CY), Czech Republic (CZ), Germany (DE), Denmark (DK), Estonia (EE), Greece (EL), Spain (ES), Finland (FI), France (FR), Croatia (HR), Ireland (IE), Italy (IT), Hungary (HU), Latvia (LV), Luxembourg (LU), Lithuania (LT), Malta (MT), the Netherlands (NL), Poland (PL), Portugal (PT), Romania (RO), Sweden (SE), Slovenia (SI), and Slovakia (SK).

The countries that experienced the highest inflation rates were not necessarily those that experienced the highest inflation inequality. Take Italy (IT in the chart) and Germany (DE). They had roughly similar inflation rates at 12.57 percent in Italy and 11.56 percent in Germany, respectively. However, inflation inequality in Italy was 9.13 percent, the highest in Europe, while in Germany it was negative at −1.29 percent. While the same inflation rate widened the gap between the poor and the rich in Italy, it narrowed it in Germany. Why was this? Because low-income Italians faced higher inflation than high-income Italians, while high-income Germans were more exposed to inflation than low-income Germans. Bruegel investigated the reasons for these differences and found three factors at play.

The first was consumption patterns. Poor people spend more of their income on basic goods, while rich people spend more of it on luxury goods. This much we know. These differences are, however, quite accentuated across countries. In the Czech Republic, for instance, where inflation inequality fell, rich and poor people have similar consumption patterns. When gas prices went up by 52.86 percent in 2022, they impacted everyone in a similar way, as the difference in the share of gas consumption between the rich and the poor was 0.10. By contrast, in Bulgaria, where the inflation rate was similar to that of the Czech Republic, inflation inequality grew because energy consumption patterns varied much more between the rich and the poor. There, the poor spent 10 percentage points more of their total consumption on energy compared to the rich, which is one hundred times more than in the Czech Republic.

Second, as noted above, what you spend your money on, as a function of your income level, affects the inflation inequality you experience. Even if rich and poor spend similar shares of their incomes in categories such as energy or food, price changes in other categories where the rich tend to spend differently can affect inflation inequality, which explains the difference between Italy and Germany, despite similar inflation levels. In both countries, the gap between the rich and the poor was stretched because of energy inflation.

However, these differences in Germany were reduced by a category where richer Germans, like all Americans, tend to spend a large chunk of their income: motor vehicles. Motor vehicle prices grew substantially due to supply-chain disruptions, putting strains on the wallets of richer Germans. This sheds light on a new aspect of inflation inequality. Low inflation inequality does not necessarily mean that the poor are better off. Rather, in the case of Germany, inflation inequality was lower simply because richer Germans "suffered" inflation more than the rich elsewhere due to their different consumption choices.

Third, what also made a difference in inflation inequality was government policies. In the previous chapters we showed how governments can use policies to compensate inflation losers through such mechanisms as price controls, windfall taxes, or agreements with firms to cap their prices. One example cited in a Bruegel study on this topic was a comparison between Estonia and Malta, two small European countries that experienced similar levels of inflation inequality, which both tried to contain with a price cap on energy prices. When Estonia removed its cap, inflation inequality rose from 1.35 in March to 6.96 in July 2022. Meanwhile, in Malta, where the price cap was maintained, inflation inequality stayed steady between 0.20 and 0.30.

A similar study by the European Central Bank showed that price and incomes policies put in place by European governments helped reduce the inequality stemming from higher consumer prices. They estimate that without government measures, inflation in 2022 would have been 1.6 percent higher. Most strikingly, they found that such policies "closed around 60 percent of the inequality gap between lower- and higher-income households." Income support measures, such as cash transfers or income tax reductions, were three times more effective at reducing inequality than price caps, because they were more strictly targeted to poorer households, while price control measures had a lower impact and a higher fiscal cost.

In short, while inflation may have affected everyone, the poorest amongst us are still the biggest losers from inflation. That much we knew already. But the distribution of losses, and gains, is more dispersed than we usually think. Moreover, the effects of inflation on income and wealth vary widely. While we are used to thinking of a single inflation rate that applies to each country, once we unpack inflation through these different channels, we see that different classes of people across and within countries experience quite different inflation rates. But if the poor still suffer the most, and the rich get partial compensation through higher rates, who are inflation's true winners? To understand that we need to stop looking at the economy through the lens of income distribution and start looking at it as composed of firms and workers in conflict over the surplus that capitalism produces.

INFLATION AS CLASS CONFLICT:
WORKERS VS. FIRMS

At the end of 2022, macroeconomist Olivier Blanchard noted that "a point which is often lost in discussions of inflation and central bank policy" is that "inflation is fundamentally the outcome of the distributional conflict between firms, workers, and taxpayers. It stops only when the various players are forced to accept the outcome." What did Blanchard mean by describing inflation as a conflict? He is referring to the conflict between price and wage increases, which is really a conflict between workers and firms.

One of the questions that seldom gets asked, that we should probably ask more, is "what is an economy?" When you define it in terms of output, measured by gross domestic product (GDP), it is nothing more than the number of workers multiplied by the number of hours worked multiplied by the quantity and quality of capital with which they work. That's really it. And that is all you need to explain output quite well. But that process says absolutely nothing about the distribution of that output. That is, who gets to claim a share of it, and why do they get what they get?

In normal times this issue recedes into the background. We accept the microeconomic truism that "workers get paid according to their marginal contribution to what is produced." Leaving aside the issue of why bankers get paid hundreds of times more than nurses (are they really that much more productive, even at the margin?), it is only in inflationary times that this conflict comes out into the open. In inflationary times firms want to increase their prices, given what they pay out in wages, while workers want to increase their wages to keep their purchasing power. This is the source of conflict. It's also another version of the labor market story that we examined in chapter 4.

Blanchard noted that such pressures can come from exogenous sources such as energy prices unexpectedly spiking, pushing firms to increase their prices to reflect the higher costs of intermediate goods. But it may come from something deeply endogenous to capitalism itself, from workers being in a strong position to bargain for higher wages because of inflation. This is, you will recall, the mechanism behind the price-wage spiral generated from the Phillips curve.

The Phillips curve describes a world where for inflation to go down, in theory at least, we need unemployment to go up. In contrast, if unemployment is too low, workers are able to bid for higher wages because there are many other open positions for which they can apply. This "tight market" for labor pushes wages up. And as firms must offer higher wages to get the limited supply of available labor, they transfer these costs into higher prices for their goods and services to preserve their profits, generating higher inflation. In such a world, it is really difficult to determine who wins from inflation, since in the aggregate everyone loses. Everyone seems to be temporary winners and permanent losers at the same time.

This conflict is something central banks fear deeply. ECB president Christine Lagarde expressed as much in February 2023 when she said, "Looking at the labor market, wages are growing faster, supported by robust employment dynamics, with the main theme in wage negotiations becoming how wages can to some extent catch up with high inflation. And even though most measures of longer-term inflation expectations currently stand at around 2 percent, these measures warrant continued monitoring."

In other words, the European Central Bank is concerned with how workers negotiate their wages because this is an inflation catalyst that might get out of control. Once again, it's the dreaded wage-price spiral. But does this actually happen? Is the conflict between workers and firms we see today as zero-sum as the one we witnessed in the 1970s? The one that (possibly) led to a wage-price spiral back then? The decline in union density today that we described in chapter 4 suggests that this is most unlikely. But to understand what really happened in 2021 to 2023, we need to examine how workers' real wages and firms' profits changed during the 2021–2023 inflation.

WAGE-PRICE LAGGARDS?

The short answer is that wages did indeed go up during the inflation, but not enough to absorb the rising costs of inflation. In the first quarter of 2023, the average growth of nominal wages among the rich countries of the OECD was 5.6 percent. So the average worker saw a higher number on her or his paycheck. However, real wage growth was *negative*: –3.8 percent. In other words, the increase in wages that was supposed to compensate for the increase in cost of living was simply not enough to offset it. Importantly, that fall in real wages was not limited to the first quarter of 2023. The OECD also provides data on the *cumulative* change in nominal and real wages. That is, of how much nominal and real wages grew since before COVID-19, from the fourth quarter of 2019 up until the fourth quarter of

FIGURE 6.2:

CUMULATIVE CHANGE IN NOMINAL AND REAL HOURLY WAGES IN OECD COUNTRIES

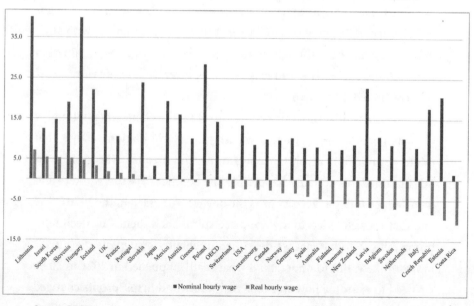

Source: OECD.

2022. If we take this into account, real wages overall are still *decreasing*, at a growth rate of –2.2 percent. Figure 6.2 shows the comparison of these two measures for OECD economies, illustrating that real-wage growth was positive only in a few countries, and even there it was well contained.

In short, if there was a conflict, workers didn't win it. The main reason being, as we have argued before, that workers today are much weaker than they were in the 1970s. As we noted earlier, trade union density has declined sharply over the past several decades, weakening workers' bargaining power. With the fall in union density, the correlation between wages and inflation has become feebler. On top of that, as David Blanchflower and Alex Bryson have argued, by increasing interest rates central banks undermine low-wage workers' ability to maintain their current level of consumption through credit. That credit gets more expensive, so such workers consume less, which further reduces labor demand by depressing the economy, which in turn increases the unemployment risk of low-income workers.

In contrast, firms (at least a lot of them) were inflation winners. We discussed greedflation, or more accurately sellers' inflation, in chapter 3, and we concluded then that the evidence for it was positive but not conclusive. That judgment stands regarding the overall drivers of inflation across countries, especially regarding inflation's origins. But in particular cases there is plenty of evidence that shows how firms used inflation to gain significantly more profits than they are used to, and that happened amid a stagnant growth in real wages. In other words, workers were too weak to claim higher wages while firms used this imbalance to charge higher prices. This really should not be a surprise. As no less than Adam Smith once argued, "High profits tend much more to raise the price of work than high wages."

Echoing Smith, the IMF estimated that for inflation in Europe, rising corporate profits accounted for almost half (45 percent) of the increase in 2022–23, as shown in Figure 6.3. The second main driver of inflation was import prices resulting from supply-chain disruptions, which accounted

CORPORATE PROFITS AND LABOR COSTS CONTRIBUTING TO INFLATION IN THE US AND ON THE EURO AREA

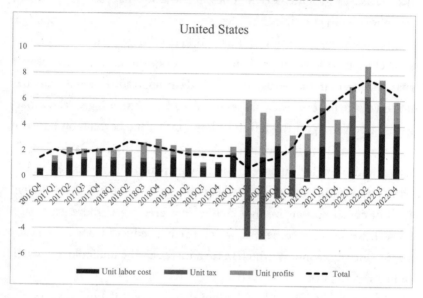

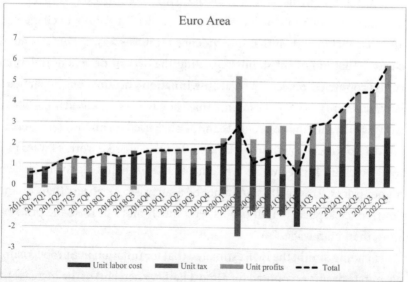

Source: Chart from Jung and Hayes (2023) based on data from Hansen et al. (2023). Unit profits refers to profits per unit of GDP, unit labor cost to labor compensation per unit of real GDP, and unit taxes to taxes less subsidies per unit of GDP.

for 40 percent of the change. By contrast, labor costs contributed only marginally to the overall increase in prices. The IMF study noted that firms "have passed on more than the nominal cost shock," meaning that their profits went beyond the price adjustment needed to cope with rising intermediate costs, with the result that companies "have fared relatively better than workers." Profits, as adjusted for inflation, were 1 percent above pre-pandemic levels, whereas labor costs were about 2 percent below the pre-COVID-19 trend. Added together, that is a big win for firms. In the United States, in contrast, profits boosted inflation earlier than in Europe, but were accompanied by higher labor costs later on.

BUT ARE FIRMS REALLY INFLATION'S CLEAR WINNERS?

While this picture makes it clear that workers were inflation's losers and that firms pushed up prices by passing on costs in 2021 to 2024, that sadly does not mean we have definitively solved the mystery of who wins once and for all. First of all, while profits have outpaced wages for now, wages may grow in the future, and by more than we would normally expect. While wages, especially in the United States, have stagnated for many years, this began to turn around in 2017 and has continued to date. Especially for the bottom two quintiles of the US income distribution, the gains have been real and large. Economists who study inequality have calculated that over the past five years wage inequality in the US has declined by almost one quarter. Add to this large numbers of retiring workers and a lack of immigrant labor and you can see why this situation where profit hikes may outpace wages might be a one-off.

Second, higher profits do not necessarily mean that firms are infla-tion winners. Counterintuitive as this may sound, the reason lies in the distinction between unit profits and profit markups. While this dis-tinction seems a mere technicality, it is crucial to understand whether firms simply protected themselves from inflation or used it to take from others. In other words, it helps us understand whether firms are simply inflation winners that succeeded in protecting themselves or are inflation abusers.

An example, we hope, clarifies the difference between profit and markup. Suppose that a firm produces a good and sells it for $120. Producing the good costs $100, so the producer gets a 20 percent *markup* that generates $20 of profits. Now, imagine that an energy shock increases the costs of producing that good by 100 percent (that's a lot of inflation, but it makes the example simpler). This will push the selling cost of that good to $240. That is, $200 of production costs plus 20 percent markup, which produces $40 of profits. Unit profits doubled from $20 to $40, but in reality the share of the price that the firm keeps for itself, *the markup*, has remained stable at 20 percent. Based on this distinction, it is difficult to cleanly infer that profit hikes caused inflation simply because firms wanted to gain from it. Companies could have simply increased their profits (in cash terms) as a reaction to higher intermediate costs, such as energy and transportation, with no net effect on their earnings coming from an increase in markups.

Given this, it is key to understand whether markups also increased, and whether they boosted inflation. Again, this is not an easy question to answer because it is very difficult to get comprehensive data on the intermediate goods that firms import, which you need to understand how much of the price change depends on the change in the cost of those intermediate goods alone. Put simply, it's easy to see that your hairdresser has changed the cost of a haircut. But it's difficult to tell how much of that depends on an increase in the cost of paying the utility bills for the shop versus an increase in the desire for a new summer cruise. Despite these difficulties, some researchers have managed to estimate firms' markups for some countries for which there is enough available data, and they found something very interesting, as we're going to show in the next section.

MARKING UP PROFITS?

Compared to Europe, the cost of energy played a more marginal role in pushing up inflation in the United States. As firms passed on those energy price increases, according to one estimate, those markups showed up as around a 10 percent rise in the average US profit share. Wages played a somewhat more important role, accounting for 25 percent of the increase in the profit share during 2020 through 2022. But the real "culprit" of inflation was markups that are not explained by passing on the costs of energy or wage increases. The same analysis estimates that these mark-ups explain almost two thirds of the growth in US corporations' profit share in 2020–2022. While the magnitude of the estimates varies across studies and the different methods they use, the underlying story is similar: a work from the Federal Reserve of Kansas City showed that markup growth likely contributed more than 50 percent of the 2021 inflation in the US, while a study from the Roosevelt Institute shows that US markups in 2021 reached their historical peak since 1955. However, markups did not grow equally across American firms: firms that had more market power—that is, less competition—were able to increase their markups more than those firms that faced higher competition.

In Europe, the situation is different. Markups did not change much in Germany and Italy, where they mostly returned to pre-pandemic levels, with the exception of a few sectors. However, in the Netherlands, markups explained more than 26 percent of the increase in prices. A study by Carsten Jung and Chris Hayes sifted this evidence by analyzing stock-market-listed firms in the US, the UK, Germany, Brazil, and South Africa. They found that, on average, firms increased their profit margins in *all* countries. While this dynamic was somewhat less apparent in Europe compared to the United States, firms did indeed increase their mark-ups beyond covering extra costs, seizing the opportunity to use higher prices to raise their prices, and thus their profits. As *The Wall*

Street Journal noted, "Companies, which in normal times are wary of angering customers with big price changes, seem to have seized on the excuse of generalized inflation to shield their margins." While some firms were just shielding themselves from rising costs, others took advantage of the situation to push their prices well past the point of shielding.

Energy companies did really well from marking up. The OECD noted that "a disproportionate part of the observed increase of unit profits in 2022 came from mining and utilities," which includes electricity, gas, and water companies. In advanced economies this sector is small (it accounts on average for about 4 percent of the economy), hence its muted effect on inflation in the US, for example. However, that sector as a whole experienced an average rise of unit profits of more than 40 percent. As we saw in the previous chapter, governments rightly targeted this sector with different measures to redistribute some of their gains to the most vulnerable.

The mechanism behind this markup-driven inflation has been detailed by Isabella Weber and Evan Wasner, whose work we encountered previously. They start from the observation that firms would normally refrain from raising prices as buyers would simply buy the same products from their competitors at a cheaper price. However, sector-wide shocks, such as COVID-19 and the Russian-Ukraine conflict, can lead firms to increase prices under a kind of implicit agreement that other firms in the same sector will follow suit. Knowing this, it becomes safe to raise prices. A crucial next step follows from this observation. While firms may initially do this to *protect* their profits, they may later on take advantage of this situation to *increase* their profits. If you tried it once and it worked—no other firm came in with cheaper prices and took your market share—why not do it again?

This is even easier when firms have a high degree of market power, which, as we've seen, occurs when a few firms dominate an entire sector. As the OECD put it, firms in less competitive markets can increase their prices

more easily and can profit from it. This mechanism connects well with the
findings of Jung and Hayes that we mentioned above. Stock market firms
tend to be larger and to have higher market power. Their study showed
that 90 percent of nominal profit increases in the UK derived from only 11
percent of the firms (while it was 19 percent in Germany and 33 percent in
the United States). This led Jung and Hayes to conclude, in line with Weber
and Wasner, that "companies with (temporary) market power seemed to
be able to protect their margins or even reap 'excess profits,' setting prices
higher than would be socially and economically beneficial."

But that may be putting it mildly. In contrast to the IMF study that
we discussed earlier, where profit-driven inflation in the US peaked in
2021 but then cooled in 2022, a more recent analysis by an NGO called
the Groundwork Collaborative has estimated that US "corporate profits
drove 53 percent of the inflation during the second and third quarters of
2023 and more than one third [of all inflation] since the start of the pandemic. Comparatively, over the past 40 years prior to the pandemic, they
drove just 11 percent of price growth."

These findings suggest another way that today's inflation differs from
the inflation of the 1970s. In the 1970s, inflation was not only the product
of an energy shock, but also the result of conflict between workers and
corporations. Today, this conflict between workers and corporations has
largely been settled and the corporations won. Notwithstanding a few
major labor agreements in 2023, US workers' overall bargaining power
has dropped. While economists and central bankers keep monitoring
unemployment, worried about the start of a wage-price spiral like the
1970s, they all struggle to find it. This is because firms now have more
market power and use it to collect more profits via increasing their markups. This is what shows up in higher inflation. Workers are the ones paying for those profits with higher prices. In sum, it's much easier today
than it was in the 1970s to tell the winners from the losers of inflation.
Firms won. Workers lost.

BANKING ON INFLATION?

One unusual type of firm, banks, deserve special attention when talking about the distributional impacts of inflation. Unlike concentrated firms in uncompetitive markets that can push up their margins, banks are generally considered inflation losers. After all, lending money is their main activity, and as we learned from the Fisher channel, creditors hate inflation as it erodes the value of their loans. Moreover, inflation creates uncertainty, which reduces investment. Without investment, there is no demand for loans, and that means banks will suffer. For these reasons, banks are always very wary of inflation. For example, in October 2023, even as US inflation fell from 8 to 3 percent, Deutsche Bank warned the Federal Reserve that the economy was still running the risk of taking a path similar to the 1970s, and that a tight monetary policy was still needed. But if banks are really inflation losers, why did governments target them, claiming that they profited from higher prices? And can inflation explain the recent banking crises the United States experienced?

While banks lose from inflation, they can benefit from central banks' response to surging prices. As we know, when inflation is high, central banks start raising interest rates. This makes loans costly, which benefits banks who can lend money at a higher price. The extent to which a bank really benefits from such higher rates, however, depends on how much the economy slows and demand falls, which they cannot control, and how much the bank can transfer those higher rates onto its loans while keeping its deposit rates low, which they can control.

Basically, if a central bank increases the cost of money by charging higher rates, then banks can transfer this cost to their borrowers by charging higher rates on the loans they issue. However, banks should also "reward" their depositors for giving them the money they lent in the first place, as it has become more valuable thanks to inflation. To do so, banks would have to increase their deposit rate. In theory, if they don't do so, depositors might decide to withdraw their money and deposit it in a bank that pays a higher rate. So did banks actually take the risk of charging higher rates while stuffing their depositors? Yes they did.

As we touched upon in chapter 3, while UK banks passed about 43 percent of their interest rate gains to their customers, French banks passed a lesser 35 percent, American banks passed on 25 percent, while German banks passed on a mere 20 percent. Other countries' banks were even more parsimonious. Italian and Spanish banks transferred a paltry 11 and 10 percent, respectively, to their customers, prompting their national governments to introduce windfall taxes to transfer some of these gains back to inflation's losers. European banks passed just 20 percent of their interest rate gains to their customers, on average.

One more factor that benefits banks is that banks are required to keep a share of their money as reserves at the central bank. The purpose of these reserve requirements is to avoid a situation where a bank runs out of money and cannot pay back its depositors. If, for some reason, depositors panic and decide to withdraw their money all at once, the bank can still rely on a fraction of the money it has kept at the central bank to be able to pay back most of the deposits it holds on its books. While traditionally these reserves were not remunerated, after the global financial crisis central banks began to pay interest on these reserve balances as a way to manage how much money circulates in the economy and where it ends up—in low-yield safe assets or higher-yield risk assets.

That policy shift has provided a very profitable side payment to banks when there is inflation because the central bank effectively gives them "inflation insurance" via "interest on excess reserves." When the central bank raises rates to counter inflation, the interest rate paid on those reserves goes up too. Paul De Grauwe and Yuemei Ji estimated that in June 2023 the interest payments from central banks to commercial banks amounted to 0.64 percent of GDP in the US (162 billion dollars), 1.13 percent in the euro area (152 billion euros), and 1.75 percent in the UK (39 billion pounds). The *Financial Times* estimated that US banks made a $1 trillion windfall from the Federal Reserve's two-and-a-half-year era of high interest rates.

BIG WINNERS IN A RISKY BUSINESS

Banks win big with inflation. They get to short their depositors, and they get paid for simply parking reserves at the central bank. But these trades against their customers and against the government are not risk-free. Recent turbulence in the US banking sector proves this. The collapse of regional banks in the United States, namely Silicon Valley Bank, First Republic, and Signature Bank, was an unintended consequence of the rapid increase in interest rates. Silicon Valley Bank was the sixteenth largest bank in the United States, and the failure of First Republic Bank and SVB represented two of the largest bank collapses in the US since the collapse of Washington Mutual in 2008. These banks failed to profit from higher interest rates as they were exposed to what is known as "interest rate risk."

The story of SVB is emblematic of this problem. As the name suggests, SVB was mostly a bank for tech start-ups from the Silicon Valley. Start-ups are abnormal customers in that their deposits are quite large, which matters because the state (in this case, the FDIC) insures only deposits below or equal to $250,000. On average, American banks have around 50 percent of their deposits insured by the FDIC. Only 7 percent of SVB's deposits were insured. This made SVB particularly vulnerable to a bank run if depositors wanted their money out. And SVB had another critical vulnerability.

SVB invested a lot of its deposits into fixed-income securities such as Treasury bonds. These securities are highly liquid debt instruments that pay a fixed interest rate on a regular basis. They are generally seen as a very safe investment. While on average banks invest around 24 percent of their assets in these types of securities, SVB decided to invest 55 percent of their assets in Treasury bonds. But if they're so safe, what's the problem with holding these securities? The issue is that bond prices and bond rates move inversely. In plain English, if interest rates go up, the value of these bonds falls because new bonds being issued today and tomorrow will pay a higher rate than previously issued ones. This will make the new bonds more attractive to investors. The demand for older bonds will then fall, causing their price (and therefore their value) to fall.

A bank that holds a lot of fixed-income bonds risks that an increase in interest rates will result in a fall in the value of its assets. This is not a problem if the bank can wait and hold those bonds until they reach maturity. However, SVB's depositors got worried and started asking for their money back before SVB's bonds matured. In order to satisfy these demands, SVB had to sell those assets at the market price and take the losses, until these losses became unsustainable. The experience of SVB suggests that while banks can lose on higher interest rates, this risk is more the exception than the norm. The IMF recently conducted a study to test banks' vulnerability to this problem and concluded that "the global banking system remains broadly resilient."

In short, while banks do not benefit directly from inflation, some (not all, as the story of SVB shows) can benefit substantially from the policy response to inflation. If a bank manages to pass only a small share of its gains to depositors, it can profit significantly. If governments are foolish enough to pay interest on excess reserves to banks, then banks can make money by simply showing up at the Fed with money that could be put to work elsewhere. But these are bugs in the system, not features. Banks are (indirectly) inflation winners and inflation users, and they may sometimes be abusers. But their wins are driven by policy, not inflation itself.

Looking at how inflation creates winners and losers brings us back to the question of whether inflation wars are class wars and whether they have to be. The short answer is that yes, inflation wars are class wars. Inflation hits the poor the most, and they get compensated the least when it falls. The knee-jerk solution of higher interest rates makes the lives of lower-income individuals and families harder. They'll face higher payments on their rents, mortgages, and debts as the purchasing power of their income falls.

In contrast, inflation helps some corporations boost their profits at the expense of consumers. They really do win. Central bank rate rises have little effect on this. All they can do is reduce firms' investment by making borrowing more expensive. But this can simply be an additional incentive for firms to focus even more on stashing profits rather than reinvesting them in the firm's growth, a choice that would ultimately produce unemployment, hurting the poor once again. Finally, higher rates benefit those banks that can hide these gains from their depositors and that are not exposed to interest rate risks. While a more solid banking sector is desirable, and higher profits help to achieve this, it is difficult to see how this giveaway from the government to banks via the central bank can help any economy recover from high prices.

So, if inflation wars are class wars, do they have to be? The answer to that is no. As we've seen in chapters 2 and 5, there are severe doubts, even among central bankers, about the effectiveness of interest rates in lowering inflation and worries about the long-term damage that they cause. Even if one believes that Volcker's hammer works to lower inflation, it is not clear why the high and asymmetric costs of lowering inflation should be borne by those least able to shoulder them, especially when there are other instruments that seem to work as well, if not even better. Subsidies could be transferred from the state to the most vulnerable to help them pay their bills. Windfall taxes could be implemented to redistribute some of the inflation winners' gains to the inflation losers. Price controls could be imposed or agreed with firms if they are designed properly and backed by the necessary political commitment. It is simply not true that there is no alternative to the distribution of resources that inflation and higher interest rates impose on our societies. The alternatives are there. They just need to be taken seriously.

Conclusion

≡≡≡

SO HAVE WE SEEN
THE LAST OF IT?

Beware of his false knowledge. It is more dangerous than ignorance.
—George Bernard Shaw

SO, WHAT DO WE REALLY KNOW
ABOUT INFLATION?

After reading this book, we would hope that the answer to that question is "quite a bit." After all, we have covered a lot of ground. But throughout our journey we have suggested that our knowledge of inflation, what it is, how it's measured, how it spreads, and how it ends, is far from complete. Indeed, one of the main arguments we have made is that our underlying theories of inflation are quite fragile and that inflation stories are as much rhetorical devices designed to shove the cost of inflation onto someone else as they are robust scientific theories backed by solid empirical evidence. Another key takeaway was that while money is certainly implicated in inflation, it is never the full, nor often the primary, culprit. A third argument we developed was that inflation is never one thing. Inflation is an experience that varies by class, race, and geography, and our attempts to define it and capture it in various indices often render its workings all the more obscure.

But perhaps our most important insight was that the inflation play-book we inherited from the 1970s and '80s might be filled with the wrong plays. If it is the case that we didn't get the current inflation right because we misunderstand the lessons of the 1970s and '80s, then it's supply shocks and concentrated markets rather than the money supply and labor's expectations that we need to focus on going forward. This in turn suggests that we may need to stay Volcker's hammer if we want to deal more effectively with the types of inflation we are likely to face in the future. When we are looking at whether inflation will return or not we have to specify the most likely causes. If we stick with money and labor markets then the answer is no, it's probably not coming back. But if we relearn the 1970s as supply shocks that concatenate and then dissipate, are we more likely than not to see more of these on the horizon? We think that the answer is yes, we shall, but first let's take the question, Was the inflation of 2021–25 just a blip—or is this the new normal?—on its own terms.

By now, you have probably noticed that we are not big fans of economic predictions. But this shouldn't prevent us from drawing some conclusions about what *could* happen to inflation in the future. We argue that while there are good reasons to think that the future could be either deflationary or inflationary, and we lay out both sides of this debate, we believe that a more inflationary future is the more likely outcome, for reasons we elaborate below.

A DEFLATIONARY FUTURE?

The first reason to think that the future will be deflationary is that the past twenty-five years have been deflationary. That's quite a trend. From the late 1980s until 2021, at least as far as the OECD countries have been concerned, inflation has been a 1980s horror story, wheeled out to scare the kids but never seen in the flesh. But then it came back. And if one of our conclusions is that the current outbreak has been, in the main, supply shocks plus a bit of price gouging by firms, then that conclusion suggests a strong element of mean reversion to where we were before, once the shocks have passed.

Another conclusion we can draw is that the future could be deflationary simply because inflations are exceptions rather than rules, for four reasons. The first is that the natural tendency of capitalism, at least over the past fifty years, is deflation, not inflation. We know that sounds weird since central bankers and politicians always bang on about being "ever vigilant" against inflation, and we have built our entire economic governance around institutions that supposedly shield us from this clear and present danger. But in fact, deflation is normal for modern capitalism. Inflation is not.

Think, for example, of the cost of buying a car over time. Imagine a 1979 Volkswagen Golf GTI. Its original price at its UK launch was £4,705, which was $9,536 in 1979 dollars. It was a fabulous car, but it didn't have airbags, ABS, Bluetooth, navigation, or even air-conditioning. The current version of the GTI is superior in every way possible to the 1979 model and costs $29,880. But when you adjust the price of the 1979 model, that is, you price 1979 dollars as 2022 dollars, that translates into $41,370 of purchasing power today.

In short, the 2022 GTI isn't just qualitatively better, it is significantly cheaper. You get more for less. Why? Because of competition between car manufacturers pushing down prices as they compete on price and quality. After all, in 2022 there are many more alternatives to the GTI than there were in 1978. Competition and technological change means that the world tends to deflate, not inflate. Think of the collapse in the price of solar panels or the cost of non-Apple mobile phones, for example. Inflation is not a constant danger that we must always guard against. That type of thinking caused the then European Central Bank resident Jean-Claude Trichet to raise interest rates in 2011 in the middle of a deflation, sending the eurozone into a near decade-long recession, which suggests that how we think about inflation can be as dangerous as inflation itself.

The second reason for seeing high inflation as an exception is that if you are suffering from a serious inflation, you are more than likely to have many other more serious problems that are in fact causing the inflation. Former Argentine economy minister Martin Lousteau tells this story of living with hyperinflation in Argentina in the 1990s. When he was a student, prices were rising so rapidly that the first thing he did when he went out for pizza with his classmates was to negotiate with the pizza restaurant whether they wanted to be paid at the start or the end of the meal, because prices would change so much in a few hours. Such an environment is hugely disruptive for business. But, as we saw in our earlier discussion of Argentina, it's also a signal that Argentina has deeper problems than the inflation itself.

Third, if the supply-shock plus price-gouging explanation of the current inflation are at least in the main correct, then not only are such shocks and responses temporally limited events, the very structure of the global economy also mitigates against them. We have largely forgotten that the decade after the financial crisis of 2008 saw the slowest economic recovery in US history, while Europe lost an entire decade of growth. Bad deflation, where the entire level of economic activity craters, was a real thing. Inflation was nowhere to be seen.

Economists who are now superconcerned with runaway deficits and stimulus-driven inflation were a few short years ago concerned with "secular stagnation." This was the idea that a dearth of investment opportunities, structurally low interest rates, and a reliance on credit bubbles to get the economy moving combined to make economic growth persistently low. The inflation of the past few years made us forget all that. If we return to the pre-pandemic trend, we will return to a path of low growth and low investment, and deflation rather than inflation. These three factors are compounded by one more factor that is barely noticed but is hugely important: that the structure of firms in capitalism, especially in the United States, has turned, as Herman Mark Schwartz puts it, "from Fordism to franchise." Schwartz demonstrates that the type of firms that made high growth and high wages possible in the postwar era—vertically integrated firms that employed large numbers of workers who could effectively demand their share of productivity gains via unions—has been replaced by an entirely different type of firm.

Today, at the top of the global food chain of corporations, sit firms that make huge profits from monopoly or quasi monopoly positions gleaned through the ownership of digital platforms or highly specific intellectual property. Such firms earn huge profits but employ very few workers. They invest little and largely derive profits from subscriptions, fees, and closed-system hardware and software. Think Apple. Below these top firms lie their key suppliers. Think Corning, which makes the glass for iPhones. They employ more people and pay good wages but are limited in their investments by everyone else in the economy below them having little money. Why is this?

Because below them are the vast majority of firms that earn almost no profits and pay low wages. Think of the folks selling iPhone cases in the local mall and the fast-food restaurants that serve them. That economic structure creates a squeeze on demand that limits investment by the more profitable firms, which in turn leads to franchise structures further down the food chain, where squeezing labor constitutes the only real source of profit. Think of the last hotel you stayed in and note that the folks cleaning the hotel are not employed by the hotel—it's all franchised out. In such a world, inflation can only come from external supply shocks and can only be temporary. There is simply not enough demand in the system to get excited about inflation.

AN INFLATIONARY FUTURE?

But even if inflations are historically rare events and the past has been deflationary rather than inflationary, that does not mean that "it will all be over soon," so you can put this book down and forget about inflation. Although one should always attach a large "Buyer beware" sign to

"This time it's different" claims, we want to entertain the strong possibility that 'this time it may actually really be different' insofar as the
inflation of the moment may be here to stay, despite the very compelling
reasons to expect deflation that we just gave you. Just like the current
inflationary episode of 2021–2025, inflation will not come as an ever-
accelerating spiral of wages and prices chasing each other up to infinity.
Rather, it may appear as a higher and more volatile baseline of costs for
all economies.

If we take a very long-term perspective on inflation in advanced
economies, we immediately notice that prices have become more stable
than they used to be. One way to see that is to look at inflation from Bank
of England data going back to the year 1200 C.E. In this graph, you can
see that periods of inflation and deflation have become less extreme in
the twentieth century. Interestingly, while as we just described, there are
strong reasons to believe we're living in a deflationary period, the past

INFLATION IN THE UK ACROSS CENTURIES

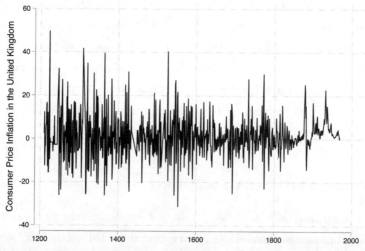

Source: Authors' elaboration based on data from Bank of England retrieved from FRED, Federal
Reserve Bank of St. Louis. Note: consumer price inflation in the United Kingdom, percent, annual
frequency, not seasonally adjusted.

several decades have been more inflationary than deflationary, at least at
the level of the UK CPI.

To understand why that might be the case, we find it helpful to think
about capitalist economies as being constituted by particular *macroeconomic regimes* in specific historical periods. That is, as particular bundles
of institutions and ideas—the hardware and software of capitalism, if you
like—that operate in particular historical periods and that endogenously
undermine themselves over time.

If we think about the period from 1945 to 1980, capitalist economies
typically promoted full employment as the overarching goal of policy,
and used a variety of means, from controlling domestic financial markets, limiting international capital flows, and encouraging the growth of
trade unions, to force business to share productivity gains with workers
in the form of rising wages. To make that work, businesses had to invest
in productivity enhancements to achieve that goal and stay in profit. The
problem with doing so was that over the long term such a setup pushed up
labor's share of GDP and lowered capital's share while encouraging inflation. This was, for us, and as we described in prior chapters, the essence
of the inflationary crisis of the 1970s.

In response, capital struck back through a disengagement with these
institutions and the promotion of a new set of political and economic
ideas that we came to know as neoliberalism, which dominated in the
period of 1980 to 2008. This "regime shift" modified the hardware of
capitalism by shifting much of the governance of the economy to independent central banks and by opening up local economies to global
economic integration, most notably with China. These changes sucked
the inflation out of these economies as millions of workers with lower
cost bases entered global supply chains and restored Western capital's
share of GDP.

But this regime was also unstable at its core. The inequality in income
and wealth that it generated was covered over by mountains of private
credit that eventually came unstuck in the financial crisis of 2008. Stabi-

lizing this, in turn, required equally massive public credit provision by central banks to keep the system going. This time around there was no regime shift, but the instruments used to keep it going, zero interest rates and massive asset purchases, further increased inequality and, through this, political polarization. By 2021, a combination of COVID-19, populist politics, and a much more strained geopolitics between China and the United States has caused the beginnings of another regime shift—one that removes much of the deflationary effects of the neoliberal regime and replaces it with a new regime that may see inflation become, once again, a permanent feature of our lives. This regime shift has three main drivers.

The first driver is climate change. For generations we have assumed that we can "take from" and "dump into" nature and never have to worry about it. In economic language, the externalities of capitalism are fully absorbed by nature. But we now know that's not true, and it is becoming less true over time. In a world where carbon, methane, acidification, and excessive heat may make water, food, and shelter increasingly expensive, that has to show up in a higher baseline set of costs.

Maximilian Kotz from the Potsdam Institute for Climate Impact Research and his colleagues from the European Central Bank have put together the first systematic assessments of how much climate change will impact inflation through the effects of climate change on agricultural markets. The results are worrying. Assuming temperature increases projected through 2035, food inflation will increase by 0.92 to 3.23 percent per year, while headline inflation (of which food inflation is an important subcomponent) will rise between 0.32 and 1.18 percent per year. Compound those numbers over a decade and we are looking at not just food inflation, but food insecurity becoming a structural fact for many economies going forward. Europe's recent and persistent droughts and crop failures are really just the thin end of the wedge in that regard.

The second driver is the new geopolitics of the 2020s. As the developed world "deglobalizes" due to security competition between the United States and China, while at the same time attempting to reindustrialize in order to capture the green technology/climate change adaption market, the costs of new local production will rise while the price of such output will likely fall as supply gluts fail to find end users who sit behind protectionist barriers. The most recent version of this problem, the panic over China's exports of electric vehicles, is the canary in the coal mine for the bigger issue of every country trying to be an exporter while no one wants to be the importer. Meanwhile, the cost of the critical minerals needed for this reindustrialization drive are only going to go up in the absence of major technological breakthroughs, and they tend to be located in places where such geopolitical competition is most intense.

Globalization, which was essentially moving huge parts of Western productive capital to China to take advantage of massive amounts of cheap labor, was inherently deflationary. That thirty-year period, and the ability to undertake secure just-in-time manufacturing in China, seems to be ending. As a result, the deflationary pressure that came from incorporating China into the global economy is over too. Add to this the reality of a world that is utterly dependent on fossil fuels for growth lacking sufficient local fossil fuels due to these new geopolitics, and we find another reason to expect climate pressures to increasingly show up as inflationary pressures.

The third driver is what we might call the new demographic realities of the already rich world. Quite simply, we are all getting older. The baby boomers are finally leaving our labor markets in their droves and there simply are not enough replacement workers to fill their shoes. It has been estimated that baby boomers in the United States increased inflation by 6 percentage points when they were young, in the period from 1955 to 1975, but decreased it by 5 percentage points when they entered the workforce in 1975 to 1990. In short, as the baby boomers leave, so does their deflationary effect. Empirical evidence shows that if there are too many people who are either too young or too old to work so the workforce shrinks, this has inflationary pressures.

On top of the longer-term consequences of demography, COVID-19 caused the labor force participation rate to fall precipitously at the turn of the decade, at the same time as immigration became extremely politicized in many countries. Labor participation has picked up since COVID-19 and, as we've noted previously, despite increasing interest rates, employment in the United States has continually gone up since 2022, not down, which suggests employers are still finding it hard to find workers. Inflation has taken a huge bite out of real (inflation adjusted) wages, but even these are now back to where they were pre-pandemic.

All of this suggests to us that inflation may be baked into the DNA of the emergent macroeconomic regime. We may lack a word for it, but we are surely entering a world that is quite different from the world of relatively stable prices we were used to. The green transition—despite how slowly it's happening and recent backsliding—China's changing role in the world economy, a new geopolitics of manufacturing, and the aging populations of the Western world (and some Eastern worlds) are all shaping this new macroeconomy.

As the famous baseball player Yogi Berra opined, it's hard to make predictions, especially about the future. You can't really describe how something works if you haven't seen it yet. There are good reasons to believe that the future could be deflationary or inflationary (while it is very unlikely that it will be hyperinflationary). Our hunch is that there is a good chance we are going to see more of inflation in the future, and we hope that this book has provided you with the tools to understand who's going to win, lose, use, and abuse inflation in that new world.

A CAUTIONARY TALE AND A
SUPPLY-SIDE SURPRISE

We close this book with a cautionary tale and a hopeful observation. We begin with the cautionary tale, which brings us back to the 1970s one last time. Looking back on the inflation of the '70s, the philosopher Brian Barry argued that "the orthodox interpretation of welfare economics has

great difficulty in identifying a welfare loss from inflation at all com-
mensurate with that often loosely attributed to it." Indeed, a little inflation can go a long way toward diffusing social tensions. Sweden used to
occasionally allow nominal wage setting in the economy to run ahead of
productivity growth in order to sell workers the illusion that their wages
were rising. They were not. Their real wages (adjusted for inflation) were
still below productivity, which boosted firm profitability, while keeping
social peace. Was that such a bad thing, at least in that context? It certainly doesn't sound so deadly. Why, then, the panic around inflation?
Perhaps because it's always been more than the economic costs. It's about
the (im)morality that it supports.

As we noted in a prior chapter, back in the 1970s economists such
as Milton Friedman and James Buchanan attacked price controls and
the growing role of the state in the economy. They were also deeply concerned with inflation, but not just for the economic damage that they
saw it causing. For such commentators, "inflation destroys expectations
and creates uncertainty; it increases the sense of felt injustice and causes
alienation. It prompts behavioral responses which reflect a generalized shortening of time horizons. 'Enjoy, enjoy!' . . . becomes a rational
response . . . where the plans made yesterday seem to have been made in
folly." Milton Friedman insisted that when inflation appears " 'prudent'
behavior becomes reckless and 'reckless' behavior becomes prudent."
The society is polarized; one group is set against another. Political unrest
increases. The capacity of any government to govern is reduced at the
same time that the pressure for strong action grows." When one considers that the average OECD inflation rate for the 1970s as a whole was 10
percent a year, such moralizing suggests that our inflation worries are
as much about the behavior that it allows than the costs it imposes. But
those costs are important in another way.

As we argued previously, inflation acts like a tax on future profits
as well as on present consumption. If you are an investor with a five-
year time horizon and the expected rate of return on your investment

is 5 percent when adjusted for inflation, if inflation goes to 10 percent, your borrowing costs just jumped up and your expected profits collapsed. This is why inflations destroy investment. In an inflationary world, it is individually irrational to invest since inflation crushes expected future returns. But it's collectively disastrous if the whole investment community thinks that way, as that will bring about a general collapse in investment and produce the recession that everyone is individually trying to avoid. Meanwhile, if labor is organized and can press for higher wages, the squeeze on profits gets even more extreme.

This might go some way to explaining why the moralistic jeremiads of the more "capital friendly" economists quoted above were unleashed back when labor was organized, and why today we still worry about wage-price spirals that are nowhere to be found. Such commentators worry that inflation is a sign of social decay as much as it is a problem of income or distribution. It's not. But that story is a powerful one that makes us take inflation very seriously, which is exactly what those with assets at risk want us to do. Inflation stories shift the costs of inflation around. They also question the morality of those who would tolerate it, which reinforces the claims of those who have most to lose in inflationary periods.

The hopeful observation, in turn, concerns Denmark. If you have ever been there or read anything about the place you will know that it's a leading decarbonizer and a very equal society in comparison to most. It was also a top inflation performer in the COVID-19 era. Danish inflation peaked at 10 percent in mid 2022 and fell below 1 percent in April 2024. How did it manage to do that? Part of the answer might be bicycles.

When the oil shocks of 1974 and 1979 hit, Denmark responded, in part, by getting on bikes. This was combined with very high taxes on cars, which together made Demark one of the most cycling-dependent places in the developed world. Add to that heavy investment in renewables, and what you have is an example of a society that has consciously altered its supply side to be more robust to inflationary shocks. That's not just good, it's clever. It tells us that inflation is not just something that we have to suffer even if there is going to be more of it around in the future. It tells us that the best way to deal with a demand shock or a supply shock is to change the supply side of the economy to accommodate it. That sounds hard, but sometimes, as the Danes showed, it's really not. It just needs imagination and a recognition that there's more to fighting inflation than monetary austerity. Adaptation can be a more effective and longer-term solution than simply jacking up rates.

SO WHERE DO WE GO FROM HERE?

If we start to view our world less as a series of island-type economies with overheating labor markets and more as a tightly coupled system of highly integrated economies that share the same supply-side vulnerabilities, a few things follow.

The first is that we need a new inflationary playbook. We need to learn the lessons of the current inflation on its own terms and not in the ever present rearview mirror of the 1970s. We have suggested why that period is misunderstood and why the lessons drawn from it are misplaced. If this period of inflation shows us that it is global factors that ignite inflation and that a large part of its persistence is explained by the behavior of firms, then we need to learn that lesson and act accordingly. This is not a pitch for controls as much as it is a call for a "Swiss-Army-knife" approach to the problem of supply-driven inflation. Buffer stocks, windfall taxes, and yes, even controls should be seen without prejudice.

Second, if we manage to do that, then perhaps we can update our inflation stories. Going forward, if we are right about declining demographics and restrictive immigration policies interacting to produce fewer prime-age workers, then looking to the labor market for inflationary pressures may become more central to our explanation than they are at the moment, but for reasons quite different from the traditional wage-price spiral explanations.

The current moment also suggests that we can probably downgrade excessive spending from the prime suspect to being just one of the accused. And yet, as climate shocks become more extreme and increasingly impact our abilities to farm and to work, governments will be under tremendous pressure to spend more money on climate adaptation, much later than they should have and at much greater expense. As such, it would be foolish to discount state spending as a future driver of inflation, even if only in reaction to wider environmental changes. As for a focus on firms as inflation drivers, if markets continue to become increasingly concentrated with fewer firms producing more of our consumption goods, it would be naive to not expect such firms to both defend their margins and, where possible, extend them.

Third, whatever form the emergent macroeconomic regime eventually takes will profoundly affect future inflationary dynamics. The most likely form is a neo-nationalist order that lives behind tariff walls. A return to the deflationary days of high globalization is simply not in the cards. Such regimes are likely to take a jaundiced view of "experts" and technocratic governance. This puts independent central banks and bold transnational schemes such as the European Green Deal in the crosshairs. While temporarily thwarted by tactical alliances of the left and center, the recent shift to the right in European politics, possibly mirrored in the United States in November 2024, may curtail climate action and thereby help accelerate it. Populist economics, if it has a credo, seems to be cheap debt plus tariffs plus preferences for national firms. It's hard to see how such a mix would not be inflationary.

Fourth, given all this, we must ask if our current anti-inflationary institutions are up to the task ahead of them. Will central banks be able to face down their populist masters and raise rates when they think it's necessary? Or does the inflation of the 2020s already show us the limits of such institutions and such strategies? We think it does. But what that means for dealing with inflation going forward is far from clear. What is clear is that we will still be dealing with it going forward.

In conclusion then, try to remember two things. First, regardless of how it plays out in the future, in an inflationary world if you are not an inflation user, then one way or another you are being used. Second, that inflation does not make everyone a loser. Despite what they tell you, some folks do win.

Acknowledgments

We would like to acknowledge the support given to us, first and foremost, by our publisher, Norton, and especially our editor, Merry Sun, and our copyeditor, Jane Cavolina. Making a book happen is much more than just the writing of the book. We would also like to thank the following people who read the manuscript and in doing both made it better while saving us from ourselves: Danny Blanchflower, David Lebow, Eric Lonergan, Alan McIntyre, Oddny Helgadottir, Brett Christophers, Alex Smith, Dan Driscoll, and Mark Vail. The best bits of this book bear your imprints. Additionally, we would like to thank Niels-Jakob Hansen, Frederik G. Toscani, Jing Zhou, Frederic Bossay, Fiorella De Fiore, Deniz Igan, Albert Pierres-Tejada, and Daniel Rees for sharing the data from their papers with us, as well as all the authors that made their data public, allowing us to reproduce some of the charts in this book.. Any remaining imperfections and errors remain our fault.

Notes

≡

Introduction: Why We Need to Rethink What We Think About Inflation

1 **"We listen to opinions"**: Adam Grant, adamgrant.net, https://adamgrant
.net/book/think-again/#:~:text=In%20our%20daily%20lives%2C%20
too,than%20an%20opportunity%20to%20learn.

1 **books on austerity**: Robert Skidelsky and Nicolò Fraccaroli, *Austerity vs
Stimulus: The Political Future of Economic Recovery* (Cham, Switzerland: Pal-
grave Macmillan, 2017); Mark Blyth, *Austerity: The History of a Dangerous
Idea* (New York: Oxford University Press, 2015).

2 **"the rate of increase"**: Ceyda Oner, "Inflation: Prices on the Rise," IMF
Finance & Development, https://www.imf.org/en/Publications/fandd/issues/
Series/Back-to-Basics/Inflation.

2 **"we need five years"**: Jordan Weissmann, "Why Larry Summers Thinks We
Need Massive Unemployment to Beat Inflation," *Slate*, July 7, 2022, https://
slate.com/business/2022/07/larry-summers-massive-unemployment-fed
-inflation.html.

2 **arguments in favor of austerity**: Jean Claude Trichet, "Stimulate No More:
Now Is the Time to Tighten," *Financial Times*, July 22, 2010, https://www.ft
.com/content/1b3ae97e-95c6-11df-b5ad-00144feab49a.

3 **"everyone" would have to suffer**: As Stephen Cecchetti et al. put it, "we
find no instance in which a significant central bank-induced disinflation
occurred without a recession." S. Cecchetti, M. Feroli, P. Hooper, F. Mishkin and K. Schoenholtz, "DP18068 Managing Disinflations," CEPR Discussion Paper No. 18068 (Paris & London: CEPR Press, 2023), https://cepr.org/
publications/dp18068.

3 **"The further we looked"**: David Byrne, "Twistin' in the Wind" on *Uh Oh*, LuakaBop/Warner Bros., 1992.

3 **"inflation is always"**: Milton Friedman, quoted in "The Real Story Behind Inflation," Heritage Foundation, 1994, https://www.heritage.org/budget-and -spending/heritage-explains/the-real-story-behind-inflation.

4 **unemployment harm outweighs the inflation harm**: Lina el-Jahel, R. Mac-culloch, and H. Shafiee, "How Does Monetary Policy Affect Welfare? Some New Estimates Using Data on Life Evaluation and Emotional Well-Being," *Journal of Money, Credit and Banking* 55, no. 8 (2022): 2001–2025, https://doi .org/10.1111/jmcb.13000; and David G. Blanchflower et al., "The Happiness Trade-Off Between Unemployment and Inflation," *Journal of Money, Credit and Banking* 46, no. S2 (October 2014): 117–41, https://doi.org/10.1111/jmcb .12154.

5 **Without investment you can't have growth:** This is what British economist John Maynard Keynes, who is considered the father of macroeconomics, called the "paradox of thrift."

5 **the proverbial drunk's lamppost:** The drunk's lamppost refers to the obser-vational bias that is summarized by a popular joke involving a policeman and a drunk man. The policeman notices that the drunk man is searching for his keys under a lamppost and asks him if he is sure he lost them there. The drunk man replies that he is not sure, but he is searching under the lamppost because that is where the light is. This joke is often used to describe the obser-vational bias economists are often subject to, which pushes them to look for solutions in familiar places rather than thinking out of the box.

8 **superprofits that it gained in 2021–23:** Aramco Media & Executive Commu-nications Department, "Aramco Announces Record Full-Year 2022 Results," Aramco, March 11, 2023, https://www.aramco.com/en/news-media/news/ 2023/aramco-announces-full-year-2022-results.

9 **"roughly 40 percent of Americans":** Julian Jacobs, "An Unequal Embrace of Digitization May Contribute to Recession Risk," Brookings, Commentary, July 26, 2022, https://www.brookings.edu/articles/an-unequal-embrace-of -digitalization-may-contribute-to-recession-risk/.

9 **prices and profits were booming:** Sabrina Valle, "Exxon Beats Estimates, Ends 2023 with a $36 Billion Profit," Reuters, February 2, 2024, https://www .reuters.com/business/energy/exxon-beats-estimates-ends-2023-with-36 -billion-profit-2024-02-02/.

Chapter 1: Five Things They Don't Tell You About Inflation

15 **"The only man":** George Bernard Shaw, *Man and Superman* (New York: Pen-guin Classics, 2000).

15 **1.4 percent in June 2024:** Data from "Switzerland Inflation Rate," Trading Economics, https://tradingeconomics.com/switzerland/inflation-cpi.

16 **in Switzerland a Big Mac costs:** Data for 2021 based on the World Bank and *The Economist*'s Big Mac Index.

16 **"nominal" rather than a "real" change:** We are going to be talking a lot about nominal versus real in what follows. The basic idea is that your "real" wage is your wage minus the effects of inflation. Say that your wage is initially $50,000. If both wages and prices rise 10 percent, then you're now paid $55,000, but your purchasing power remains the same. The nominal amount is unchanged, but in "real" terms you just took a pay cut.

16 **makes inflation's real effects different:** This is why the Biden campaign (before it ended) was dealing with "real" indicators being quite good but people's subjective estimates of those indicators being bad.

11 **the good, the bad, and the ugly:** Fabio Panetta, "Patient Monetary Policy Amid a Rocky Recovery," speech at Sciences Po, Paris, November 24, 2021, https://www.ecb.europa.eu/press/key/date/2021/html/ecb.sp211124~a0bb243dfe.en.html.

17 **the goal of most central banks:** Such a view is, however, not without its critics. Some argue that no price rises at all would be better than allowing for upward movements that may ultimately erode purchasing power.

18 **people will buy items now:** Whether they actually do this is seldom investigated. The expectations story is nonetheless central to most understandings of how inflation is generated. As we shall see later on, there is surprisingly little evidence that these models correspond to the realities of the world in which we actually live. See Jeremy B. Rudd, "Why Do We Think That Inflation Expectations Matter for Inflation (And Should We?)," Finance and Economics Discussion Paper Series 2021-062, Divisions of Statistics and Monetary Affairs, Federal Reserve Board, Washington, DC, 2021, https://doi.org/10.17016/FEDS.2021.062.

18 **such a "wage-price spiral":** European Trades Union Institute, "ECB Must Accept There Is No Wage-Price Spiral," April 11, 2024, https://www.etuc.org/en/pressrelease/ecb-must-accept-there-no-wage-price-spiral.

18 **inflation "cannot be measured by":** "What Is Inflation and How Does the Federal Reserve Evaluate Changes in the Rate of Inflation?," Board of Governors of the Federal Reserve System, last modified September 9, 2016, https://www.federalreserve.gov/faqs/economy_14419.html

19 **it is updated more frequently:** Andrew Foran, "PCE vs. CPI: What's the Difference and Why It Matters Right Now," TD Economy, October 27, 2022, https://economics.td.com/us-cpi-pce.

19 **fits with the central bank's dual mandate:** "What Is Inflation and How Does the Federal Reserve Evaluate Changes in the Rate of Inflation?"

19 **a basket of eighty thousand goods and services:** Nasiha Salwati and David Wessel, "How Does the Government Measure Inflation?," Brookings, June 28, 2021, https://www.brookings.edu/articles/how-does-the-government-measure-inflation/.

19 **Information on prices is collected:** "Measuring Inflation—The Harmonised Index of Consumer Prices (HICP)", European Central Bank, last modified May 17, 2024, https://www.ecb.europa.eu/stats/macroeconomic_and_sectoral/hicp/html/index.en.html.

19 **basket contains over seven hundred goods:** "Consumer Price Inflation Basket of Goods and Services: 2023," Office for National Statistics (ONS) news release, March 13, 2023, https://www.ons.gov.uk/economy/inflationandpriceindices/articles/ukconsumerpriceinflationbasketofgoodsandservices/2023.

19 **Consumer Prices Index:** "What Is Inflation?," Bank of England, last modified November 4, 2022, https://www.bankofengland.co.uk/explainers/what-is-inflation.

20 **"occurs when there is a broad increase":** "What Is Inflation?" European Central Bank, last modified June 11 2024, https://www.ecb.europa.eu/ecb-and-you/explainers/tell-me-more/html/what_is_inflation.en.html.

20 **a quite different impression:** Not that any normal person would ever do such a thing of course.

21 **collected into a single indicator:** In the US, the Bureau of Labor Statistics computes the Consumer Price Index for All Urban Consumers (CPI-U). In Europe, the reference index is the Harmonised Index of Consumer Prices (HICP), where "harmonised" refers to the fact that all European countries use the same methodology to produce an index that is comparable.

21 **the rate of change in this index:** We have yearly inflation when we're measuring how the CPI has changed from one year to another, or monthly inflation when we're comparing a month with the preceding month (e.g., May and June 2022) or with the same month in the preceding year (e.g., June 2022 with June 2021, to take into account seasonal changes).

23 **core inflation was higher in the United States:** "Consumer Price Index for All Urban Consumers," FRED, https://fred.stlouisfed.org/graph/?g=rocU, and Eurostat, https://ec.europa.eu/eurostat/statistics-explained/index.php?title=File:Euro_area_annual_inflation_and_its_main_components,_2022,_July_2021_and_February_2022-July_2022.png.

23 **other versions of these indexes exclude:** This is the case of the ECB's inflation measure HICPX excluding travel and clothing and footwear items. Derry O'Brien and Christiane Nickel, "The ECB's Measures of Underlying Inflation for the Euro Area," VoxEU Column, Center for Economic Policy

Research, November 20, 2018, https://cepr.org/voxeu/columns/ecbs-measures
-underlying-inflation-euro-area.

23 **Each is selective and subjective:** M. Ehrmann, G. Ferrucci, M. Lenza, and
D. O'Brien, "Measures of Underlying Inflation for the Euro Area," *ECB
Economic Bulletin* 4, April 2018, https://www.ecb.europa.eu/pub/economic
-bulletin/articles/2018/html/ecb.ebart201804_03.en.html#toc8.

23 **when you are rich you care less:** But you do care much more about its effects
on your investments. More on that later.

24 **an import ban on Mexican avocados:** Marvin Perez, "Avocado Prices
Surge to a 24-Year High," Bloomberg.com, March 29, 2022, https://www
.bloomberg.com/news/articles/2022-03-29/avocado-price-rallies-to-24-year
-high-lifting-guacamole-costs#xj4y7vzkg.

24 **"true inflation" occurs when:** Adam Tooze, "Chartbook #42—The Great
Inflation Debate," Chartbook, October 5, 2021, https://adamtooze.substack
.com/p/chartbook-42-the-great-inflation.

24 **the price of certain goods:** https://www.weforum.org/agenda/2023/02/charted
-heres-how-us-goods-and-services-have-changed-in-price-since-2000/.

24 **more dispersed over time:** Benjamin Bakkum, "Prices -> An Uncertain
Future," Macro Chronicles, May 20, 2021, https://www.macrochronicles
.com/blog/prices-an-uncertain-future/.

25 **the *base effect* of inflation measurement:** Mike Konczal, J. W. Mason,
and Lauren Melodia, "The Illusion of Inflation: Why This Spring's Numbers Will Look Artificially High," Roosevelt Institute, April 8, 2021, https://
rooseveltinstitute.org/2021/04/08/the-illusion-of-inflation-why-this
-springs-numbers-will-look-artificially-high/.

26 **Alberto Cavallo has used data:** Alberto Cavallo, "Inflation with Covid Consumption Baskets," IMF Economic Review. prepublished online August 31,
2023, https://www.nber.org/system/files/working_papers/w27352/w27352.pdf.

26 **prices for transport services in German inflation indexes:** Francesco
Grigoli and Evgenia Pugacheva "COVID-19 Inflation Weights in the UK and
Germany," *Journal of Macroeconomics* 79 (March 2024): 103543.

26 **The weights of spending categories:** For Germany and the United Kingdom see: Francesco Grigoli and Evgenia Pugacheva, "COVID-19 Inflation
Weights in the UK and Germany," *Journal of Macroeconomics* 79 (March
2024): 103543. For the United States see: Alberto Cavallo, "Inflation with
Covid Consumption Baskets," *IMF Economic Review* 72 (2024), 902–17.

27 **inflation in Germany accelerated sharply:** Tooze, "Chartbook #42—The
Great Inflation Debate."

27 **living in a more digitized world:** We thank Eric Lonergan for this point.

28 **most likely to respond to interest rates:** Unless you are in the US on a fixed-

rate 30-year mortgage. As long as you don't sell, you are impervious to rate increases.

28 **The costs of shelter:** Jared Bernstein, Ernie Tedeschi, and Sarah Robinson, "Housing Prices and Inflation," White House Council of Economic Advisers, blog, https://www.whitehouse.gov/cea/written-materials/2021/09/09/housing-prices-and-inflation/. See also Christopher D. Cotton, "A Faster Convergence of Shelter Prices and Market Rent: Implications for Inflation," Federal Reserve Bank of Boston, Current Policy Perspectives, June 17, 2024: https://www.bostonfed.org/publications/current-policy-perspectives/2024/a-faster-convergence-of-shelter-prices-and-market-rent-implications-for-inflation.aspx#:~:text=Given%20that%20shelter%20comprises%2036.1,PCE%2C%20respectively%2C%20from%20June%202024.

28 **measures the price of *consumption*:** But then why are cars and other durable goods included in the CPI? Cars are very expensive, and we don't buy them that frequently. So, buying a car could also be considered as an investment rather than a consumption. The difference between housing and cars is that the former depreciates more slowly, meaning that they tend to last for longer and therefore to be purchased less frequently. Moreover, despite depreciation, houses increase in value over time. Most cars do not. When they do they are thought of as assets and are sometimes treated differently for tax purposes. For example, owning a "classic" car can count as an asset.

29 **CPI includes a proxy measure of shelter:** Alexander Conner, Sophia Campbell, Louise Sheiner, and David Wessel, "How Does the Consumer Price Index Account for the Cost of Housing?," Brookings, January 31, 2024, https://www.brookings.edu/blog/up-front/2022/05/18/how-does-the-consumer-price-index-account-for-the-cost-of-housing/. It should be noticed that experts are still debating the best way to include housing in the CPI. A recent study from the National Academy of Sciences, for instance, still considered the Owners' Equivalent Rent as the primary approach to estimate the price of housing services for owned properties. See: National Academy of Sciences, Engineering, and Medicine, "Modernizing the Consumer Price Index for the 21st Century," Washington DC: The National Academy Press, 2022. https://doi.org/10.17226/26485.

30 **between 1953 and 1983:** Bernstein, Tedeschi, and Robinson, "Housing Prices and Inflation."

30 **removing house prices:** *The Economist* explains, "Why Don't Rising House Prices Count Towards Inflation?," *The Economist*, July 29, 2021, https://www.economist.com/the-economist-explains/2021/07/29/why-dont-rising-house-prices-count-towards-inflation.

30 **CPI Shelter, 1970–2024:** Bernstein, Tedeschi, and Robinson, "Housing Prices and Inflation."

31 **at around 15 percent per year:** Data on house prices are based on the Case-Shiller index as reported by the White House CEA. Inflation is based on the CPI for urban consumers based on data from the BLS.

31 **take so-called house price inflation:** But remember, "house-price inflation" is not an inflation.

31 **inflation targets remain unchanged:** Tyler Powell and David Wessel, "Why Is the New Zealand Government Telling Its Central Bank to Focus on Rising House Prices?," Brookings, April 2, 2021, https://www.brookings.edu/blog/up-front/2021/04/02/why-is-the-new-zealand-government-telling-its-central-bank-to-focus-on-rising-house-prices/.

31 **house prices in New Zealand increased by 41 percent:** Jayden Fennell, "Revealed—How Much NZ Housing Values Fell in 2022," *NZ Adviser,* January 6, 2023, https://www.mpamag.com/nz/news/general/revealed-how-much-nz-housing-values-fell-in-2022/431922.

31 **include the costs of homeownership:** "ECB's Governing Council Approves Its New Monetary Policy Strategy," European Central Bank, press release, July 8, 2021, https://www.ecb.europa.eu/press/pr/date/2021/html/ecb.pr210708~dc78cc4b0d.en.html.

32 **the cost of actual rents:** Stanislas Jourdan, "It Is Time to Include Housing Prices into the ECB's Inflation Index," Positive Money Europe, January 16, 2020, https://www.positivemoney.eu/2020/01/housing-prices-inflation-index/.

32 **estimate of owner-occupied housing cost:** Daniel Gros, "Persistent Low Inflation in the Euro Area: Mismeasurement Rather Than a Cause for Concern?," CEPS—Monetary Dialogue, February 2018, https://www.europarl.europa.eu/RegData/etudes/IDAN/2018/614214/IPOL_IDA(2018)614214_EN.pdf.

32 **Bank of England sets its target:** The Bank of England targets the CPI index compiled by the British Office for National Statistics (ONS). However, the ONS also compiled the CPIH index, which includes owner occupier's housing costs. In July 2022, the CPI index was 10.1 percent, while the CPIH was 8.8 percent. "Consumer Price Inflation, UK: July 2022," Office for National Statistics (ONS) news release, August 17, 2022, https://www.ons.gov.uk/economy/inflationandpriceindices/bulletins/consumerpriceinflation/july2022.

33 **index to adjust tax brackets:** The precise name is Chained Consumer Price Index for All Urban Consumers, or C-CPI-U.

33 **"Because the chained CPI climbs":** Michael Ng and David Wessel, "The Hutchins Center Explains: The Chained CPI," Brookings, updated June 9, 2023, https://www.brookings.edu/blog/up-front/2017/12/07/the-hutchins-center-explains-the-chained-cpi/.

34 **The Fed bases its decisions:** Salwati and Wessel, "How Does the Government Measure Inflation?"

35 **actually increasing the Official Bank Rate:** Bank of England, "Official Bank Rate History," accessed May 28, 2023, https://www.bankofengland.co.uk/boeapps/database/Bank-Rate.asp.

35 **raised rates to offset the bet:** Mark Tran, "Brown Confirms Inflation Target Change," *The Guardian*, December 10, 2003, https://www.theguardian.com/uk/2003/dec/10/budget2004.budget3.

35 **house prices will push the HICP inflation index up:** Martin Arnold, "ECB 'Cannot Ignore' House Price Surge in Inflation Assessment, Says Executive," *Financial Times*, February 15, 2022, https://www.ft.com/content/d874327c-ce79-4772-b63f-b8f56e30be8d.

Chapter 2: Why Do We Do What We Do When We Have Inflation?

37 **"History is the same thing":** Interview in *Der Spiegel*, June 20, 2005.

38 **this set of rate hikes:** At the time, the European Central Bank didn't exist yet, and interest rates in Europe were set independently by each national central bank.

38 **Central Bank Interest Rates:** Bank for International Settlements, Central Bank Policy Rates database, https://data.bis.org/topics/CBPOL.

39 **the US economy boomed:** As of May 2024, unemployment in the US is 4 percent. This is significantly lower than the spike in unemployment driven by the pandemic, which reached 14.9 percent in April 2020. When the Fed started hiking rates in March 2021, unemployment was already down to 6.1 percent and kept falling to 3.6 percent in March 2022. Unemployment started to grow at a slow pace from April 2023, when it was 3.4 percent, up to the current 4 percent in May 2024. Data from the US Bureau of Labor Statistics taken from "United States Unemployment Rate," Trading Economics, https://tradingeconomics.com/united-states/unemployment-rate#:~:text=June%20of%202024.-,Unemployment%20Rate%20in%20the%20United%20States%20increased%20to%204%20percent,macro%20models%20and%20analysts%20expectations.

40 **achieving an immaculate disinflation:** See, for example, Jessica Smialek, "Is American Beholding Immaculate Disinflation?" *New York Times*, November 17, 2023, https://www.nytimes.com/interactive/2023/11/17/business/what-is-immaculate-disinflation.html; and Jeffrey Frankel, "Does the Fed Deserve Credit for the Disinflation?," Belfer Centre, *Views on the Economy and the World* blog post, November 19, 2023, https://www.belfercenter.org/publication/does-fed-deserve-credit-disinflation.

40 **"Federal Reserve was itself":** Arthur F. Burns, "The Anguish of Central Banking," lecture, Sixteenth Per Jacobsson Lecture, Belgrade, Yugoslavia,

September 30, 1979, https://fraser.stlouisfed.org/files/docs/publications/
FRB/pages/1985-1989/32252_1985-1989.pdf.

41 **began to rapidly raise rates:** Initially, Volcker's approach didn't rely only
on interest rate hikes. In 1980, the Fed imposed credit controls, meaning
that banks that would lend too much were going to be sanctioned. The
sanction applied also to certain types of loans. This would have helped contain consumer borrowing. This strategy worked too well, in the sense that
consumption dropped, but way more than desired, provoking a short-lived
recession. The reason was that credit controls were unclear and confused
banks, making consumers reluctant to borrow. Volcker quickly abandoned
this policy.

41 **insistence on driving rates up in order:** We discuss in chapter 5 why this
might not be the right lesson to take from that period.

42 **"the extension of conservative politics":** Adam Tooze, "The 1970s Weren't
What You Think," *Foreign Policy*, July 1, 2022, https://foreignpolicy
.com/2022/07/01/global-economy-policy-financial-crisis-1970s/.

42 **Many S&Ls became insolvent:** Greta Krippner, *Capitalizing on Crisis: The
Political Origins of the Rise of Finance* (Cambridge, MA: Harvard University
Press, 2011).

43 **recent study by the Federal Reserve:** Òscar Jordà, Sanjay R. Singh, and Alan
M. Taylor, "Does Monetary Policy Have Long-Run Effects?," *FRBSF Economic Letter* 2023-23, September 5, 2023, https://www.frbsf.org/economic
-research/publications/economic-letter/2023/september/does-monetary
-policy-have-long-run-effects/.

44 **dumping money into an economy:** The so-called neutrality of money thesis.
It's a bit like adding a zero to a currency. Are you really ten times richer once
that happens? Maybe for a few hours, but prices will adjust pretty quickly (at
least in theory).

45 **two key sources of uncertainty:** Isabel Schnabel, "The Risks of Stubborn
Inflation," speech at Euro50 Group conference on "New Challenges for
the Economic and Monetary Union in the Post-Crisis Environment," Luxembourg, June 19, 2023, https://www.ecb.europa.eu/press/key/date/2023/
html/ecb.sp230619_1~2c0bdf2422.en.html?utm_source=substack&utm_
medium=email.

46 **when the government sets a price:** The government has the option of providing a subsidy to suppliers to allow them to produce enough goods to avoid
this issue. However, this would create a substantial public expenditure burden. See here for more details: Undral Batmunkh and Tobias Pfutze, "Temporary Price Controls as a Second-Best Option to Control Sudden Spikes
in the Prices of Basic Necessities," *World Bank Malaysia Hub Research and
Policy Briefs*, no. 56 (May 24, 2022), https://documents1.worldbank.org/

curated/en/099305005242213626/pdf/IDU07fa7a81307124043c40a3bf06151
15439fa4.pdf.

47 **firms with "market power":** Think Apple Computers or iPhones or forty
types of cereal sold by two companies.

47 **"ordering a freeze":** Gene Healy, "Remembering Nixon's Wage and
Price Controls," Cato Institute, August 16, 2011, https://www.cato.org/
commentary/remembering-nixons-wage-price-controls.

47 **This decision followed a period:** The decision was also accompanied by the
decision to abandon the Bretton Woods system, through which foreign currencies were convertible to the USD at a fixed rate.

48 **mandated that pay rises could be:** Which is one of the main problems in
estimating the effect of markups, which we discuss in chapter 6.

49 **meat prices grew:** Mark Blyth, *Great Transformations: Economic Ideas and
Institutional Change in the Twentieth Century* (Cambridge: Cambridge University Press, 2002), 136.

49 **Arab-Israeli War of 1973:** Benjamin Hunt, "Oil Price Shocks and the U.S.
Stagflation of the 1970s: Some Insights from GEM," *Energy Journal* 27, no. 4
(2006), https://journals.sagepub.com/doi/pdf/10.5547/ISSN0195-6574-EJ
-Vol27-No4-3

49 **Orban imposed price caps:** Some evidence on this topic is collected here:
Ryan Bourne, "National Conservatives Can't Find a Good Excuse for Viktor Orbán's Inflation Disaster," Cato Institute, February 2, 2023, https://
www.cato.org/commentary/national-conservatives-cant-find-good-excuse
-viktor-orbans-inflation-disaster.

50 **price controls proved a failure:** Ian Johnston and Marton Dunai, "Europe's
Politicians Impose Price Caps to Address Soaring Food Costs," *Financial
Times*, May 21, 2023, https://www.ft.com/content/133ca49d-b25a-47ee-9bfa
-d8c2f62a5f3b.

50 **In Spain, in contrast, the government introduced:** Jorge Uxó González,
"Inflation and Counter-Inflationary Policy Measures: The Case of Spain," IMK
Study, no. 83-5 (2022), Macroeconomic Policy Institute (IMK) at the Hans
Boeckler Foundation, https://www.econstor.eu/bitstream/10419/270347/1/
p_imk_study_83-05_2022.pdf.

51 **Hungary gets most of its gas:** Reuters, "Hungary Agrees on Option for More
Russian Gas Shipments, Oil Transit Fees," April 11, 2023, https://www.reuters
.com/business/energy/hungary-agrees-option-more-russian-gas-shipments
-oil-transit-fees-2023-04-11/.

51 **Spain has a GDP per capita:** International Monetary Fund's DataMap-
per for year 2023, https://tradingeconomics.com/spain/real-gdp-per-capita
-eurostat-data.html#:~:text=Spain%20%2D%20Real%20GDP%20per%20
capita%20was%20EUR25210.,EUROSTAT%20on%20June%20of%202024.

51 **In July 2023, food inflation:** Eurostat, "EU Food Inflation: Oils and Fats Up 23% in March 2023," May 8, 2023, https://ec.europa.eu/eurostat/web/products-eurostat-news/w/ddn-20230508-2.

52 **a freeze on rents:** Lukanyo Mnyanda, "Are Scotland's Rent Controls Working?," *Financial Times*, August 3, 2023, https://www.ft.com/content/2152bba5-9da4-446f-b780-2fa4fe5e3c7d.

53 **an increase of the mortgage rate:** Of course many of these landlords did not have mortgages and simply used the moment as an excuse to raise prices far beyond historic norms—an example of what Isabella Weber and her colleagues call "sellers' inflation," which we discuss below.

53 **landlords can regularly hike rents:** Office of National Statistics (UK) Data Visualizations: House Prices in Edinburgh, June 11, 2024, https://www.ons.gov.uk/visualisations/housingpriceslocal/S12000036/#.

53 **Wholesale gas prices rocketed:** Isabella M. Weber, Thore Beckmann, and Jan-Erik Thie, "The Tale of the German Gas Price Brake: Why We Need Economic Disaster Preparedness in Times of Overlapping Emergencies," *Intereconomics* 58, no. 1 (2023), 11.

54 **price controls for German gas:** The original proposal had been made by Sebastian Dullen and Isabella Weber in a series of op-eds in 2022. The term "stupid" came from Paul Krugman's reply to Weber's proposal on Twitter. He later apologized. As Dullen and Weber note, the response of economists to this later proposal "was overwhelmingly critical." See Weber, Beckmann, and Thie, "The Tale of the German Gas Price Brake."

54 **the cap reduced German inflation:** Weber, Beckmann, and Thie, "The Tale of the German Gas Price Brake," 1.

54 **originally estimated to cost:** "German Gas Price Brake Will Be Much Cheaper Than Expected," IFO Institute press release, August 9, 2023, https://www.ifo.de/en/press-release/2023-08-09/german-gas-price-brake-will-be-much-cheaper-expected.

54 **Germany bought social peace:** And given the nature of the price being controlled—very large volumes of an explosive commodity—a black market was unlikely to form in this case.

54 **A subsidy is not:** Noah Smith, *Noapinion* blog, January 9, 2023, https://www.noahpinion.blog/p/price-controls-too-early-for-a-victory,

55 **the state is intervening:** The main difference between price controls and subsidies is that the former is a form of regulation that limits an action while the other puts in place incentives to encourage a certain action.

55 **fear that price controls represent:** For representative examples, see Christopher J. Neely, "Why Price Controls Should Stay in the History Books," Federal Reserve Bank of St. Louis, March 24, 2022, https://www.stlouisfed.org/publications/regional-economist/2022/mar/why-price-controls-should-stay

-history-books, and Zachary Carter, "What if We Are Thinking About Inflation All Wrong?," *New Yorker*, June 6, 2023, https://www.newyorker.com/
news/persons-of-interest/what-if-were-thinking-about-inflation-all-wrong.

55 **China has historically used:** Isabella Weber, *How China Escaped Shock Ther-
apy* (New York: Routledge, 2021).

55 **In the electricity market:** European Union Agency for the Cooperation of
Energy Regulators, *ACER Annual Report on the Results of Monitoring the
Internal Electricity and Natural Gas Markets in 2020—Energy Retail Markets
and Consumer Protection Volume*, November 9, 2021, https://www.ceer.eu/
national-report/national-reporting-2021/. We thank Brett Christophers for
this observation.

56 **energy profit tax of 45 percent:** HM Revenue and Customs, "Electricity
Generator Levy on Exceptional Electricity Generation Receipts," policy
paper, December 20, 2022, https://www.gov.uk/government/publications/
electricity-generator-levy/electricity-generator-levy-on-exceptional
-electricity-generation-receipts. The threshold set by the British government
was seventy-five pounds per MWh. Any receipt that exceeds this amount
over the period January 1, 2023 and March 31, 2028 will be considered an
"exceptional receipt" and will be taxed accordingly.

56 **energy companies delayed paying tax:** The point that energy companies
could appeal against the tax on extra profits because it could be considered
unconstitutional has been made by many Italian commentators. This point
is reminiscent of the 2008 Robin Hood Tax introduced by the Italian government to tax the extra profit of certain energy companies due to high oil
prices. At the time, the Italian Constitutional Court rejected the Robin Hood
Tax because it considered it against the Italian Constitution due to its design
and the way it defined profits. This led some commentators to believe that
the same will happen to the recent windfall tax on energy companies. See for
instance, Fabio Ghiselli, "Tax on Extra Profits, Pros and Cons of Extraordinary Tax Measures," Econopoly, August 10, 2023, https://www.econopoly
.ilsole24ore.com/2023/08/10/extraprofitti-governo-tassa/.

57 **the spread or pass-through:** The pass-through rates of Italian banks was
low compared to those of other banks in the euro area, which are all subject
to the European Central Bank's policy, and therefore share the same central
bank rate. The pass-through rate of Italian banks was 11 percent, against an
average of 20 percent in the euro area. Pass-through rates were way higher
in Germany (20 percent), the Netherlands (26), and France (35), as well
as in the US (25) and the UK (43), which had different central banks but
faced similar policy changes. Lorenzo Moretti and Donato Di Carlo, "Italy:
Banking on the Wrong Tax," LUHNIP Policy Brief 1/2023 (Rome, Italy:
Luiss Institute for European Analysis and Policy, November 20, 2023),

https://leap.luiss.it/wp-content/uploads/2023/11/LUHNIP-Policy-Brief-1
.23-OK.pdf.

57 **taxing banks' windfall profits:** The measure was somewhat more moderate
in Spain, which imposed a 4.8 percent windfall tax on banks' net interest
income and net commissions above 800 million euros.

57 **not inflation-control devices:** But if you view inflation as coming in large
part from "sellers' inflation," then once implemented windfall taxes can act as
inflation-control devices. We thank Brett Christophers for this observation.

57 **introduced a 40 percent tax:** "I Pro e i Contro della Tassa Sugli 'Extraprof-
itti' delle Banche" [The Pros and Cons of the Tax on Banks' "Extra Profits"],
Pagella Politica, August 9, 2023, https://pagellapolitica.it/articoli/pro-contro
-tassa-extraprofitti-banche.

58 **the weight of energy and food:** More technically, the weight of food in the
2022 HICP was 33.2 percent for the first quintile and 16.5 percent for the fifth
quintile. For energy, it was 14.6 percent in the first quintile and 6.7 percent
in the fifth quintile. These results are based on a study by the Bank of Italy:
Francesco Corsello and Marianna Riggi, "Inflation Is Not Equal for All,"
VoxEU Column, Center for Economic Policy Research, November 26, 2023,
https://cepr.org/voxeu/columns/inflation-not-equal-all.

58 **didn't quite go as planned:** Moretti and Di Carlo, "Italy: Banking on the
Wrong Tax."

58 **government revised the policy:** The pool of banks was restricted by increasing the threshold of banks' interest margins, above which a bank would have
been subject to the tax. The threshold was increased from 3 percent to 5
percent for the interest margins recorded in 2022 compared to 2021, and
from 6 percent to 10 percent for the interest margins recorded in 2023 compared to 2022. In addition, the policy fine-tuned the tax based on the size of
financial institutions by capping the maximum impact of the tax to 0.1 percent of a bank's assets and 25 percent of its equity. Source: Lorenzo Moretti
and Donato Di Carlo, "Italy: Banking on the Wrong Tax," LUISS Institute
for European Analysis and Policy, LUHNIP Policy Brief 1/2023, https://leap
.luiss.it/wp-content/uploads/2023/11/LUHNIP-Policy-Brief-1.23-OK.pdf.

59 **seventy-five French food producers:** Benoit Van Overstraeten and Leigh
Thomas, "France Strong-Arms Big Food Companies into Cutting Prices,"
Reuters, June 9, 2023, https://www.reuters.com/markets/europe/frances-le
-maire-says-75-food-firms-cut-prices-2023-06-09/.

60 **"a bit, but not too much":** Leigh Thomas and Richa Naidu, "France Says Nestle, Unilever, Pepsico Among Firms Not Toeing the Line on Prices," Reuters,
August 31, 2023, https://www.reuters.com/business/retail-consumer/france
-reaches-agreement-with-food-retailers-producers-cut-prices-le-maire
-2023-08-31/.

60 **still 11 percent higher:** "In August 2023, Consumer Prices Increased by 4.8% Year on Year," Informations Rapides No 218, Insee, August 31, 2023, https://www.insee.fr/en/statistiques/7662184.

60 **Carrefour decided not to sell:** Adrienne Klasa and Madeleine Speed, "French Retailer Carrefour Drops Pepsico Products over High Prices," *Financial Times*, January 4, 2024, https://www.ft.com/content/acdb9c48-1a8b-40b5-8418-394be39067da.

60 **China does this with a whole host:** Isabella Weber and Hao Qi, "The State-Constituted Market Economy: A Conceptual Framework for China's State-Market Relations," University of Massachusetts Amherst, Economics Department Working Paper Series 319, January 1, 2022, https://doi.org/10.7275/kj02-f646.

61 **release 50 million oil barrels:** "President Biden Announces Release from the Strategic Petroleum Reserve as Part of Ongoing Efforts to Lower Prices and Address Lack of Supply Around the World," White House, press release, November 23, 2021, https://www.whitehouse.gov/briefing-room/statements-releases/2021/11/23/president-biden-announces-release-from-the-strategic-petroleum-reserve-as-part-of-ongoing-efforts-to-lower-prices-and-address-lack-of-supply-around-the-world/.

61 **injection of 180 million barrels:** "Biden Administration Responds to Putin's Price Hike by Awarding First Barrels from Historic Strategic Petroleum Reserve Release & Deploying Affordable Clean Energy," White House, press release, April 21, 2022, https://www.whitehouse.gov/briefing-room/statements-releases/2022/04/21/fact-sheet-biden-administration-responds-to-putins-price-hike-by-awarding-first-barrels-from-historic-strategic-petroleum-reserve-release-deploying-affordable-clean-energy/.

61 **effective in lowering the price of oil:** "The Price Impact of the Strategic Petroleum Reserve Release," U.S. Department of the Treasury, press release, July 26, 2022, https://home.treasury.gov/news/press-releases/jy0887.

61 **stockpiling oil is not costless:** Just to give a sense of some costs, there are 111 federal employees and 887 contractors and subcontractors working on the maintenance of the US Strategic Reserve, according to the Department of Energy, https://www.energy.gov/ceser/spr-faqs.

62 **fiscal measures that supported:** Corsello and Riggi, "Inflation Is Not Equal for All." In their study, Corsello and Riggi estimate that without monetary policy tightening, the inflation gap between the first and last household quintiles in Italy would have been roughly 3 percentage points lower at its peak.

62 **an effective anti-inflationary arsenal:** Although in a new paper Tom Krebs and Isabella Weber argue that controls can in fact be an optimal policy when endogenous uncertainty over future prices is pervasive, as it can bring price expectations back into line and change production incentives. Since this

work is primarily theoretical, we do not engage with it directly here, although it is persuasive in its own terms. See: Krebs and Weber, "Can Price Controls Be Optimal? The Economics of the Energy Shock in Germany," University of Massachusetts Amherst, March 2024, Working Paper Series no. 597, PERI, https://peri.umass.edu/images/publication/WP597.pdf.

Chapter 3: Inflation Stories and the Politics of Blame

66 **by generating a recession:** Jordan Weissmann, "Why Larry Summers Thinks We Need Massive Unemployment to Beat Inflation," *Slate*, July 7, 2022, https://slate.com/business/2022/07/larry-summers-massive-unemployment -fed-inflation.html.

66 **today's rising prices resemble:** Paul Krugman, "History Says Don't Panic About Inflation," *New York Times*, November 11, 2021, https://www.nytimes .com/2021/11/11/opinion/inflation-history.html.

67 **"will set off inflationary pressures":** Larry Summers, quoted in John Cassidy, "Is Larry Summers Really Right About Biden and Inflation?," *New Yorker*, April 8, 2022, https://www.newyorker.com/news/our-columnists/is -larry-summers-really-right-about-inflation-and-biden.

67 **blaming a Democratic president:** Senator Mitch McConnell, quoted in "Explainer: Republicans Blame Biden for Inflation, But Are They Right?," Reuters, November 1, 2021, https://www.reuters.com/world/us/republicans -blame-biden-inflation-are-they-right-2021-11-01/.

68 **multiplier is very difficult to estimate:** For a survey of such estimates see Olivier Blanchard and Daniel Leigh, "Growth Forecast Errors and Fiscal Multipliers," *American Economic Review* 103, no. 3 (2013): 117–20, https:// www.aeaweb.org/articles?id=10.1257/aer.103.3.117.

68 **similar voices estimate the multiplier:** See, for example, Veronique de Rugy and Jack Salmon, "Declining Fiscal Multipliers and Inflationary Risks in the Shadow of Public Debt," Mercatus Policy Brief, August 22, 2022, https:// www.mercatus.org/research/policy-briefs/declining-fiscal-multipliers-and -inflationary-risks-shadow-public-debt.

69 **these estimates are too uncertain:** Òscar Jordà et al., "Why Is US Inflation Higher Than in Other Countries?," *FRBSF Economic Letter 2022-07*, Federal Reserve Bank of San Francisco, March 28, 2022, https://www.frbsf.org/ economic-research/publications/economic-letter/2022/march/why-is-us -inflation-higher-than-in-other-countries/.

69 **$1.8 trillion of the $5 trillion:** "How Much Money Did the Pandemic Programs Pay Out?," PandemicOversight.Gov, November 1, 2021, https://www .pandemicoversight.gov/news/articles/how-much-money-did-pandemic -unemployment-programs-pay-out.

70 **three waves of stimulus checks:** "Update: Three Rounds of Stimulus Checks: See How Many Went Out and for How Much," PandemicOversight.Gov, February 17, 2022, https://www.pandemicoversight.gov/data-interactive-tools/data-stories/update-three-rounds-stimulus-checks-see-how-many-went-out-and.

70 **the cash will be spent now:** In econospeak, the poor have a higher marginal propensity to spend than the rich. They get cash, they spend it.

70 **a counterfactual where no checks were spent:** Moreover, one can also point out that, according to Oxfam, two thirds of all new wealth gains since 2020 have gone to the top 1 percent. As such, it's reasonable to argue that the velocity of money as the driver of inflation did not take off across the whole economy. It was confined to the wealth gains of the very top strata. We thank Alex Smith for this observation. Anthony Kamande, "Survival of the Richest," Methodology Note, OXFAM, January 2023, https://oxfamilibrary.openrepository.com/bitstream/handle/10546/621477/mn-survival-of-the-richest-methodology-160123-en.pdf.

70 **"Credit card balances declined":** Federal Reserve Bank of New York, *Quarterly Report on Household Debt and Credit 2020: Q2*, August 2020, https://www.newyorkfed.org/medialibrary/interactives/householdcredit/data/pdf/hhdc_2020q2.pdf.

70 **"balances are $157 billion lower":** Federal Reserve Bank of New York, *Quarterly Report on Household Debt and Credit 2021: Q1*, May 2021, https://www.newyorkfed.org/medialibrary/interactives/householdcredit/data/pdf/hhdc_2021q1.pdf.

70 **spent on credit card reduction:** Thesia I. Garner, Adam Safir, and Jake Schild, "Receipt and Use of Stimulus Payments in the Time of the Covid-19 Pandemic," *Prices and Spending* 9, no. 10 (August 2020), https://www.bls.gov/opub/btn/volume-9/receipt-and-use-of-stimulus-payments-in-the-time-of-the-COVID-19-pandemic.htm.

71 **used the cash to avoid mortgage delinquency:** "Background," Center for Microeconomic Data, Federal Reserve Bank of New York, accessed June 4, 2024, https://www.newyorkfed.org/microeconomics/hhdc/background.html.

71 **so-called excess savings:** Federal Reserve Bank of San Francisco, "Pandemic-Era Excess Savings," undated, https://www.frbsf.org/research-and-insights/data-and-indicators/pandemic-era-excess-savings/.

71 **checks being spent on bitcoins:** "Nearly 1 in 10 Americans Have Used Stimulus Checks to Invest in Crypto," Harris Poll, March 17, 2021, https://theharrispoll.com/briefs/stimulus-check-spending/.

72 **much-talked-about Phillips curve:** James Forder has thrown serious doubt on this "official history" of the Phillips curve. He argues that the notion of the curve acting as a menu for policy was never true. Moreover, the idea that Friedman and Phelps came along and "'demolished" the curve by add-

ing expectations is an after-the-fact construction of textbooks from the late 1970s onward. His take-home is that the Phillips curve became historical fact after the fact because it was useful to have as a straw man to argue against. As he put it in a recent interview, "There's an extraordinary number of facile little pieces written by central bank research department people . . . that ran through the myth as . . . historical fact . . . sometimes explicitly saying . . . this is why we need an independent central bank." Seen in this way, Summers's rhetorical use of the Phillips curve to argue for a "necessary" recession is typical of the way it is invoked. See Seth Ackerman, "The Myth at the Heart of Modern Economics," Jacobin, April 2023, https://jacobin.com/2023/04/phillips-curve-myth-unemployment-inflation-wages-milton-friedman-economics.

72 **when unemployment goes up, inflation goes down:** This reasoning might lead the reader to wonder if there is an optimal balance between inflation and unemployment. Mainstream economists think so. According to this view, there is a "natural" rate of unemployment at which inflation does not accelerate, called the NAIRU, which stands for Non-Accelerating Inflation Rate of Unemployment. The idea is that even in the strongest labor market, there will always be some low degree of unemployment as people switch jobs, are looking for a job after school, or lack the necessary skills to find employment. In this framework, unemployment engages in this spiral with inflation only as it decreases and deviates from the NAIRU. The task of policymakers is then to increase unemployment as far as to bring it back to its natural rate. The problem with the NAIRU is that for the past twenty years it has jumped around all over the place at a near constant rate of inflation, which implies that for long periods of time there is no trade-off. As Eric Lonergan pointed out to us, an even bigger problem is that the NAIRU framework implicitly argues that there is a level of unemployment at which inflation spirals upward. But that is empirically false. Those who stick with this framework argue that such a level exists, but we just don't know where it is. But if we don't know where it is, how can we use it for policy? Further, if it lies at extremely low levels, wouldn't the economy adapt to accommodate it through capital substitution of labor and other mechanisms?

73 **Unemployment more than doubled:** Board of Governors of the Federal Reserve System (US), "Federal Funds Effective Rate," FRED, Federal Reserve Bank of St. Louis, updated July 4, 2024, https://fred.stlouisfed.org/series/FEDFUNDS.

73 **a massive recession was the necessary pain:** Here we are providing a simplified description of the Phillips curve. The original wage-led Phillips curve was helpful to describe the inflation of the 1960s. In the 1970s, the Phillips curve was adapted to account for inflation expectations and supply-side

shocks (the original curve was demand driven only). Despite these differences, the unemployment-inflation trade-off at the heart of the Phillips curve remained the same.

73 **important differences between the 1970s and today:** Jongrim Ha, M. Ayhan Kose, and Franziska Ohnsorge, "From Low to High Inflation: Implications for Emerging Market and Developing Economies," CEPR Policy Insight, no. 115, Center for Economic Policy Research, March 30, 2022, https://ideas .repec.org/p/koc/wpaper/2202.html.

74 **one in six jobs in the United States:** Thomas Oatley and Mark Blyth, "The Death of the Carbon Coalition," *Foreign Policy*, February 12 2021, https:// foreignpolicy.com/2021/02/12/carbon-coalition-median-voter-us-politics/.

75 **workers bargain over money:** John Maynard Keynes, *The General Theory of Employment, Interest, and Money* (New York: Harcourt 1964), chapter 2.

76 **not to adjust to prices going up:** Which is really what Governor Andrew Bailey was suggesting in his infamous quote about UK workers not asking for wage increases. See William Schomberg and Alistair Smout, "Bank of England Calls for Wage Restraint to Keep Grip on Inflation," Reuters, February 4, 2022, https://www.reuters.com/world/uk/boes-bailey-says-wage -restraint-key-keeping-grip-inflation-2022-02-04/.

76 **balance of power between capital and labor:** Frederic Boissay et al., "Are Major Advanced Economies on the Verge of a Wage-Price Spiral?" *BIS Bulletin*, no. 53, Bank for International Settlements, May 4, 2022, https://www.bis .org/publ/bisbull53.pdf.

76 **swing of profits away from wages:** Sangmin Aum and Yongseok Shin, "Why Is the Labor Share Declining?," Federal Reserve Bank of St. Louis, *Review* 102, no. 4 (Fourth Quarter 2020), https://research.stlouisfed.org/publications/ review/2020/10/22/why-is-the-labor-share-declining.

76 **$2.5 trillion poorer:** Carter C. Price and Kathryn A. Edwards, "Trends in Income from 1975 to 2018," Working Paper no. WR-A516-1, RAND Corporation, September 14, 2020, https://doi.org/10.7249/WRA516-1.

77 **profits, not wages:** Isabel Schnabel, "The Globalisation of Inflation," speech at conference organized by the Österreichische Vereinigung für Finanzanalyse und Asset Management, Vienna, May 11, 2022, https://www.ecb.europa .eu/press/key/date/2022/html/ecb.sp220511_1~e9ba02e127.en.html.

77 **wage-price spirals are quite rare:** Jorge A. Alvarez et al., "Wage-Price Spirals: What Is the Historical Evidence?," IMF Working Paper 2022/221, Research Department, International Monetary Fund, Washington, DC, November 2022, https://www.imf.org/en/Publications/WP/Issues/2022/11/11/Wage -Price-Spirals-What-is-the-Historical-Evidence-525073.

77 **Bank for International Settlements:** Boissay et al., "Are Major Advanced Economies on the Verge of a Wage-Price Spiral?"

17 **European Central Bank:** Niccolo Battistini and coauthors, from the European Central Bank, noted that wages have not been increasing since the recent surge in inflation. They argued that "the muted developments in the wage share . . . may stem from several long-term economic changes affecting, for instance, the production structure (e.g., lower energy dependence, deeper integration in global value chains), labour market institutions (e.g., less widespread wage indexation, a lower degree of unionisation) and monetary policy (e.g., a clearer strategy aimed at controlling inflation)." See N. Battistini, H. Grapow, E. Hahn, and M. Soudan, "Wage Share Dynamics and Second-Round Effects on Inflation After Energy Price Surges in the 1970s and Today," Box 2, ECB Economic Bulletin, Issue 5/2022, https://www.ecb.europa.eu/pub/pdf/ecbu/eb202205.en.pdf.

77 **The Decline of Trade Unions:** Boissay et al., "Are Major Advanced Economies on the Verge of a Wage-Price Spiral?"

79 **due to "special factors":** Alan S. Blinder and Jeremy B. Rudd, "The Supply-Shock Explanation of the Great Stagflation Revisited," in *The Great Inflation: The Rebirth of Modern Central Banking* (Chicago: University of Chicago Press, 2013), 119–75.

79 **running the United States economy superhot:** Jonathan Kirshner, "The Education of Ben Bernanke," review of Ben Bernanke, *21st Century Monetary Policy: The Federal Reserve from the Great Inflation to COVID-19*, in *Boston Review*, August 18, 2022, https://www.bostonreview.net/articles/the-education-of-ben-bernanke/.

79 **Incorporating women and minorities:** As Michael Green explained, while increasing labor supply should lower labor costs, in the late 1960s that did not happen because we have to think of labor as a demand factor as well as a supply factor. Specifically, "women and minorities (especially women) [in this period] did not form households at anywhere near the rate of white males prior to the 1960s. Civil rights opened the door for them to rent/buy their own homes. Household formation surged, especially women/minority headed. The lack of capital deepening (alongside a less experienced labor force) harmed productivity and the introduction of the Clean Air Act further pushed jobs abroad. The hiking of interest rates just expedited this dynamic and led to manufacturing offshoring and a lack of investment." Michael Green, personal communication.

79 **current inflation is a transitory phenomenon:** But the data for 2024 might temper that conclusion. This is an issue that we return to, appropriately, in the conclusion.

79 **Proponents of this story:** Paul Krugman, "Wonking Out: I'm Still on Team Transitory," *New York Times*, September 10, 2021, https://www.nytimes.com/2021/09/10/opinion/transitory-inflation-COVID-consumer-prices

.html; Martin Sandbu, "The Case for 'Team Transitory' Lives On," *Financial Times*, June 1, 2023, https://www.ft.com/content/8009bc16-68a5-4d2b-bdfe-31c5b99ea0b8.

79 **today's inflation is more like:** Sandbu, "The Case for 'Team Transitory' Lives On." Interestingly, those on team transitory do not usually see the 1970s as a case that they themselves should embrace for reasons we discuss below.

80 **assumes that people know all this:** Quite why they would know this when no one, even professional forecasters, can predict the future path of inflation again remains a mystery.

80 **self-fulfilling inflation spiral:** We tried to find empirical evidence that this in fact really happens. There is not much of it, and most of what there is comes from the COVID crisis rather than inflation per se. See T.-H. Cham et al., "Should I Buy or Not? Revisiting the Concept and Measurement of Panic Buying," *Current Psychology* 42, (2023): 19116–136, https://doi.org/10.1007/s12144-022-03089-9. The take-home seems to be that it does happen, but only in quite extreme conditions (like COVID) or in economies where inflation is already sufficiently entrenched that panic buying is a response rather than a cause of inflation. See also Alberto Cavallo and Oleksiy Kryvtsov, "What Can Stockouts Tell Us About Inflation? Evidence from Online Micro Data," *Journal of International Economics* 146 (December 2023), https://doi.org/10.1016/j.jinteco.2023.103769.

81 **medium-term inflation expectations:** Paul Krugman, "Inflation: A Revolution of Falling Expectations," *New York Times*, July 19, 2022, https://www.nytimes.com/2022/07/19/opinion/inflation-prices-fed.html.

81 **while supply factors account for a large share:** Jongrim Ha, M. Ayhan Kose, and Franziska Ohnsorge, eds., *Inflation in Emerging and Developing Economies: Evolution, Drivers, and Policies* (Washington, DC: World Bank, 2019).

82 **demand- and supply-driven contributors:** Adam Hale Shapiro, "Decomposing Supply and Demand Driven Inflation," Federal Reserve Bank of San Francisco Working Paper 2022-18, FRBSF, San Francisco, CA, October 2022, https://www.frbsf.org/wp-content/uploads/sites/4/wp2022-18.pdf.

82 **Bernanke and Blanchard decomposed US inflation:** Ben Bernanke and Oliver Blanchard, "What Caused the U.S. Pandemic-Era Inflation?," conference draft, prepared for "The Fed: Lessons Learned from the Past Three Years," Brookings Institute's Hutchins Center on Fiscal & Monetary Policy, Washington DC, May 23, 2023, https://www.brookings.edu/wp-content/uploads/2023/04/bernanke-blanchard-conference-draft_5.23.23.pdf.

82 **Car prices indeed go up:** And if automotive firms know this, they can further restrict supply and reap windfall profits as prices are bid up, which seems to be exactly what US automakers did during the pandemic. See Matt Phillips, "Fewer Autos and Bigger Profits for Carmakers," Axios, January

6, 2023, https://www.axios.com/2023/01/06/fewer-autos-and-bigger-profits
-for-carmakers.

83 **keeps inflation expectations anchored:** See, for instance, Alan S. Blinder,
"Central-Bank Credibility: Why Do We Care? How Do We Build It?," *American Economic Review* 90 no. 5 (2000): 1421–31.

83 **concept of inflation expectations:** For instance, in a recent press conference the chair of the Federal Reserve, Jerome Powell, stated that "we can't allow inflation expectations to become unanchored. It's just something that we can't allow to happen." See Chris Anstey, "What Powell Is Monitoring as the Fed Hikes Rates," Bloomberg.com, June 24, 2022, https://www
.bloomberg.com/news/newsletters/2022-06-24/what-s-happening-in-the
-world-economy-powell-s-dashboard-as-he-hikes-rates.

83 **the view that expectations matter:** Jeremy B. Rudd, "Why Do We Think That Inflation Expectations Matter for Inflation? (And Should We?)," Finance and Economics Discussion Series 2021-062, Board of Governors of the Federal Reserve System, Washington, DC, September 23, 2021, 18, https://www
.federalreserve.gov/econres/feds/files/2021062pap.pdf.

83 **shows the contrary:** Economists tried to make sense of the fact that individuals did not really act as they expected. This led some economists to put people into a group defined as "near-rational," which are those who either ignore their inflation expectations or do not take them into account when taking a price/wage decision; see George A. Akerlof, William T Dickens, and George L. Perry, "Near-Rational Wage and Price Setting and the Long-Run Phillips Curve," *Brookings Paper on Economic Activity*, no. 1 (2000): 1–44, https://doi
.org/10.1353/eca.2000.0001.]

83 **focus on medium-term expectations:** Krugman, "Inflation: A Revolution of Falling Expectations."

83 **When asked about their beliefs,** Peter Andre, Carlo Pizzinelli, Christopher Roth, and Johannes Wohlfart, "Subjective Models of the Macroeconomy: Evidence from Experts and Representative Samples," *Review of Economic Studies* 89(6), November 2022, 2958-2991: https://academic.oup.com/restud/
article/89/6/2958/6531988.

83 **the general population thinks the opposite:** Similar findings are found in the following articles: Alberto Binetti, Francesco Nuzzi, and Stefanie Stantcheva, "People's understanding of inflation," *Journal of Monetary Economics*, (August 2024), 103652: https://www.sciencedirect.com/science/article/
pii/S0304393224001053#sec4. Peter Andre, Carlo Pizzinelli, Christopher Roth, and Johannes Wohlfart, "Subjective Models of the Macroeconomy: Evidence from Experts and Representative Samples," *Review of Economic Studies* 89(6), November 2022, 2958-2991: https://academic.oup.com/restud/
article/89/6/2958/6531988.

84 **Their belief is grounded in the idea:** Peter Andre, Carlo Pizzinelli, Christopher Roth, and Johannes Wohlfart, "Subjective Models of the Macroeconomy: Evidence from Experts and Representative Samples," *Review of Economic Studies* 89, no. 6 (November 2022): 2958–91, https://academic.oup.com/restud/article/89/6/2958/6531988.

84 **experts' inflation forecasts:** Jonathan Benchimol, Makram El-Shagi, and Yossi Saadon, "Do Expert Experience and Characteristics Affect Inflation Forecasts?," *Journal of Economic Behavior & Organization* 201 (September 2022): 205–26, https://www.sciencedirect.com/science/article/pii/S0167268122002219?dgcid=coauthor#sec0013.

84 **inflation expectations are actually quite chaotic:** Peter Andre et al., "Subjective Models of the Macroeconomy: Evidence from Experts and Representative Samples," *Review of Economic Studies* 89, no. 6 (November 2022): 2958–91, https://www.restud.com/paper/subjective-models-of-the-macroeconomy-evidence-from-experts-and-representative-samples/.

84 **such managers are poorly informed about inflation dynamics:** Saten Kumar et al., "Inflation Targeting Does Not Anchor Inflation Expectations: Evidence from Firms in New Zealand," conference draft, *Brookings Papers on Economic Activity*, September 10–11, 2015, 4, https://www.brookings.edu/wp-content/uploads/2015/09/KumarTextFall15BPEA.pdf.

85 **inflammatory name of *greedflation*:** Isabella M. Weber and Evan Wasner, "Seller's Inflation, Profits and Conflict: Why Can Large Firms Hike Prices in an Emergency," University of Massachusetts Amherst, January 2023, Economics Department Working Paper Series, https://scholarworks.umass.edu/econ_workingpaper/343/.

86 **Charge twice what the other guy charges:** Unless you are providing a luxury version of pizza in a very rich neighborhood. Here a higher price might result in more sales, a phenomenon known as a "Giffen good."

87 **Thomas Philippon has shown:** Thomas Philippon, *The Great Reversal: How America Gave Up on Free Markets* (Cambridge, MA: Harvard University Press, 2017).

87 **Brett Christophers has shown:** Brett Christophers, *Rentier Capitalism* (New York: Verso, 2020).

87 **9.4 percent of the increase in inflation:** Weber and Wasner, "Sellers' Inflation, Profits and Conflict."

87 **increased by 49 percent:** Tom Perkins, "Revealed: Top US Corporations Raising Prices on Americans Even as Profits Surge," *The Guardian*, April 27, 2022, https://www.theguardian.com/business/2022/apr/27/inflation-corporate-america-increased-prices-profits/.

87 **American Economic Liberties Project:** Matt Stoller, "Corporate Profits Drive 60% of Inflation Increases," *BIG by Matt Stoller*, December 29, 2021,

https://mattstoller.substack.com/p/corporate-profits-drive-60-of-inflation?r=
5205r&s=r&utm_campaign=post&utm_medium=web&utm_source=direct.

88 **survey conducted by Digital.com:** "More than a half of retail businesses are using inflation to price gouge," Global Trade magazine website, originally appeared on Digital.com, November 30, 2021, https://www.globaltrademag.com/more-than -half-of-retail-businesses-are-using-inflation-to-price-gouge/.

89 **growing profits fueled inflation in Europe:** Elke Hahn, "How Have Unit Profits Contributed to the Recent Strengthening of Euro Area Domestic Price Pressures?," *ECB Economic Bulletin* 4/2023, European Central Bank, April 2024, https://www.ecb.europa.eu/pub/economic-bulletin/ focus/2023/html/ecb.ebbox202304_03~705befadac.en.html;   Niels-Jakob Hansen, Frederik Toscani, and Jing Zhou, "Europe's Inflation Outlook Depends on How Corporate Profits Absorb Wage Gains," *IMF Blog*, International Monetary Fund, June 26, 2023, https://www.imf.org/en/ Blogs/Articles/2023/06/26/europes-inflation-outlook-depends-on-how -corporate-profits-absorb-wage-gains.

89 **corporate profit seeking is responsible:** Estimates based on Stoller, "Corporate Profits Drive 60% of Inflation Increases."

89 **American economy is more concentrated:** To understand how we got here, see Philippon, *The Great Reversal: How American Gave Up on Free Markets*.

89 **price-gouging perspective is particularly appealing:** The argument on the Democrats liking the price-gouging story also features in German Lopez, "Inflation and Price Gouging," *New York Times*, June 14, 2022, https://www .nytimes.com/2022/06/14/briefing/inflation-supply-chain-greedflation.html.

89 **six in ten individuals:** Stephen Rogers, Justin Cook, and Leon Pieters, "When Rising Prices Break Consumers' Trust," *Deloitte Insights*, May 20, 2022, https://www2.deloitte.com/us/en/insights/industry/retail-distribution/ consumer-behavior-trends-state-of-the-consumer-tracker/price-gouging -and-rising-us-inflation.html. See also Pamela N. Danziger, "Inflation and Price Gouging May Flip Luxury Consumers' Purchase Switch Off," *Forbes*, June 2, 2022, https://www.forbes.com/sites/pamdanziger/2022/06/02/inflation -and-price-gouging-may-flip-luxury-consumers-purchase-switch-off/.

90 **higher interest rates will generate higher inflation:** Peter Andre et al., "Subjective Models of the Macroeconomy: Evidence from Experts and Representative Samples"; David G. Blanchflower et al., "The Happiness Trade-Off Between Unemployment and Inflation," *Journal of Money, Credit and Banking* 46, no. S2 (October 2014): 117–41, https://doi.org/10.1111/jmcb.12154.

90 **price controls were part of the solution:** Isabella Weber, "Could Strategic Price Controls Help Fight Inflation?," *The Guardian*, December 29, 2021, https://www.theguardian.com/business/commentisfree/2021/dec/29/ inflation-price-controls-time-we-use-it.

90 **tax away the price hike:** Robert Kuttner, "Inflation and Price-Gouging," *American Prospect*, February 7, 2022, https://prospect.org/blogs-and -newsletters/tap/inflation-and-price-gouging/.

90 **net income increased 90 percent:** Samer Al-Atrush, "Saudi Aramco Hits Fresh Profit Record as High Energy Prices Deliver Windfall," *Financial Times*, August 14, 2022, https://www.ft.com/content/3c6a0c9a-0e4c-4494 -88f8-d4c44cd04aa8?emailId=62fa6ba1ba0c8e002316012f&segmentId=278 5c52b-1c00-edaa-29be-7452cf90b5a2; Vivienne Walt, "Saudi Arabia Has the Most Profitable Company in the History of the World, with $3.2 Trillion to Invest by 2030. Who Will Say No to That Tidal Wave of Cash?," *Fortune*, August 1, 2023, https://fortune.com/2023/08/01/saudi-aramco-profitable-oil -company-trillions/.

90 **raising interest rates would do little:** Romain A. Duval et al., "Market Power and Monetary Policy Transmission," IMF Working Paper No. 2021/184, International Monetary Fund, July 9, 2021, https://www.imf.org/en/Publications/ WP/Issues/2021/07/09/Market-Power-and-Monetary-Policy-Transmission -461332

91 **"an accelerant of price increases":** The quote is from Lindsay Owens, executive director of left-leaning Groundwork Collaborative, in Lopez, "Inflation and Price Gouging."

91 **might explain some part:** Lopez, "Inflation and Price Gouging."

91 **neither as strong nor as automatic:** Lopez, "Inflation and Price Gouging."

91 **stock markets plummeted:** Jeff Cox, "This Was the Worst First Half for the Market in 50 Years and It's All Because of One Thing—Inflation," CNBC, June 30, 2022, https://www.cnbc.com/2022/06/30/the-markets-worst-first -half-in-50-years-has-all-come-down-to-one-thing.html.

91 **This was the case with health care:** In fairness, health-care prices in the US are not market prices and do not operate according to supply and demand. They are fully administered prices agreed among the different parts of the industry.

92 **sellers' inflation occurs:** Weber and Wasner, "Sellers' Inflation, Profits and Conflict," 5.

92 **while profits are up:** J. P. Morgan Research, "Inflation and the Auto Industry: When Will Car Prices Drop?," Global Research, *J.P. Morgan Insights*, February 22, 2023, https://www.jpmorgan.com/insights/global-research/autos/ when-will-car-prices-drop.

92 **interaction of demography and globalization:** Charles Goodhart and Manoj Pradham, *The Great Demographic Reversal: Ageing Societies, Waning Inequality, and an Inflation Revival* (London: Palgrave Macmillan, 2020).

94 **the "jeopardy thesis":** BBC News, "Cost of Living: Labour to Call Vote on Windfall Tax on Big Oil and Gas Companies," May 16, 2022, https://www .bbc.com/news/uk-politics-61456268.

Chapter 4: When Inflation Goes Hyper

97 **"There is a big logical jump":** Ha-joon Chang, *Bad Samaritans: The Myth of Free Trade and the Secret History of Capitalism* (New York: Bloomsbury Press, 2007), 141.

17 **three types of inflation:** Fabio Panetta, "Patient Monetary Policy Amid a Rocky Recovery," speech at Sciences Po, Paris, 24 November 2021, https://www.ecb.europa.eu/press/key/date/2021/html/ecb.sp211124~a0bb243dfe.en.html.

98 **monthly change in prices:** Phillip Cagan, "The Monetary Dynamics of Hyperinflation," in *Studies in the Quantity Theory of Money,* ed. Milton Friedman (Chicago: University of Chicago Press, 1956), 25–117.

98 **price of a gallon of milk:** Arnold C. Harberger also defined the concepts of chronic inflation and acute inflation, which is a "rapid burst of inflation." See Harberger, "A Primer on Inflation," Journal of Money Credit and Banking 10, no. 4 (November 1978): 505–21, quoted in Emilio Ocampo, "Fighting Inflation in Argentina: A Brief History of Ten Stabilization Plans," Working Paper no. 613, Finance Department, UCEMA/NYU Stern, Buenos Aires, June 2017.

98 **eight cases of hyperinflation:** Jens R. Clausen et al., "Lessons from High Inflation Episodes for Stabilizing the Economy in Zimbabwe," IMF Working Papers 2007 no. 099, International Monetary Fund, Washington DC, 2007, https://doi.org/10.5089/9781451866636.001.A001.

98 **"there is no well-defined threshold":** Phillip Cagan, "Hyperinflation," in J. Eatwell, M. Milgate, P. Newman, eds., *Money* (London: Palgrave Macmillan, 1989), 179.

98 **"a very rapid rise":** Michał Kalecki, "A Model of Hyperinflation," *Manchester School* 30, no. 3 (September 1962): 275.

99 **"a very rapid increase":** Sébastien Charles and Jonathan Marie, "Hyperinflation in a Small Open Economy with a Fixed Exchange Rate: A Post Keynesian View," *Journal of Post Keynesian Economics* 39, no. 3 (2016): 361–86, https://doi.org/10.1080/01603477.2016.1200950.

99 **"hyperinflations are always caused":** See Peter Bernholz, *Monetary Regimes and Inflation: History, Economics and Political Relationship* (Northampton, MA: Edward Elgar, 2003), 11.

99 **"balance of payments" view:** There are three reasons why a country can get into such a crisis. First, a disequilibrium in the current account balance; second, self-fulfilling expectations; third, a sudden stop of capital inflows.

102 **Argentinian central bank abandoned:** Nicolás Cachanosky and Federico Julián Ferrelli Mazza, "Why Did Inflation Targeting Fail in Argentina?," *Quarterly Review of Economics and Finance* 80, May 2021, 102–16, https://doi.org/10.1016/j.qref.2021.01.014.

102 **you can't trust politicians:** It's the last part of the sentence that is particularly contestable.

103 **Central Bank Independence Reform:** Daron Acemoglu et al., "When Does Policy Reform Work? The Case of Central Bank Independence," *Brookings Papers on Economic Activity*, Spring 2008: 351–418, https://www.brookings .edu/wp-content/uploads/2008/03/2008a_bpea_acemoglu.pdf.

103 **the difference in disinflation performance:** Rodolfo Dall'Orto Mas, Benjamin Vonessen, Christian Fehlker, and Katrin Arnold, "The Case for Central Bank Independence: A Review of Key Issues in the International Debate," European Central Bank Occasional Paper 248, October 2020, https://www .ecb.europa.eu/pub/pdf/scpops/ecb.op248~28bebb193a.en.pdf.

104 **Venezuelan inflation had reached:** Source: ECLAC data presented in Leonardo Vera, "Venezuela 1999–2014: Macro-Policy, Oil Governance and Economic Performance," *Comparative Economic Studies* 57, no. 3 (September 2015), 539–68, https://doi.org/10.1057/ces.2015.13

104 **the jaw-dropping rate:** Giovanni B. Pittaluga, Elena Seghezza, and Pierluigi Morelli, "The Political Economy of Hyperinflation in Venezuela," *Public Choice* 186, no. 3–4 (2021): 337–50.

104 **cost of the café con leche:** Data are from the Bloomberg Café con Leche Index. This index measures the cost of a single cup of coffee in Venezuela. Bloomberg created this index as a helpful substitute to official statistics since the Venezuelan government stopped publishing official statistics on inflation. See "Venezuelan Café con Leche Index," Bloomberg.com, December 15, 2016, https://www.bloomberg.com/features/2016-venezuela-cafe-con-leche -index/?terminal=true.

104 **annual inflation rate of 224 percent:** Photographer Carlos Garcia Rawlins found an even more creative way to display the struggle that hyperinflation means to Venezuelans. In his project, he took pictures of basic goods next to the amount of banknotes needed to buy those items. The pile of banknotes needed to buy a chicken is taller than the chicken itself. See Claire Heffron, "These Photos Reveal the Huge Amounts of Cash Venezuelans Need to Buy Daily Essentials," euronews, August 21, 2018, https://www .euronews.com/2018/08/20/these-photos-reveal-the-huge-amounts-of-cash -venezuelans-need-to-buy-daily-essentials

105 **called "Bolivarian Missions":** See Pittaluga, Seghezza, and Morelli, "The Political Economy of Hyperinflation in Venezuela."

105 **pension rights were extended:** These policies were continued by the current president, Nicolas Maduro, who succeeded Chavez after his death in 2013.

105 **excessive monetary growth:** See Pittaluga, Seghezza, and Morelli, "The Political Economy of Hyperinflation in Venezuela," which shows economet-

·ric evidence in favor of the fiscal view based on the case of Venezuela and using data for the years 2010–2017.

105 **the export of oil:** Amelia Cheatham and Diana Roy, "Venezuela: The Rise and Fall of a Petrostate," Council on Foreign Relations, updated December 22, 2023, https://www.cfr.org/backgrounder/venezuela-crisis.

106 **called "Dutch disease":** See Javier Corrales and Michael Penfold, *Dragon in the Tropics: Hugo Chavez and the Political Economy of Revolution in Venezuela* (Washington, DC: Brookings Institution Press, 2011), and Marta Kulesza, "Inflation and Hyperinflation in Venezuela (1970s–2016): A Post-Keynesian Interpretation," Working Paper No. 93/2017, Berlin Institute for International Political Economy (IPE), November 2017, https://www.ipe-berlin.org/fileadmin/institut-ipe/Dokumente/Working_Papers/IPE_WP_93.pdf.

107 **oil price crisis:** Pedro Palma, "La Política Cambiaria en Venezuela," in Asdrúbal Baptista, *Veinticinco Años de Pensamiento Económico Venezolano* (Caracas, Venezuela: Academia Nacional de Ciencias Económicas, 2008), 463–532.

107 **public revenues collapsed:** Oil revenues in 2009 fell by almost 40 percent. See Leonardo Vera, "Venezuela 1999–2014: Macro-Policy, Oil Governance and Economic Performance," *Comparative Economic Studies* 57 (2015): 539–68.

107 **maintain fixed parity:** Kulesza, "Inflation and Hyperinflation in Venezuela (1970s–2016); Vera, "Venezuela 1999–2014."

107 **bolivar rapidly depreciated:** More precisely, the government introduced a two-tier system. A basket of selected goods, such as food and drugs, would have a more favorable exchange rate of 2.15 bolivars per dollar, whereas for all the other goods the exchange rate was 5.3 bolivars per dollar.

108 **workers managed to partially offset the costs:** Kulesza, "Inflation and Hyperinflation in Venezuela (1970s–2016)," based on data from ECLAC. This dynamic is the same as we described in chapter 3 as genre two of inflation stories, which argued that inflation is generated by a wage-price spiral. It is, however, also consonant with genre four, where firms take advantage of the increase in import prices to engage in price gouging.

108 **imposing price controls:** Vera, "Venezuela 1999–2014."

109 **black market for dollars:** Reportedly, groups of middle-aged women made their income by regularly crossing the border to use ATMs in Colombia, where they could withdraw dollars safely and then profit by selling greenbacks at a markup back in Venezuela. Michelle Carmody, "What Caused Hyperinflation in Venezuela: A Rare Blend of Public Ineptitude and Private Enterprise," The Conversation, January 5, 2019, https://theconversation.com/what-caused-hyperinflation-in-venezuela-a-rare-blend-of-public-ineptitude-and-private-enterprise-102483.

109 **seven million Venezuelans fled:** For a general overview see https://en
.wikipedia.org/wiki/Venezuelan_refugee_crisis.

110 **thirty US dollars:** "Zimbabwe Rolls Out Z$100tr Note," BBC, January 16,
2009, http://news.bbc.co.uk/2/hi/africa/7832601.stm.

110 **79.6 *billion* percent:** Steve H. Hanke and Alex Kwok, "On the Measurement of Zimbabwe's Hyperinflation," *Cato Journal* 29, no. 2 (Spring/Sum-
mer 2009): 359, https://www.cato.org/sites/cato.org/files/serials/files/cato
-journal/2009/5/cj29n2-8.pdf.

110 **highest monthly inflation rate:** Hanke and Kwok, "On the Measurement of
Zimbabwe's Hyperinflation."

110 **income of black workers was one tenth:** Godfrey Kanyenze, "The Performance of the Zimbabwean Economy, 1980–2000," in Staffan Darnolf and
Liisa Laakso, eds., *Twenty Years of Independence in Zimbabwe: From Liberation to Authoritarianism* (Basingstoke and New York: Palgrave Macmillan, 2003), 37, https://www.sahistory.org.za/sites/default/files/file%20
uploads%20/staffan_darnolf_liisa_laakso_twenty_years_of_inbook4you
.pdf#page=53. Kanyenze refers to those estimates as coming from a World
Bank report: "Zimbabwe—A Strategy for Sustained Growth," World Bank,
Washington DC, 1987, https://documents.albankaldawli.org/en/publication/
documents-reports/documentdetail/675471468334173934/main-report.

111 **black population engaged in subsistence farming:** Jayson Coomer and
Thomas Gstraunthaler, "The Hyperinflation in Zimbabwe," *Quarterly Journal of Austrian Economics* 14, no. 3 (Fall 2011): 311–46.

111 **large-scale land redistribution:** Kiren Aziz Chaudhry, "The Myths of the
Market and the Common History of Late Developers," *Politics and Society* 21,
no. 3 (1993): 245–73, and Ha-Joon Chang, *Kicking Away the Ladder: Development Strategy in Historical Perspective* (London: Anthem Press, 2002).

111 **East-Asian "developmental states":** Alice Amsden, "The State and Taiwan's
Economic Development" in Peter Evans et al., *Bringing the State Back In?*
(Cambridge: Cambridge University Press, 1985), 77–106.

111 **knowledge and skills needed:** This is arguably true for both the land reform
implemented in the first five years of independence as well as in regard to the
fast-track program introduced in June 2000 to mitigate protests.

112 **a particularly important protest group:** Norma Kriger, "Zimbabwe: Political Constructions of War Veterans," *Review of African Political Economy* 30,
no. 96 (June 2003): 323–28, http://www.jstor.org/stable/4006770.

113 **government borrowed money:** Coomer and Gstraunthaler, "The Hyperinflation in Zimbabwe."

113 **stock market collapse:** Chidochashe L. Munangagwa, "The Economic
Decline of Zimbabwe," *Gettysburg Economic Review* 3, no. 9 (2009), https://
cupola.gettysburg.edu/ger/vol3/iss1/9.

113 **ballooned the fiscal deficit:** Munangagwa, "The Economic Decline of Zimbabwe."

113 **suspended their lending:** Andrew Meldrum, "Zimbabwe Loans Cut Off as Leak Shows War Costs," *The Guardian* (US edition), October 6, 1999, https://www.theguardian.com/world/1999/oct/07/andrewmeldrum; Amy Copley, "Africa in the News: IMF Drops Zimbabwe Sanctions, DRC and Guinea-Bissau Dissolve Governments, and Pew Releases African Attitudes Survey," *Brookings*, November 18, 2016, https://www.brookings.edu/blog/africa-in-focus/2016/11/18/africa-in-the-news-imf-drops-zimbabwe-sanctions-drc-and-guinea-bissau-dissolve-governments-and-pew-releases-african-attitudes-survey/.

113 **money was released as export credit:** "IMF Staff Concludes Staff Visit to Zimbabwe," International Monetary Fund, press release no. 22/310, September 19, 2022, https://www.imf.org/en/News/Articles/2022/09/19/pr22310-zimbabwe-imf-staff-concludes-virtual-staff-visit.

113 **devalued the currency:** Coomer and Gstraunthaler, "The Hyperinflation in Zimbabwe."

115 **Zim dollars soon lost value:** Joseph Cotterill, "Ecocash Defies Zimbabwe Order to Suspend Mobile Money Transactions," *Financial Times*, June 27, 2020, https://www.ft.com/content/f0d7ab8a-ea25-4599-b5ab-17cf4c1919a0.

115 **hyperinflation is still a problem:** "IMF Staff Concludes Staff Visit to Zimbabwe."

116 **Argentina has never quite recovered:** Carmen M. Reinhart and Kenneth S. Rogoff, *This Time It's Different: Eight Centuries of Financial Folly* (Princeton, NJ: Princeton University Press 2011).

117 **Argentina's average inflation rate:** Emilio Ocampo, "A Brief History of Hyperinflation in Argentina," Working Paper No. 787, University of CEMA, Buenos Aires, April 2021, 22, https://www.econstor.eu/bitstream/10419/238412/1/787.pdf.

117 **hovered around 90 percent:** Instituto Nacional de Estadistica y Censos de la Republica Argentina, *Índices y Variaciones Porcentuales Mensuales e Interanuales Según Divisiones de la Canasta, Bienes yServicios, Clasificación de Grupos. Diciembre de 2016–Abril de 2024*, May 2024, https://www.indec.gob.ar/indec/web/Nivel4-Tema-3-5-31.

117 **"four sorts of countries":** "How Argentina and Japan Continue to Confound Macroeconomists," *The Economist*, March 28, 2019, https://www.economist.com/finance-and-economics/2019/03/28/how-argentina-and-japan-continue-to-confound-macroeconomists.

117 **causes of Argentina's inflation:** Analyses of this debate can be found in Peter J. Montiel, "Empirical Analysis of High-Inflation Episodes in Argentina, Bra-

zil, and Israel," Staff Papers (International Monetary Fund) 36, no. 3 (1989): 527–49, https://doi.org/10.2307/3867046; Robert C. Vogel, "The Dynamics of Inflation in Latin America, 1950–1969," *American Economic Review* 64, no. 1 (March 1974): 102–14.

118 **"intensity of Argentina's hyperinflationary episodes":** Ocampo, "A Brief History of Hyperinflation in Argentina."

118 **excessive growth of the money supply:** See Vogel, "The Dynamics of Inflation in Latin America, 1950–1969." See also Adolfo C. Diz, "Money and Prices in Argentina, 1935–1962," in *Varieties of Monetary Experience*, ed. David Meiselman (Chicago: University of Chicago Press, 1970), 111–22.

118 **date back to 1945:** Ocampo, "Fighting Inflation in Argentina." There was no inflation problem in Argentina before that date: between 1900 and 1945 average annual inflation was 1.5 percent.

118 **historic high of 3,046 percent:** "Inflation, GDP deflator (annual %)—Argentina," World Bank, accessed June 10, 2024, https://data.worldbank.org/indicator/NY .GDP.DEFL.KD.ZG?locations=AR.

119 **Convertibility Plan of 1991:** The plan is explained in detail in a short paper coauthored by Cavallo himself and by the undersecretary of Macroeconomic Programming, Joaquin Cottani. Domingo Cavallo and Joaquin Cottani, "Argentina's Convertibility Plan and the IMF," *American Economic Review* 87, no. 2 (May 1997): 17–22.

119 **convertible one-to-one peg:** Apparently this plan by Cavallo was influenced by the Rentenmark issuance that stabilized the German hyperinflation that we discuss next. We thank Eric Lonergan for this insight.

119 **imports get more expensive:** The magnitude of this effect is measured by the exchange-rate pass-through. In a nutshell, the exchange-rate pass-through computes how much foreign prices react to a change in the exchange rate. This indicator is often given by the ratio between the percentage change of prices of imported goods in domestic currency and the percentage change of the exchange rate.

120 **around 80 percent of Argentina's debt:** Adam Tooze, *Crashed: How a Decade of Financial Crisis Changed the World* (New York: Viking, 2018). We discuss why this is the case below.

120 **in dollar-denominated deposits:** The rationale is simple. Suppose you want to deposit your pesos in a bank today. You can decide to deposit them as pesos or as US dollars, where the conversion of pesos into dollar is given by today's exchange rate. If you fear that the peso could lose value relative to the dollar in a few years, then you prefer to deposit your money in a dollar-denominated deposit and "fix" their value.

120 **peg its currency to the dollar:** In addition, the exchange-rate parity had two short-term domestic advantages. It made imports cheaper and it lowered the

cost of foreign real estate—the latter being an advantage only for a small class
of wealthier Argentineans.

121 **"fiscal" and "balance of payments" views:** Montiel, "Empirical Analysis of
High-Inflation Episodes in Argentina, Brazil, and Israel."

121 **Argentine anti-inflationary plans:** Ocampo, "Fighting Inflation in Argentina."

122 **external factors played a prominent role:** Ocampo, "Fighting Inflation in
Argentina."

122 **exchange-rate pass-through:** Amit Ghosh, "Exchange Rate Pass Through,
Macro Fundamentals and Regime Choice in Latin America," *Journal of Macroeconomics* 35 (March 2013): 163–71, https://doi.org/10.1016/j.jmacro.2012
.09.00.

123 **Latin America, was incorporated:** Jazmin Sierra, "The Politics of Growth
Model Switching: Why Latin America Tries, and Fails, to Abandon Commodity Driven Growth," in *Diminishing Returns: The New Politics of Growth
and Stagnation*, eds. Lucio Baccaro, Mark Blyth, and Jonas Pontusson (New
York: Oxford University Press, 2022), 167–89.

123 **70 percent of jobs:** Martin Castelllano, "Winners and Losers in Latin America's Commodity Markets," America's Quarterly, March 16, 2022, https://
www.americasquarterly.org/article/winners-and-losers-in-latin-americas
-commodities-market/.

124 **drive to industrialize:** Wolfgang Streeck and Kozo Yamamura, eds., *The Origins of Nonliberal Capitalism: Germany and Japan in Comparison* (Ithaca,
NY: Cornell University Press, 2005).

124 **Japan exported that model to Korea:** Atul Kohli, *State Directed Development: Political Power and Industrialization in the Global Periphery* (Princeton, NJ: Princeton University Press, 2004).).

124 **Taiwan did more or less:** Alice Amsden, "The State and Taiwan's Economic
Development," in Evans et al., *Bringing the State Back In?*

126 **German hyperinflation of the 1920s:** For an overview see https://en
.wikipedia.org/wiki/Hyperinflation_in_the_Weimar_Republic.

126 **"too much money" inflation:** The discussion of this case draws upon prior
work by Mark Blyth in *Austerity: The History of a Dangerous Idea* (New York:
Oxford University Press, 2015).

129 **"Inflation proved to be":** Albrecht Ritschl, "The German Transfer Problem,
1920–33: A Sovereign-Debt Perspective," *European Review of History: Revue
Européenne d'histoire* 19, no. 6: 943–64, https://doi.org/10.1080/13507486
.2012.739147.

129 **consequence of hyperinflation as policy:** Barry Eichengreen, *Golden Fet-
ters: The Gold Standard and the Great Depression, 1919–1939* (New York:
Oxford University Press, 1992), 139.

129 **printed new money:** See Gerald Feldman, *The Great Disorder: Politics, Eco-*

nomics and Society 1914–1924 (New York: Oxford University Press, 1997) for the definitive account of the German inflation.

129 **this monetary reform succeeded:** Gustavo Franco, "The Rentenmark Miracle," Texto para Discussão no. 159, Pontifícia Universidade Católica do Rio de Janeiro (PUC-Rio), Departamento de Economia, Rio de Janeiro, 1987.

129 **powered the German economy out of crisis:** Ritschl, "The German Transfer Problem, 1920–33," 7.

131 **bring the Nazis to power:** Blyth, *Austerity*, 196.

132 **new normal state of affairs:** See for example, just before inflation appeared Larry Summers wrote: "Accepting the Reality of Secular Stagnation," International Monetary Fund, March 2020, https://www.imf.org/en/Publications/fandd/issues/2020/03/larry-summers-on-secular-stagnation; while Olivier Blanchard said this in 2019: Greg Robb, "Leading Economist Says High Public Debt 'Might Not Be So Bad,'" MarketWatch, January 7, 2019, https://www.marketwatch.com/story/leading-economist-says-high-public-debt-might-not-be-so-bad-2019-01-07; and then said this in 2023: Alice Gledhill, "Public Debt Spiral Must Be Averted at All Costs, Blanchard Says," Bloomberg.com, November 7, 2023, https://www.bloomberg.com/news/articles/2023-11-07/public-debt-spiral-must-be-averted-at-all-costs-blanchard-says?embedded-checkout=true.

Chapter 5: Why Didn't We See This One Coming?

133 **"The task of the historian":** Herbert Butterfield, *The Whig Interpretation of History* (New York, W. W. Norton, 1965).

133 **"So in summary, Your Majesty":** Letter to the Queen from British Academy, July 22 2009, https://www.ma.imperial.ac.uk/~bin06/M3A22/queen-lse.pdf.

134 **Isabella Weber published an op-ed:** For a discussion of the whole episode, see Zachary Carter, "What if We Are Thinking About Inflation All Wrong?," *New Yorker*, June 6, 2023, https://www.newyorker.com/news/persons-of-interest/what-if-were-thinking-about-inflation-all-wrong.

135 **economics is a language of power:** Elizabeth Popp Berman, *Thinking Like an Economist: How Efficiency Replaced Equality in U.S. Public Policy* (Princeton, NJ: Princeton University Press 2022).

135 **"Price controls have had":** Christopher J. Neely, "Why Price Controls Should Stay in the History Books," St. Louis Federal Reserve Bank, March 24, 2022, https://www.stlouisfed.org/publications/regional-economist/2022/mar/why-price-controls-should-stay-history-books.

136 **postwar Keynesian consensus:** John Maynard Keynes, *The General Theory of Employment, Interest, and Money* (New York: Harcourt, 1964).

137 **suggested a political problem:** Michał Kalecki, "Political Problems of Full Employment," *Political Quarterly*, 1943.

137 **maintaining full employment:** Michael Stewart, *Keynes and After* (London: Penguin Books, 1985), 152.

137 **protect private markets:** Mark Blyth, Great Transformations: Economic Ideas and Institutional Change in the Twentieth Century (Cambridge: Cambridge University Press, 2002).

138 **stability of trade-off:** Milton Friedman, "The Role of Monetary Policy" AEA address, published in *American Economic Review* 58, no. 1 (March 1968), https://www.andrew.cmu.edu/course/88-301/phillips/friedman.pdf.

138 **rational expectations economists:** Blyth, *Great Transformations*, 142–44.

139 **give these responsibilities to "conservative" central bankers:** Kenneth Rogoff, "The Optimal Degree of Commitment to an Intermediate Monetary Target," *Quarterly Journal of Economics* 100, no. 4 (1985): 1169–89.

140 **Reagan famously observed, the problem:** Ronald Reagan, Inaugural Address, January 20, 1981, https://www.reaganfoundation.org/ronald-reagan/reagan-quotes-speeches/inaugural-address-2/.

140 **Economics is not exceptional:** It is exceptional in that PhD training in economics does not usually include taking classes in economic history. As such, the discipline's learning from the past is packed into textbooks and is expressed in short form, which makes it particularly prone to a rather whiggish official version of events.

141 **"Everything depends upon Vietnam":** Blyth, *Great Transformations*, 131 fn17.

142 **"a street-walker who":** Blyth, *Great Transformations*, 135 fn33.

48 **Nixon's price controls:** Hugh Rockoff, *Drastic Measures: A History of Wage and Price Controls in United States* (Cambridge: Cambridge University Press, 1986).

143 **a step too far normatively:** Rockoff, *Drastic Measures*.

143 **anticipatory or rational expectations:** On the rise of that "rational expectations" framework in macroeconomics see Blyth, *Great Transformations*, 142–44.

144 **"end of the Nixon wage-price controls":** Alan S. Blinder, "The Anatomy of Double-Digit Inflation in the 1970s," in *Inflation: Causes and Effects*, ed. Robert E. Hall (Chicago: University of Chicago Press, 1982), 262, italics added.

144 **from mandatory to voluntary controls:** Blinder, "The Anatomy of Double-Digit Inflation in the 1970s," 267.

144 **"once again, three factors":** Blinder, "The Anatomy of Double-Digit Inflation in the 1970s," 269, italics added.

144 **"the CPI energy component":** Blinder, "The Anatomy of Double-Digit Inflation in the 1970s," 271.

144 **"the deceleration of mortgage costs":** Alan S. Blinder, "The Anatomy of Double-Digit Inflation in the 1970s," in Robert E. Hall, *Inflation: Causes and Effects* (Chicago, University of Press,1981), 274.

145 **"many people continue":** Blinder, "The Anatomy of Double-Digit Inflation in the 1970s," 275.

145 **" 'old fashioned' supply-shock":** Alan S. Blinder and Jeremy B. Rudd, "The Supply-Shock Explanation of the Great Stagflation Revisited," in *The Great Inflation: The Rebirth of Modern Central Banking*, eds. Michael D. Bordo and Athanasios Orphanides (Chicago: University of Chicago Press, 2013), 123.

145 ***"more than 100 percent* of the rise":** Blinder and Rudd, "The Supply-Shock Explanation of the Great Stagflation Revisited," 152.

145 **"anyone who tries to explain":** Blinder and Rudd, "The Supply-Shock Explanation of the Great Stagflation Revisited," 145, italics added.

146 **"better monetary policy":** Ben Bernanke, "The Great Moderation," speech at the Eastern Economic Association Meeting, Washington, DC, February 20, 2004, https://www.federalreserve.gov/BOARDDOCS/SPEECHES/2004/20040220/default.htm.

146 **Gordon Brown drew:** Deborah Summers, "No Return to Boom and Bust: What Brown Said When He Was Chancellor," *The Guardian*, September 11, 2008, https://www.theguardian.com/politics/2008/sep/11/gordonbrown.economy.

146 **"central problem of depression prevention":** Robert E. Lucas, "Macroeconomic Priorities," *American Economic Review* 93, no. 1 (March 2003), https://www.princeton.edu/~markus/misc/Lucas2003.pdf.

147 **distributional impacts of inflation:** Donald T. Brash, speech to the Trans-Tasman Business Circle, Sydney, March 30, 2001, "Central Banks: What They Can and Cannot Do," https://www.bis.org/review/r010402c.pdf.

147 **"I, and people like me":** Brash, "Central Banks: What They Can and Cannot Do."

147 **Inflation targeting, at least in theory:** The creation of an inflation target actually happened more by accident than by design. After decades of volatile prices, the finance minister, Roger Douglas, was also strongly committed to making inflation reduction his main objective. He wanted to persuade New Zealanders that the government and the central bank were both unhappy with high inflation. On April 1, 1988, he went on TV, and to make his point clearer, he stated that his ideal inflation rate was "around zero to one percent," https://www.rba.gov.au/publications/confs/2018/mcdermott-williams.html#fn13 .

148 **the finance minister to instruct:** The prereform Reserve Bank of New Zealand Act clearly stated that the central bank was to "give effect to the

monetary policy of the Government," https://www.rba.gov.au/publications/confs/2018/mcdermott-williams.html#fn10 .

148 **"policy target agreement":** In practice, none were ever removed.

149 **Bundesbank's inflation performance:** See for example, Andreas Beyer et al., "Opting Out of the Great Inflation: German Monetary Policy After the Breakdown of Bretton Woods," Working Paper Series, no. 1012, March 2009, https://www.ecb.europa.eu/pub/pdf/scpwps/ecbwp1020.pdf.

149 **central banks around the world set inflation targets:** Scott Roger, "Inflation Targeting at 20—Achievements and Challenges," IMF Working Papers Series 2009, International Monetary Fund, Washington DC, 2009, https://www.elibrary.imf.org/view/journals/001/2009/236/article-A001-en.xml.

149 **success of inflation targeting:** Prakash Loungani, "Lars Svensson: Central Banking Revolutionary," *IMF Finance & Development*, March 2023, https://www.imf.org/en/Publications/fandd/issues/2023/03/PIE-central-banking-revolutionary-lars-svensson.

149 **twenty-six countries adopted:** Roger, "Inflation Targeting at 20—Achievements and Challenges."

149 **gained more political independence:** Davide Romelli, "The Political Economy of Reforms in Central Bank Design: Evidence from a New Dataset," *Economic Policy* 37, no. 112 (October 2022): 641–88, https://doi.org/10.1093/epolic/eiac011.

149 **dispatched training manuals:** For a discussion of how central banking ideas were spread around Eastern Europe by Western central banks see Juliet Johnson, *The Priests of Prosperity: How Central Bankers Transformed the Postcommunist World* (Ithaca, NY: Cornell University Press 2016).

149 **became the most zealous:** The peak of which was probably the head of the Romania central bank in 2004 declaring that "we have had enough of the socialist dictates of the IMF" when they warned about their current account getting out of whack. See Cornel Ban, *Ruling Ideas: How Global Neoliberalism Goes Local* (New York: Oxford University Press, 2016).

151 **"inflation and inflation expectations":** B. S. Bernanke, T. Laubach, F. S. Mishkin, and A. S. Posen, *Inflation Targeting: Lessons from the International Experience* (Princeton, NJ: Princeton University Press, 1999).

151 **three sets of reasons:** See Evan F. Koenig, George A. Kahn, and Robert Leeson, *The Taylor Rule and the Transformation of Monetary Policy* (Stanford, CA: Hoover Institution Press, 2012).

152 **variant of the structural change view:** A point also made by Charles Goodhart, whom we encountered in chapter 4 on inflation stories.

152 **"a better explanation":** Robert Skidelsky, *Money and Government: A Challenge to Mainstream Economics* (London: Allen Lane, 2018).

152 **incorporation of low-cost producers:** Stephen D. King, *We Need to Talk About Inflation: 14 Urgent Lessons from the Last 2,000 Years* (New Haven, CT: Yale University Press, 2023).

153 **"end of history":** Francis Fukuyama, *The End of History and the Last Man* (New York: Free Press, 1992).

153 **occurrence of macroeconomic shocks:** James H. Stock and Mark W. Watson, "Disentangling the Channels of the 2007–09 Recession," Brookings Papers on Economic Activity, Spring 2012, 81–156, https://www.federalreservehistory .org/essays/great-moderation.

153 **"Shocks are not measured directly":** Charles Bean, cited in Craig S. Hakkio, "The Great Moderation, 1982–2007," Federal Reserve History, https://www .federalreservehistory.org/essays/great-moderation.

153 **did occur during the Great Moderation:** Hakkio, "The Great Moderation, 1982–2007."

154 **higher degrees of central bank independence:** Alberto Alesina, "Macroeco- nomics and Politics," in *NBER Macroeconomics Annual*, ed. Stanley Fischer (Cambridge, MA: MIT Press, 1988); Alberto Alesina, "Politics and Business Cycles in Industrial Democracies," *Economic Policy* 8 (Spring 1989), 58–98; Alberto Alesina and Vittorio Grilli, "The European Central Bank: Reshaping Monetary Policy in Europe," in *Establishing a Central Bank: Issues in Europe and Lessons from United States*, eds. Matthew Canzoneri, Vittorio Grilli, and Paul Masson (Cambridge: Cambridge University Press and CEPR, 1992); Alberto Alesina and Lawrence H. Summers, "Central Bank Independence and Macroeconomic Performance: Some Comparative Evidence," *Journal of Money, Credit, and Banking* 25, no. 2 (May 1993), 151–62.

101 **Central Bank Independence:** Alesina and Summers, "Central Bank Inde- pendence and Macroeconomic Performance: Some Comparative Evidence.

154 **"the 'great moderation' ":** Mario Draghi, "Central Bank Independence," Lamfalussy Lecture, National Bank of Belgium, Brussels, October 26, 2018, https://www.bis.org/review/r181029d.pdfhttps://www.bis.org/review/ r181029d.pdf.

155 **"cross-country correlations":** Andrew Haldane, "What Has Central Bank Independence Ever Done for Us?," speech at the UCL Economists' Society Economics Conference, November 28, 2020, https://www.bankofengland .co.uk/-/media/boe/files/speech/2020/what-has-central-bank-independence -ever-done-for-us-speech-by-andy-haldane.pdf.

155 ***"will not forget the lessons":*** Ben Bernanke, "The Great Moderation: Remarks at the Meeting of the Eastern Economic Association," February 2004, https:// fraser.stlouisfed.org/title/statements-speeches-ben-s-bernanke-453/great -moderation-8893, italics added.

157 **research on the Phillips curve:** See, for example, David Ratner and Jae

Sim, "Who Killed the Phillips Curve," Finance and Economics Discussion Series 2022-028, Board of Governors of the Federal Reserve System, Washington, DC, May 2022, https://www.federalreserve.gov/econres/feds/who-killed-the-phillips-curve-a-murder-mystery.htm; Pierpaolo Benigno and Gauti B. Eggertsson, "It's Baaack: The Surge in Inflation in the 2020s and the Return of the Non-Linear Phillips Curve," Working Paper 31197, NBER Working Paper Series, https://www.nber.org/system/files/working_papers/w31197/w31197.pdf; see also Jonathon Hazel et al., "The Slope of the Phillips Curve: Evidence from the US States," *Quarterly Journal of Economics* 137, no. 3 (August 2022): 1299–1344, https://doi.org/10.1093/qje/qjac010. Jay Powell testified as much to Congress in 2019: "Federal Reserve Chair Jerome Powell Testifies Before Two Congressional Committees," C-SPAN, July 10, 2019, https://www.c-span.org/video/?462331-1/federal-reserve-chair-jerome-powell-testifies-state-economy&start=,"7535.

157 **The 1970s spike in rates:** Paul Schmelzing, "Eight Centuries of the Risk-Free Rate: Bond Market Reversals from the Venetians to the 'Var Shock,'" Bank of England Staff Working Paper No. 686, October 2017, https://www.bankofengland.co.uk/-/media/boe/files/working-paper/2017/eight-centuries-of-the-risk-free-rate-bond-market-reversals-from-the-venetians-update.pdf.

158 **underpinning of expectations:** Jeremy B. Rudd, "Why Do We Think That Inflation Expectations Matter for Inflation? (And Should We?)," Finance and Economics Discussion Series 2021-062, Board of Governors of the Federal Reserve System, Washington, DC, September 23, 2021, 18, https://www.federalreserve.gov/econres/feds/files/2021062pap.pdf.

158 **R* (known as "R star"):** See the lecture by Claudio Borio on this issue, "Navigating by R*: Safe or Hazardous?," BIS, September 15, 2021, https://www.bis.org/speeches/sp210915.pdf.

159 **"it is not easy":** Surjit Bhalla, Karan Bhasin, and Prakash Loungani, "Macroeconomic Effects of Formal Adoption of Inflation Targeting," IMF Working Paper 2023/007, January 13, 2023, https://www.elibrary.imf.org/view/journals/001/2023/007/article-A001-en.xml.

159 **"undue political influence":** Ben S. Bernanke, "Central Bank Independence, Transparency, and Accountability," speech at the Institute for Monetary and Economic Studies International Conference, Bank of Japan, Tokyo, Japan, May 25, 2010, https://www.federalreserve.gov/newsevents/speech/bernanke20100525a.htm.

159 **"For much of the 1990s":** Draghi, "Central Bank Independence."

160 **Christopher Crow and Ellen Meade:** "Central Bank Independence and Transparency: Evolution and Effectiveness," *European Journal of Political Economy* 24 (2008): 763–77.

160 **link between independence and low inflation:** Ana Carolina Garriga and
Cesar M. Rodriguez, "More Effective Than We Thought: Central Bank Independence and Inflation in Developing Countries," *Economic Modelling* 85
(2023): 87–105, https://doi.org/10.1016/j.econmod.2019.05.009; Daron Acemoglu, Pablo Querubin, Simon Johnson, and James A. Robinson, "When
Does Policy Reform Work? The Case of Central Bank Independence," *Brookings Papers on Economic Activity*, Spring 2008, https://www.brookings.edu/
wp-content/uploads/2008/03/2008a_bpea_acemoglu.pdf; Cristina Bodea
and Raymond Hicks, "Price Stability and Central Bank Independence:
Discipline, Credibility, and Democratic Institutions," *International Organization* 69, no 1 (Winter 2015): 35–61, https://www.cambridge.org/core/
journals/international-organization/article/price-stability-and-central
-bank-independence-discipline-credibility-and-democratic-institutions/60
5F4E0E40C7366B2B9413103B409BFA.

160 **central bank independence is associated:** S. Posen, "Declarations Are Not
Enough: Financial Sector Sources of Central Bank Independence," *NBER
Macroeconomics Annual 10* (Cambridge, MA: MIT Press, 1995), 253–74.

160 **still subject to pressures:** Adam Carola Binder, "Political Pressure on Central Banks," *Journal of Money, Credit and Banking* 53, no. 4 (2021): 715–
44; Nicolò Fraccaroli, Alessandro Giovannini, Jean-François Jamet, and
Eric Persson, "Ideology and Monetary Policy. The Role of Political Parties'
Stances in the European Central Bank's Parliamentary Hearings," *European
Journal of Political Economy* 74 (September 2022), https://www.sciencedirect
.com/science/article/abs/pii/S0176268022000234.

160 **the appointments of central bank governors:** Sotirios Kokas, Thomas Lam-
ber, Alexander Michaelides, and Vasso Ioannidou, "(In)dependent Central
Banks," CEPR Discussion Paper 17802, CEPR Press, Paris & London, 2023,
https://cepr.org/publications/dp17802.

Chapter 6: Are Inflation Wars Class Wars?

163 **"A change in the value":** John Maynard Keynes, *Essays in Persuasion* (White-
fish, MT: Kessinger Publishing, 2010), 44.

163 **"There's class warfare":** Ben Stein, "In Class Warfare, Guess Which Class Is
Winning," *New York Times*, November 26, 2006.

163 **"Are trade wars class wars?":** Matthew Klein and Michael Pettis, *Trade Wars
Are Class Wars* (New Haven, CT: Yale University Press, 2020).

165 **"difference between inflation and unemployment":** We won't dive into a
comparison between the social relevance of inflation and unemployment,
which is beyond the scope of this book, but we recommend the response to
Bernanke's sentence by Claudia Sahm, Stay-at-Home Macro (SAHM), "Unem-

ployment Affects Everybody Too," May 23, 2022, https://stayathomemacro
.substack.com/p/unemployment-affects-everybody-too. The quote by Bernanke is taken from this article.

165 **someone lent you $100:** That is, the real interest rate is equal to the nominal
interest rate.

166 **"enriches . . . the idle":** David Ricardo, "The High Price of a Bullion, A Proof
of the Deprecation of Bank Notes," in *The Works and Correspondence of
David Ricardo*, vol. 3, *Pamphlets and Papers 1809–11*, ed. P. Sraffa (Indianap-
olis, IN: Liberty Fund, 2005), 47–128.

166 **"the main losers":** Matthias Doepke and Martin Schneider, "Inflation and
the Redistribution of Wealth," *Journal of Political Economy* 114, no. 6 (December 2006), https://www.journals.uchicago.edu/doi/abs/10.1086/508379.

167 **a class-specific tax:** Mark Blyth, Great Transformations: Economic Ideas
and Institutional Change in the Twentieth Century (Cambridge: Cambridge
University Press, 2002), chapter 5.

167 **led Paul Krugman to wonder:** Paul Krugman, Twitter post, December 11, 2021,
11:58 PM, https://twitter.com/paulkrugman/status/1469728251643838467.

167 **"thereby exacerbating inflation inequality":** Gregor Semieniuk et al.,
"Distributional implications and share ownership of record oil and gas
profits," University of Massachusetts Economics Department Working
Paper Series (forthcoming).

168 **"The sorry old truth":** "Inflation Usually Hits America's Poor Hardest. Not
This Time," *The Economist*, February 2, 2023, https://www.economist.com/
graphic-detail/2023/02/02/inflation-usually-hits-americas-poor-hardest
-not-this-time.

168 **the middle class:** Xavier Jaravel, "Inflation Inequality: Measurement, Causes,
and Policy Implications," *Annul Review of Economics* 13 (2021): 599–629.

169 **American's extreme dependence on cars:** The relative lack of a welfare state
in the US to cushion income losses, COVID notwithstanding, plays a role
here too.

169 **Black and Hispanic Americans suffered the most:** Rajashri Chakrabarti, Dan
Garcia, and Maxim Pinkovskiy, "Inflation Disparities by Race and Income
Narrow," Federal Reserve Bank of New York, Liberty Street Economics,
January 18, 2023, https://libertystreeteconomics.newyorkfed.org/2023/01/
inflation-disparities-by-race-and-income-narrow/?utm_source=newsletter
&utm_medium=email&utm_campaign=newsletter_axiosmacro&stream=
business.

170 **mostly hit lower-income households:** Antonio F. Amores et al., "Inflation,
Fiscal Policy and Inequality," Occasional Paper Series No. 330, European
Central Bank, undated, https://www.ecb.europa.eu/pub/pdf/scpops/ecb
.op330~2e42ffb621.en.pdf.

170 **inflation inequality in the euro area:** Evangelos Charalampakis et al., "The Impact of the Recent Rise in Inflation on Low-Income Households," ECB Economic Bulletin 7 (2022), https://www.ecb.europa.eu/pub/economic -bulletin/focus/2022/html/ecb.ebbox202207_04~a89ec1a6fe.en.html

170 **prices went up most for food and energy:** Francesco Corsello and Marianna Riggi, "Inflation Is Not Equal for All: The Heterogenous Effects of Energy Shocks," Banca d'Italia, Working Paper No. 1429, November 2023, https:// www.bancaditalia.it/pubblicazioni/temi-discussione/2023/2023-1429/index .html?com.dotmarketing.htmlpage.language=1.

171 **Inflation and Inflation Inequality:** Grégory Claeys Conor McCaffrey, and Lennard Welslau, "Does Inflation Hit the Poor Hardest Everywhere?," November 29, 2022, Bruegel blog post, https://www.bruegel.org/blog-post/ does-inflation-hit-poor-hardest-everywhere.

172 **differences in Germany:** Roberto A. DeSantis et al., "Motor Vehicle Sector: Explaining the Drop in Output and the Rise in Prices," ECB Economic Bulletin 7 (2022), https://www.ecb.europa.eu/pub/economic-bulletin/focus/2022/ html/ecb.ebbox202207_02~5bde8eeff0.en.html.

173 **policies put in place by European governments:** Amores et al., "Inflation, Fiscal Policy and Inequality."

174 **"a point which is often lost":** Olivier Blanchard, Twitter post, December 30, 2022, 6:24 PM, https://twitter.com/ojblanchard1/status/16089671762325258 24?lang=en.

175 **"looking at the labor market":** Christine Lagarde, speech at the plenary session of the European Parliament, Strasbourg, February 15, 2023, https:// www.ecb.europa.eu/press/key/date/2023/html/ecb.sp230215~a512d68d9f .en.html

175 **the dreaded wage-price spiral:** Remember the "special factors" argument from earlier does just as good a job in explaining the inflation of the 1970s.

176 **Cumulative Change in Nominal and Real Hourly Wages:** S. Araki, et al., "Under Pressure: Labour Market and Wage Developments in OECD Countries," in *OECD Employment Outlook 2023: Artificial Intelligence and the Labour Market*, chapter 2 (Paris: OECD Publishing, 2023), https://www .oecd-ilibrary.org/sites/08785bba-en/1/3/1/index.html?itemId=/content/ publication/08785bba-en&_csp_=9f4368ffe3fc59de4786c462d2cdc236&ite mIGO=oecd&itemContentType=book.

177 **central banks undermine low-wage workers' ability:** Danny Blanchflower and Alex Bryson, "Recession and Deflation," IZA Institute of Labor Economics Discussion Paper Series, No. 15695, November 2022, https://docs.iza.org/ dp15695.pdf.

177 **firms used inflation to gain:** For example, see "Firms' Profits: Cure or Curse?," European Stability Mechanism, May 12, 2023, https://www.esm

.europa.eu/blog/firms-profits-cure-or-curse; Elke Hahn, "How Have Unit Profits Contributed to the Recent Strengthening of Euro Area Domestic Price Pressures?," ECB Economic Bulletin 4 (2023), https://www.ecb.europa.eu/ pub/economic-bulletin/focus/2023/html/ecb.ebbox202304_03~705befadac .en.html; and "European Economic Forecast, Spring 2023," especially "*Box I.2.3:* Profit Margins and Their Role in Euro Area Inflation," 29, https://ec .europa.eu/economy_finance/forecasts/2023/spring/Box_I_2_3-Profit%20 margins%20and%20their%20role%20in%20euro%20area%20inflation.pdf.

177 **"High profits tend much more":** Quoted in Roni Hirsch, "Risk and Trouble: Adam Smith on Profit and the Protagonists of Capitalism," *American Journal of Political Science* 65, no. 1 (2020): 166–79, https://doi.org/10.1111/ajps.12556.

179 **"have fared relatively better":** Niels-Jakob Hansen, Frederik Toscani, and Jing Zhou, "Euro Area Inflation After the Pandemic and Energy Shock: Import Prices, Profits and Wages," IMF Working Paper 23/131, International Monetary Fund, June 2023, 2, https://www.imf.org/en/Publications/WP/ Issues/2023/06/23/Euro-Area-Inflation-after-the-Pandemic-and-Energy -Shock-Import-Prices-Profits-and-Wages-534837.

178 **Corporate Profits and Labor Costs:** Carston Jung and Chris Hayes, "Inflation, Profits and Market Power: Towards a New Research and Policy Agenda," IPPR, December 7, 2023, https://www.ippr.org/files/2023-12/1701878131_ inflation-profits-and-market-power-dec-23.pdf, using data from Niels-Jakob Hansen, Frederik Toscani, and Jing Zhou, "Europe's Inflation Outlook Depends on How Corporate Profits Absorb Wage Gains," IMF Blog, June 26, 2023, https://www.imf.org/en/Blogs/Articles/2023/06/26/europes-inflation -outlook-depends-on-how-corporate-profits-absorb-wage-gains.

179 **profits boosted inflation earlier:** Hansen; Toscani; and Zhou, "Euro Area Inflation after the Pandemic and Energy Shock: Import Prices, Profits and Wages."

179 **wage inequality in the US has declined:** Thomas Blanchet, Emmanuel Saez, and Gabriel Zucman, "Real-Time Inequality," NBER Working Paper 30229, (2022), DOI 10.3386/w30229.

180 **it is difficult to cleanly infer:** For instance, a recent paper by the OECD observed that "an increase in unit profits (profits per unit of value added) does not necessarily entail higher profit margins (profits as a proportion of sales) as the increase of input costs (including intermediate consumption) can result in profits per unit of value-added moving differently to profits on gross output (or sales), OECD Economic Outlook 2023, no. 1. The citation is from Box 1.2, https://www.oecd-ilibrary.org/sites/ce188438-en/1/3/1/ index.html?itemId=/content/publication/ce188438-en&_csp_=f8e326092 da6dbbbef8fbfa1b8ad3d52&itemIGO=oecd&itemContentType=book#:~ :text=Moreover%2C%20an%20increase%20in%20unit,profits%20on%20 gross%20output%20(or.

180 **managed to estimate firms' markups:** Servaas Storm, "Profit Inflation Is Real," Institute for New Economic Thinking, June 15, 2023, https:// www.ineteconomics.org/perspectives/blog/profit-inflation-is-real#:~:text =Higher%20unit%20labor%20costs%20are,already%20clear%20from%20 Figure%205). Mike Konzcal and Niko Lusiani, "Prices, Profits, and Power: An Analysis of 2021 Firm-Level Markups," Roosevelt Institute, June 2022, https://rooseveltinstitute.org/wp-content/uploads/2022/06/RI_Prices ProfitsPower_202206.pdf. A. Glover, J. Mustre-del-Río, and A. von Ende-Becker, "How Much Have Record Corporate Profits Contributed to Recent Inflation?," Federal Reserve Bank of Kansas City Economic Review, 2023, https://doi.org/10.18651/ER/v108n1GloverMustredelRiovonEndeBecker.

181 **The cost of energy:** Servaas Storm, "Profit Inflation Is Real," Institute for New Economic Thinking, June 15, 2023, https://www.ineteconomics.org/ perspectives/blog/profit-inflation-is-real#:~:text=Higher%20unit%20 labor%20costs%20are,already%20clear%20from%20Figure%205).

38 **25 percent:** https://www.ineteconomics.org/perspectives/blog/profit-inflation -is-real.

181 **the underlying story is similar:** A. Glover, J. Mustre-del-Río, and A. von Ende-Becker, "How Much Have Record Corporate Profits Contributed to Recent Inflation?," Federal Reserve Bank of Kansas City Economic Review, 2023, https:// doi.org/10.18651/ER/v108n1GloverMustredelRiovonEndeBecker; Mike Konzcal and Niko Lusiani, "Prices, Profits, and Power: An Analysis of 2021 Firm-Level Markups," Roosevelt Institute, June 2022, https://rooseveltinstitute.org/ wp-content/uploads/2022/06/RI_PricesProfitsPower_202206.pdf.

181 **markups did not grow equally:** Konzcal and Lusiani notice that the growth in markups in 2021 was mostly driven by the firms in the ninetieth and seventy-fifth percentiles of the markup distribution among US firms. Konzcal and Lusiani, "Prices, Profits, and Power."

181 **did not change much in Germany and Italy:** Markups increased in the nontradable sector (such as construction) in Germany, and in the energy sector in Italy. See Fabrizio Colonna, Roberto Torrini, and Eliana Viviano, "The Profit Share and Firm Markup: How to Interpret Them," Banca d'Italia, Occasional Paper No. 770, May 31, 2023, https://www.bancaditalia.it/pubblicazioni/ qef/2023-0770/index.html?com.dotmarketing.htmlpage.language=1.

181 **in the Netherlands, markups explained:** Servaas Storm, "Profit Inflaton Is Real," Institute for New Economic Thinking, June 15, 2023, https://www .ineteconomics.org/perspectives/blog/profit-inflation-is-real.

181 **increased their profit margins in *all* countries:** They estimate an increase in average pretax profit margins of 2.6 percentage points in the UK, 0.9 in the US, 0.5 in Germany, 6.9 in Brazil, and 7.5 in South Africa. See Jung and Hayes, "Inflation, Profits and Market Power."

182 **"Companies, which in normal times":** Jon Sindreu, "'Greedflation' Is Real—and Probably Good for the Economy," *Wall Street Journal*, May 25, 2023, https://www.wsj.com/articles/greedflation-is-realand-probably-good-for-the-economy-6c475b8e.

182 **Energy companies did really well:** Servaas Storm identified the oil company ExxonMobil as the US company that raised the markup the most (45 percent), followed by automobile companies (23–28 percent) and Chesapeake Energy (18 percent), Storm, "Profit Inflation Is Real."

182 **"a disproportionate part":** OECD Economic Outlook 2023.

182 **mechanism behind this markup-driven inflation:** Isabella M. Weber and Evan Wasner, "Seller's Inflation, Profits and Conflict: Why Can Large Firms Hike Prices in an Emergency," University of Massachusetts Amherst, January 2023, Economics Department Working Paper Series, https://scholarworks.umass.edu/econ_workingpaper/343/.

182 **firms in less competitive markets:** "Competition and Inflation," OECD Competition Policy Roundtable Background Note, 2022; https://www.oecd.org/competition/competition-and-inflation.htm; OECD Economic Outlook 2023.

183 **"companies with (temporary) market power":** Jung and Hayes, "Inflation, Profits and Market Power: Towards a New Research and Policy Agenda," 5.

183 **"corporate profits drove 53 percent":** Liz Pancotti and Lindsay Owens, "Inflation Revelation: How Outsized Corporate Profits Drive Rising Costs," Groundwork Collaborative, https://groundworkcollaborative.org/wp-content/uploads/2024/01/24.01.17-GWC-Corporate-Profits-Report.pdf.

184 **a tight monetary policy:** Jennifer Sor, "Inflation Could Come Roaring Back 1970s-Style. Here Are 4 Reasons Why Markets Should Be Concerned, According to Deutsche Bank," *Business Insider*, October 10, 2023, https://www.businessinsider.com/inflation-us-economic-outlook-fed-interest-rates-stagflation-recession-deutsche-2023-10.

185 **UK banks passed about 43 percent:** Owen Walker, "UK Banks Lead Global Rivals in Passing on Interest Rate Benefits to Savers," *Financial Times*, July 23, 2023, https://www.ft.com/content/1d2949d6-00d1-4c18-af81-01439fa7cfc5.

185 **One more factor that benefits banks:** Paul De Grauwe and Yuemei Ji, "Monetary Policies That Do Not Subsidise Banks," CEPS, 2023, https://cdn.ceps.eu/wp-content/uploads/2023/07/Towards-monetary-policies-that-do-not-subsidise-banks_July2023.pdf.

185 **interest payments from central banks:** De Grauwe and Ji, "Monetary Policies That Do Not Subsidise Banks."

185 **Stephen Gandel and Joshua Frankling:** "Fed's high-rates era handed $1tn windfall to US bank," *Financial Times*, September 22, 2024, https://www.ft.com/content/4c013d3b-796b-47a3-a964-02f753d39846.

186 **collapse of regional banks:** Differently from the regional US banks, Credit Suisse was already suffering from a series of scandals and losses stemming from bad management. The trigger for Credit Suisse's rapid fall was the announcement by the Saudi National Bank that it would stop giving money to the Swiss bank due to regulatory obstacles. Credit Suisse did not have the same interest rate exposure of SVB.

186 **Silicon Valley Bank:** A chart by Mike Bostock showing all the bank failures in the US became popular online, leading many to think that the collapses of the three regional banks were the largest ever in recent US history after the failure of Washington Mutual in 2008. While the chart is very useful in depicting the size and relevance of these collapses, this interpretation is not fully correct. First, the chart displays bank failures using FDIC data, which comprises only banks supervised by the FDIC. As Adam Tooze observed, this excludes the collapse of Lehman Brothers, whose $639 billion assets dwarfed the assets of the three regional banks (the sum of their assets is $548 billion). Second, the chart does not include investment banks. See Adam Tooze, "Chartbook #214—Why the 2023 Banking Crisis Does Not Look Like 2008, or Why One Run Is Not Like Another," Chartbook, May 10, 202, https://adamtooze.substack.com/p/chartbook-214-why-the-2023 -banking.

186 **7 percent of SVB's deposits:** Noah Smith, "Why Was There a Run on Silicon Valley Bank?," *Noapinion*, March 2023, https://www.noahpinion.blog/p/ why-was-there-a-run-on-silicon-valley?utm_source=substack&utm_ campaign=post_embed&utm_medium=email.

186 **made SVB particularly vulnerable:** Another major vulnerability is that SVB's activities were so concentrated in one sector, the tech start-up sector. For a bank it is more convenient to diversify its portfolio to hedge itself against sector-specific shocks. Higher interest rates were problematic for the tech industry, which heavily relies on venture funding. By the end of 2022, venture funding dried up and hit a nine-year low. This pushed many start-ups to rely on their deposits at SVB to pay their employees' salaries and other expenses. See Smith, "Why Was There a Run on Silicon Valley Bank?"

187 **SVB had to sell those assets:** First Republic had a similar exposure on jumbo mortgages, which is another form of long-term low-rate assets that is vulnerable to interest rate risk. Good summaries of SVB's failure can be found here: Vidhura S. Tennekoon, "Analysis: Why Silicon Valley Bank and Signature Bank Failed So Fast," PBS News, March 14, 2023, https://www.pbs.org/ newshour/economy/why-silicon-valley-bank-and-signature-bank-failed-so -fast; Smith, "Why Was There a Run on Silicon Valley Bank?"; Tooze, "Chartbook #214—Why the 2023 Banking Crisis Does Not Look Like 2008, or Why One Run Is Not Like Another."

187 **"remains broadly resilient"**: https://www.imf.org/-/media/Files/Publications/ GFSR/2023/October/English/ch2.ashx.

Conclusion: So Have We Seen the Last of It?

189 **"Beware of his false knowledge"**: George Bernard Shaw, *Man and Superman* (New York: Penguin Classics, 2000).

192 **many other more serious problems**: It's a bit like saying a fever is a problem, which it is, but a fever caused by COVID is not a problem. COVID is the problem.

192 **this story of living with hyperinflation**: Martin Lousteau, personal communication.

192 **concerned with "secular stagnation"**: See for example Lawrence H. Summers, "Accepting the Reality of Secular Stagnation," International Monetary Fund, March 2020, https://www.imf.org/en/Publications/fandd/issues/ 2020/03/larry-summers-on-secular-stagnation.

192 **the structure of firms in capitalism**: Herman Mark Schwartz, "From Fordism to Franchise: Intellectual Property and Growth Models in the Knowledge Economy," in *Diminishing Returns: The New Politics of Growth and Stagnation*, eds. Lucio Baccaro, Mark Blyth and Jonas Pontusson (New York: Oxford University Press, 2022), 74–97.

195 **particular *macroeconomic regimes***: Mark Blyth and Matthias Matthijs, "Black Swans, Lame Ducks, and the Mystery of IPE's Missing Macro-Economy," *Review of International Political Economy* 24, no. 2 (2017): 203– 31, https://doi.org/10.1080/09692290.2017.1308417.

195 **hardware and software of capitalism**: Mark Blyth and Eric Lonergan *Angrynomics* (London: Agenda Publishing, 2020), chapter 3.

195 **came to know as neoliberalism**: Mark Blyth, *Great Transformations: Economic Ideas and Institutional Change in the Twentieth Century* (Cambridge: Cambridge University Press, 2002).

195 **This "regime shift"**: On China and deflation see Charles Goodhart and Manjoy Pradhan, *The Great Demographic Reversal: Aging Societies, Waning Inequality, and an Inflation Revival* (New York: Palgrave Macmillan, 2020).

196 **the instruments used to keep it going**: Blyth and Lonergan, *Angrynomics*.

196 **food inflation will increase**: Maximilian Kotz, Frederike Kuik, and Christine Nickel, "Global Warming and Heat Extremes to Enhance Inflationary Pressures," *Nature Communications: Earth and Environment* 5, no. 1 (March 2024): 2.

197 **the deflationary pressure**: Goodhart and Pradhan, *The Great Demographic Reversal*.

197 **we are all getting older:** Mikael Juselius and Elöd Takáts, "Age and Infla-

tion," *IMF Finance & Development* 53, no. 1 (March 2016), https://www.imf
.org/external/pubs/ft/fandd/2016/03/juselius.htm.

197 **as the baby boomers leave:** Mikael Juselius and Elöd Takáts, "Inflation
and Demogaphy Through Time," *Journal of Economic Dynamics and Control* 128 (July 2021), https://www.sciencedirect.com/science/article/abs/pii/
S0165188921000713.

198 **a cautionary tale:** This cautionary tale is drawn from Blyth, *Great
Transformations.*

198 **"orthodox interpretation of welfare economics":** Brian Barry, "Does
Democracy Cause Inflation? Political Ideas of Some Economists," in *The
Politics of Inflation and Economic Stagnation: Theoretical Approaches and
International Case Studies,* eds. Leon N. Lindberg and Charles S. Maier
(Washington, DC: Brookings Institution, 1985), 282.

199 **Sweden used to occasionally allow:** We thank Jonas Pontusson for this
insight. Personal communication.

199 **doesn't sound so deadly:** As Barry noted in this regard, "If one is going to
maintain such a linkage between socio-cultural change and inflation the
causal arrows probably work the other way round, that inflation acts as a
safety valve, blurring the impact of incompatible demands." Barry, "Does
Democracy Cause Inflation? Political Ideas of Some Economists," 288.

199 **"'Enjoy, enjoy!' . . . becomes a rational response":** Buchanan and Wagner,
Democracy in Deficit (New York: Academic Press, 1977), quoted in Barry,
"Does Democracy Cause Inflation? Political Ideas of Some Economists," 284,
and quoted in Blyth, *Great Transformations,* 150.

199 **"prudent behavior becomes reckless":** "Inflation and Unemployment: The
New Dimensions of Politics," in Milton Friedman, *Monetarist Economics*
(London: Institute of Economic Affairs, 1991), 105, quoted in Blyth, *Great
Transformations,* 150.

200 **it's a leading decarbonizer:** See "Consumer Price Index," Statistics Denmark,
https://www.dst.dk/en/Statistik/emner/oekonomi/prisindeks/forbruger
prisindeks.

Index

Page numbers in *italics* refer to illustrations.
Page numbers after 203 refer to notes.